ACADEMICS
ON THE LINE

The Faculty Strike at
San Francisco State

Arlene Kaplan Daniels
Rachel Kahn-Hut
and Associates

ACADEMICS
ON THE LINE

Jossey-Bass Inc., Publishers

615 Montgomery Street · San Francisco · 1970

ACADEMICS ON THE LINE
The Faculty Strike at San Francisco State
Arlene Kaplan Daniels, Rachel Kahn-Hut, and Associates

Jossey-Bass, Inc., Publishers
615 Montgomery Street
San Francisco, California 94111

Library of Congress Catalog Card Number 79-128702

International Standard Book Number ISBN 0-87589-071-7

Manufactured in the United States of America
Composed and printed by York Composition Company, Inc.
Bound by Chas. H. Bohn & Co., Inc.

JACKET DESIGN BY WILLI BAUM, SAN FRANCISCO

FIRST EDITION

Code 7023

THE JOSSEY-BASS SERIES IN HIGHER EDUCATION

General Editors

JOSEPH AXELROD
*San Francisco State College and
University of California, Berkeley*

MERVIN B. FREEDMAN
*San Francisco State College and
Wright Institute, Berkeley*

108528

Preface

Academics on the Line began as the brainchild of some itinerant sociologists caught in the strike at San Francisco State: Sherri Cavan, John Irwin, Rachel Kahn-Hut, John Kinch, Magali Larson, George Rothbart, Arlene Daniels. As we rushed from off-campus classes to picketing assignments, we drew together to discuss the significance of the events in which we were participating. In this way we tried to continue our professional associations despite the loss of a campus base where we normally met. We were drawn together by our common fear that there might be no college left when the struggle subsided. And even if the college should survive it was questionable if we strikers would ever be permitted to return.

It was this band of sociologists, then, which formulated the notion of preparing a series of articles to publicize our view of events which occurred at State during and following the student-faculty strike in 1968–1969. At that time, because a battle-scarred campus was still relatively novel, we wanted to tell others far from the scene just what we were observing and experiencing. Ultimately the idea of presenting papers from our sociological perspective was broadened to include the views and experiences of other faculty who went on strike. And the original idea was transformed into a plan to write a book; two of us became the editors formally in charge of completing the project.

Our efforts were significantly aided and encouraged by colleagues and friends from all parts of the academic community. We would like to thank several of them for their thoughtful suggestions on the organization and focus of this collection of papers: Arturo Biblarz and James Benét from our own contributors at State, Neil Friedman at Brandeis, Robert Laufer at the University of Wisconsin, Harvey Molotch and Thomas Scheff at the University of California, Santa Barbara. We are also grateful to Edgar Austin of the University of Maryland, Far East Division, for his conscientious assistance in editing. Thanks are due Lauren Chaitkin, Carol Grenall, and Donna Jenkins for assistance in the preparation of various drafts of the manuscript.

We dedicate this book to the students who forced us to face the social and political implications of higher education and to all the members of the campus who walked the picket lines at San Francisco State College in 1968–1969.

San Francisco   ARLENE KAPLAN DANIELS
August 1970   RACHEL KAHN-HUT

Contents

Contributors

The contributors are all members of the American Federation of Teachers, and currently all but one are faculty members in the California State college system. All but three were at San Francisco State College through the events described in *Academics on the Line* and are there now.

Kenwood Bartelme is a professor of psychology.

Arturo Biblarz is a professor of sociology.

James Benét is the education editor of *Newsroom,* a nightly program presented on The National Educational Television affiliate in San Francisco, and was formerly a professor of journalism.

Sherri Cavan is a professor of sociology.

Arlene Kaplan Daniels is a professor of sociology.

Rachel Kahn-Hut is a professor in sociology.

John W. Kinch is chairman of the department of sociology.

Theodore Kroeber is a professor of psychology and a member of the SFSC Academic Senate.

Magali Sarfatti Larson is a lecturer in sociology.

Nancy McDermid is a lawyer, a professor in the Speech Department, and a member of the SFSC Academic Senate.

Patrick J. McGillivray is a professor of sociology at Sacramento State College and is vice-president of the College Council of the AFT.

Herbert Naboisek is a professor of psychology.

Stanley Ofsevit is a lecturer in social work education.

George S. Rothbart is a professor of sociology.

Worth S. Summers is a professor of sociology at Sacramento State College.

Herbert Wilner is a professor of English and creative writing.

ACADEMICS
ON THE LINE

The Faculty Strike at
San Francisco State

On the Line

Arlene Kaplan Daniels, Rachel Kahn-Hut

In the strike at San Francisco State College in 1968–1969 a large number of students, faculty, and other campus workers opposed the will of the trustees and administrators of the state college system. Before the strike, when the authors of this book were only a miscellaneous collection of ordinary college professors, we would hardly have contemplated so desperate a course of action. Old and young, tenured and part-time, locals and cosmopolitans, activist and apolitical, we were clearly a disparate group of academicians; most of us did not even know one another. This book is an attempt to explain why we left our traditional, scholarly niches, joined the American Federation of Teachers, Local 1352, and went out on strike. Part I describes SFSC before and during the strike, and it suggests the process by which we came to that act of striking for which we were labeled radicals. The second part pre-

1

sents an analysis of the problems of higher education which, though
not original to the crisis on our campus, were clarified and reaffirmed
by it. The third part describes and analyzes the pressures which forced
the faculty to recognize its powerlessness. The last part considers the
consequences of the crisis—the assessments made once the headline-
making events were over. Many of these assessments concerned the
role of the university in society.

The scholar has always been considered an observer of the
human scene rather than a participant in it. And academicians usually
prefer the self-image of critical bystander to that of active participant
in society—or perhaps that of pure rather than applied scientist. And
the public view reflects this preference in the stereotype of the scholar
as an absent-minded professor, a man remote from the practical affairs
of life. But obviously, with this perspective we cannot explain why
professors tried to close down the classrooms at San Francisco State
College.

In order to understand this behavior one must consider the
changes which have occurred in the structure of the university since
its early days. The institutions of higher learning today are certainly
not comprised, as they once may have been, of bands of wandering
scholars, free to study as they wish and relatively independent of the
political and economic life of the wider community. Today these institutions—and the lives of their faculty and students—are inextricably
enmeshed in the larger society. What happens in the world has re-
verberations on the campus, and what occurs on the campus affects
the course of events in the larger world.[1]

These connections cannot help but influence the activities of the
university. Most forms of higher education involve an enormous and
proliferating bureaucracy supported by extensive assets and investments.[2] Noneducational industries are affected by the manipulation of
these assets. Furthermore, all organizations of higher education—private and state—depend on continuing support from corporate and
governmental agencies for their maintenance and survival; and so they
are vitally affected by shifts and changes in this support. Public institu-

[1] C. Jencks and D. Riesman, *The Academic Revolution* (Garden City,
N.Y.: Doubleday, 1968).

[2] J. Ridgeway, *The Closed Corporation: American Universities in Crisis*
(New York: Random House, 1968).

tions are particularly vulnerable to pressures from their sources of support because of the contention that they should serve the interests of the public. For example, public officials may meddle in curriculum planning—as the governor of California did when he complained that the colleges spent too much money for "esoteric" courses. And academic policy may have to bow to political expedience in setting admission requirements. The governor and legislature may decide to limit student enrollment by increasing tuition and decreasing scholarship funds. This strategy will then take precedence over an academic policy of favoring higher entrance requirements as the means to limit enrollment.

Thus outside social pressures may have their effect not only upon the management of the universities but also upon the selection of the individuals who constitute them. These pressures also affect the meaning of the university for its constituents. The students who attend college are not expected to put aside worldly interests while they devote their time to scholarship and learning; instead they come to prepare for occupations. They are inclined, therefore, to find irrelevant many educational tasks which have been traditionally considered essential for intellectual development. The students resist, and slowly these "esoteric" topics disappear from the curriculum.

Faculty members also are less interested in the pursuit of pure knowledge. Today university accomplishments can bring status, security, and other rewards in the larger society. And so many academics devote themselves to prestigious activities (research, publication) which gain them these rewards both in and outside the university. Sometimes these activities are pursued instead of less noticeable though ultimately valuable ones: teaching or inquiry into unpopular areas of scholarship and research.[3] For all these reasons, it would be foolish to believe that institutions of higher education develop independently of worldly considerations.

But this interdependence of the practical and the academic worlds does not mean that the public welfare is always well served at the university. Often university experts serve some interests in the society better than others. Citizens may be hard pressed to find dis-

[3] T. Caplow and R. McGee, *The Academic Marketplace* (New York: Basic Books, 1958). T. Veblen, *The Higher Learning in America* (New York: Huebsch, 1918).

4 On the Line

interested scholarship and expertise at the university when they really
need it. For example, the state attorney general's office could not find
on any of the university campuses a qualified geologist who was willing
to speak for the public interest when oil began leaking off shore in
Santa Barbara. All the experts were supported at least partially (in
grants, equipment, and jobs for their students)' by the same oil com-
panies which were under fire as the perpetrators of serious ecological
damage.[4]

Still, it is not surprising that the general public is slow to consider the significance of these events. Harvard and the other Ivy
League schools provide the ideal-typical image of the university/college
isolated from public control while engaged in the unbiased pursuit of
knowledge. The image persists, even though everyone knows that no
college attains this ideal. And it persists despite the documentation to
indicate that higher education in America has never been independent
and has always served special interests.[5] It is easy to see why we continued to believe that the exploration of knowledge has been relatively
unhampered by political or economic considerations on the campus.
It required the disruption of our campus before many of us understood the extent and danger of some of the connections between the
university/college system and the outside world.

These alliances are dangerous because they favor established
groups in the society—those who already possess elite perspectives and
interests. Despite its lofty claims, academia does not seriously recognize
its educational responsibilities; teaching students has low priority—the
rewards go to those who do research and publish. Consequently, few
academics have been interested in the problem of how to teach those
who have difficulties or are resistant. They have ignored those previously deprived of quality education until forced to consider them by
threats and riots.

And we were no better than or different from our colleagues.
Our attention was drawn to these issues only when our students rose
up in protest. From their outcry we finally understood the consequences of the involvement we had unwittingly accepted in elitist per-

See H. Molotch, "Santa Barbara: Oil in the Velvet Playground,"
Ramparts, November 1969, *8*, 43–52.
[5] See R. Hofstadter, *The Rise of Anti-Intellectualism in America* (New
York: Knopf, 1963).

spectives. We had always assumed that we knew what was best for students. We had not been concerned that much of the campus community is excluded from decisions about its own vital concerns because we were so sure we understood what they were. Our complacency was based upon the assumption that our students were similar to us, that they shared some of our interests and goals in education. And we thought we were providing an education useful for what they wanted to do. We were operating with a model of society in which upward mobility was relatively simple. Any hard-working and reasonably intelligent student could succeed. And any well-motivated student would naturally seize the opportunities education affords to escape the ghetto or the lower classes from which he came. We could understand the problem of such mobility in terms of divided loyalties.[6] But we could not yet understand how this mobility might create antagonism, for it can be perceived as a means to drain the ghettos of their best leaders. And this was how some of our students saw it; they did not want to escape from their background as many of us have done; they wanted to return and change it.

The blindness on our part developed from other inequities. A concerned segment of the ethnic and the very poor communities in the broader society has no word in the management of the college or in the formulation of its goals. Many of their children are excluded by our admission standards and by the costs of higher education. Furthermore, the interests and needs of these communities are not voiced in the governing or policy-making bodies of higher education, for they have no spokesmen there. Although the state college Board of Trustees define their responsibility as the expression of the public view, they understand only a small portion of that public. All but one of these trustees are white businessmen, and what they understand best are the needs of the business and governmental sectors. They see, for example, how vital it is for the college to continue educating technicians, middle-level administrators, and semiprofessionals. And they understand the demands from working-class families that their children be provided with opportunities for mobility into the Establishment. But they have little understanding of the demands of citizens who want to modify rather than enter the existing system. Because these

---

[6] See R. Hoggart, "The Scholarship Boy." In *The Uses of Literacy* (Harmonsworth, Middlesex, England: Penguin, 1960).

citizens know from experience that equal opportunity is a myth, they
see the split between the idea and the reality of the democratic system
clearly. They have quite different values and immediate goals from
those understood by the trustees; they are not interested in the continuance of a system of higher education which neglects their goals or
considers their interests irrelevant. Yet they pay taxes in support of an
institution which maintains the power of those already advantaged—
for it is primarily the children of the middle and upper classes who
benefit from the public education system.[7]

During the discussions about the student strike many of us
came to understand some of the social effects or consequences of our
academic perspective. And so we realized that we had a responsibility
greater than that to our currently enrolled students; we were also
responsible to the student body at large, to those who would enter as
students in the future, and to a larger, concerned public not otherwise
represented in the deliberations. Meeting our classes might not have
first priority under these circumstances. And so our definition of how
to resolve the conflicts on the campus expanded. We became interested
not only in how best to resume classes but also in how to create a context in which resolution of fundamental college problems was possible.
These basic conflicts had been lying below the surface for some time
though they emerged clearly only in the crisis. They involved the
contradictory goals of many groups. Were the academics to educate
the masses or to preserve elitist standards? Must education explain
and justify the status quo or may it raise questions about its legitimacy? Would the administration recognize that it supported institutionalized racism or would it refuse to change? Could the trustees
serve both public and corporate interests? How was a resolution of the
crisis to be determined among various partisan groups within the
community? We felt that education as a public service could become
the focus of campus life only if these issues were finally faced.

We came to understand that these issues are not restricted to
State or to the California system of higher education. Specific issues
may trigger revolt (ROTC, admission policies, campus recruiters,
dormitories, food, ethnic studies departments). But the flaws in the

[7] See Chapter Four in this book and B. Barlow and P. Shapiro, "The
Struggle for San Francisco State." In J. McEvoy and A. Miller (Eds.), *Black
Power and Student Rebellion* (Belmont, Calif.: Wadsworth, 1969).

underlying structure of the university must be examined to explain how these problems mushroom into widespread student rebellion.

As these issues became clear to us, we felt that the faculty should be allowed to bring its growing awareness into the decision-making process of our particular campus. We realized that violence would remain a possibility until the underlying problem—the political role of the college—was faced directly. The constant potential for disturbance did not arise from the efforts of outside subversives as the trustees supposed but from a refusal by the authorities to face the causes for unrest, to recognize the legitimacy of the grievances, and to try to remove them. This view seemed to be understood by neither the administration nor the state officials who determine educational policy for the college. These officials seemed to believe that the campus would return to its educational enterprise when the disturbances were efficiently suppressed—even through the use of police power. Their attitude did not change despite the fact that violence increased rather than diminished under daily police surveillance.[8]

In such a situation, one does not remain pure and unpolitical by withdrawing from the fray; to do so is to take a political stand by default in support of the status quo. And so we refused to join the inactive group. We wanted to fight against the misuse of higher education and support the attempt to make it more flexible.

But how does a professor join the political battle for his campus, especially when his colleagues are in disagreement and confusion? The Academic Senate, comprised of the elected representatives of the faculty, had no legal power; the trustees ignored the deliberations of this body, and its rulings were easily overturned by administrative edict. Most of the remaining faculty organizations quietly folded under the pressure of the crisis; they offered no further suggestions or policies. Many professors returned passively or sullenly to their traditional, advisory role, recognizing their inability to determine the future of the campus. Some of us refused to give in so easily. If we could gain no hearing by using the traditional tactics of professors, we would try to strengthen our voices by using the tactics of employees. Instead of succumbing to the edicts of the administrative and legislative bodies, we turned to the teachers' union, the only professional

[8] For a description of this pattern see R. Stark, "Berkeley: Protest + Police = Riot." In McEvoy and Miller, *op. cit.*

organization which was still standing and willing to assert a faculty viewpoint. Those of us who joined the union saw our action as a step toward assuming the greater professional responsibility often asked of academicians. We wanted to take a role in formulating policy for higher education. In our view, as long as we were part of an educational system biased against specific public groups, we did not want to teach. And we would not accept the definition of education thrust upon us—a definition which suggested that we could and should do so.

There were many reasons for looking to the union. First, the union recognizes that decisions in higher education, as elsewhere, are made not abstractly but on the basis of political pressures. No other form of faculty association now exists which is willing to exert serious pressure for improvement of the educational system. And no other faculty organization exists which can defend beleaguered instructors once they are under attack from trustees and administration for demanding reforms. We learned about the necessity for an organization of workers when we discovered how little advantage our professional status gave us in negotiating with our employers. Paradoxically, then, it is through the workers' tactic of union organization that a professional view may be asserted in decisions on higher education.

Second, we joined the union because we wanted to work within the established and recognized forms of protest. Participation in a regularly sanctioned labor strike seemed a more reasonable form of protest than some more anarchistic or violent alternatives. We assumed that the right of workers to strike for better working conditions was already well accepted in America. We thought the community would certainly understand and respect this form of protest more easily than destructive demonstrations or guerrilla attacks. Although our action was widely publicized as radical, we saw the strategy as fairly conservative.

Ironically, this attempt to remain within established procedures brought the union members additional opprobrium. The union was accused of riding the student strike for selfish advantage. Technically, we could be accused of placing wage and hour grievances before the demand that the students receive a just hearing. But this strategy was required to gain the support of the San Francisco Labor Council. Without their support ours would be a wildcat strike. The council members were unwilling to support a strike for reform of higher education; but they would support one for more traditional issues: wages, hours, grievance procedures, and the like. In fact there was no difficulty in enumerating such a list; professors in the California State colleges teach longer hours for less salary than do professors in comparable institutions in other states. Though the union had long fought for these improvements, many faculty did not care enough about the matter to unionize until the student strike and the issues it raised became a serious problem. So this new enlarged union—grown from two hundred to four hundred members—reordered demands as the executives of the Labor Council suggested in order to gain strike sanction. Thus dependence on labor movement ties made us unable to focus publicly on our most crucial reasons for striking. Perhaps for this reason we never gained full support for our action from the surrounding community or from some of the campus community. Many hesitant or anxious colleagues seized upon this publicized discrepancy between idealism and self-interest to justify their inability to support and join us. In effect, then, we were caught between the campus and statewide administration, which granted us no voice but recognized the issue of the battle, and the unions, which provided us with political leverage with which to join the battle but would not recognize the issue.

The idea of unionization is often stoutly resisted by academicians for other reasons. The record of corruption, discrimination, and narrow self-interest does not inspire enthusiasm and idealism. Furthermore, no one likes the excesses to which principles of seniority may be carried in protecting and promoting incompetent workers. Thus many point to the possible dangers to intellectual standards if inept colleagues cannot be fired under the union rules. Of course this argument neglects consideration of the tenure system, which already exists. Under tenure rules it is almost impossible to dismiss anyone who has been permitted to pass the journeyman requirements. Or rather, it is almost impossible to bar any member from the "gentleman's club" once he has been elected. Although tenure is supposed to preserve professional standards, encourage academic freedom, and protect dissidents from political reprisals, it can also protect a number of incompetents who may be dishonest, careless, or lazy. Thus the worst aspects of tenure and of union seniority are quite similar.

If the negative aspects of unionism are no worse than what we already endure in academia, the positive effects are certainly far greater than what may be achieved with the narrow perspective of professionalism. Most professional organizations which extend beyond any particular college or university are organized around disciplines. Characteristically, such organizations are interested solely in the advancement of a science, an art, or a field of criticism. In this respect they are formed in the image of early scholarly societies devoted to some special inquiry; they attempt to offer a scholarly community to members rather than a political one. Thus, even the most political of these organizations—the American Association of University Professors, for example—fight for power at the departmental level. The focus is on hiring, firing, and determining curricula within that framework. These organizations are not concerned with the role of the university with respect to the broader society. Thus they differ very little from interdepartmental faculty organizations—academic senates, for example—within any particular school. If there is any difference, it is only that these latter organizations exist specifically at the pleasure of the administration or trustees. Thus they cannot provide the base from which to mount a serious and fundamental disagreement with authorities.

All of these professional organizations encourage the development of a false consciousness—in the strictest Marxian sense—among faculty. Because they focus upon the narrowly circumscribed power they do have in their professional world, participants in these organizations often fail to consider the range of powers which are denied them. Thus they confuse or overlook the distinction between their power to advise or consent and the power of the college/university governors to decide. Much of their political behavior is inappropriate or irrelevant, for they restrict their tactics against opponents to those which are useful among peers—but in a situation where they are not peers.

This paradox has remained unchallenged because most professionals do not define university administrations as sufficiently oppressive to deserve counterattack. In any case, they do not see the power of the administration as a direct threat to the power of the faculty. After all, faculty are safe inside their departmental tenure agreements, and they are also relatively protected by opportunities for mobility in their own disciplines. From these vantage points, professors do not see the system as so repressive that they are willing to chance the use of violence in order to make reforms. Most professional organizations thus base their policies on the assumption that the status quo in universities is relatively tolerable for the professors if not for their students. Of course some universities are more tolerable—and flexible —than others. Private institutions, such as Stanford and Columbia, have recently recognized the desirability of giving faculty and students a share in decision-making and have revised their structures accordingly. They are leaders in facing the problem of how to make reforms. But there are no signs of such a voluntary change from above in the California public system of higher education—in fact, the signs are quite the contrary—so that at this moment only unionization and consequent pressure from faculty seem practical means of bringing about change. And so we have turned to union organization to gain the power to press for recognition of our appropriate position in the system of higher education.

This book is the product of our commitment to the enterprise of higher education. We do not see the crisis at State as a unique event but rather as an emergent which is becoming almost typical in higher education today. And so we want to show how the educational and political issues appeared to us in that strike. We do not present elaborate social theory or technical scholarly research but our own experiences and interpretations as well as those of our colleagues in the union. We present this information to illuminate the question of what led professors to join the picket lines and of what may lead others to do the same in the future.

PART I

Part I describes San Francisco State College before and during the student-faculty strike. The essays set the scene and explain the circumstances of that strike from the perspective of faculty union members. In the first chapter, "Zen Basketball, Etc., at State," written long before the strike, Wilner presents an analysis of and explanation for the fact that SFSC had a national reputation as an exciting place to teach. This essay suggests why it was not surprising that this was the college where many faculty members went out on strike to support their students' demands for an education relevant to their lives and careers.

The remaining two chapters are autobiographical accounts written during the strike. We present them here to suggest how some of the faculty thought and acted before the strike and how they

12

PRELUDE AND
CHRONICLES

changed under the impact of the crisis. These personal experiences illustrate the sometimes painful process by which faculty members realized that they must drastically revise their philosophical and political views of education.

Both these accounts suggest that observation of the consequences of decisions made by the administration can lead to radicalization. Kahn-Hut describes how experiences in a commuter college bring into question elitist assumptions about proper educational standards and goals. At first, the growing intransigence of students seemed antithetical to proper education—as well as immature and unacceptable. But listening to the issues raised by the students forced a revision of this evaluation. She began to see the basic problem facing the campus as the intransigency of an unimaginative bureaucracy unwilling to recognize the political bias of the college program

13

rather than as the management of rebellious students. When estab-
lished authorities are themselves intransigent, there are no possibilities
for compromise. Under these circumstances, if you resist or criticize
authority any decision to oppose the status quo through untraditional
behavior is "radical."

The second account offers another example of the process
through which a faculty member lost faith in the campus administra-
tion. The turning point was the realization that authorities would
resort to violence to maintain their power to define the role of higher
education on the campus. Most of the dissident students engaged in
expressive acts: they demonstrated and were disobedient and disrup-
tive; but their behavior was largely dramatic rather than dangerous.
The authorities chose to interpret these activities as threatening serious
violence and so they summoned large numbers of police to campus.
After this response the serious violence began. Thus by defining the
situation as potentially dangerous, the administration in fact created
just what they feared might happen. As a result strong emotional
support developed for the students where only moderate sympathy
existed before. In this situation only one faculty organization—the
union—acted on the general faculty concern to keep bloodshed at a
minimum. And so the author became an active member in the union
and went on strike. She describes daily life while on strike and sug-
gests what some of the long-term positive benefits to campuses may be
from the new interdepartmental solidarity which can result from the
unionization of faculties.

CHAPTER 1

Zen Basketball, etc., at State[1]

Herbert Wilner

Of the more than eighteen thousand students now attending San Francisco State College, only a handful will join the Alumni Association after they graduate. Of the more than one thousand faculty members, most of whom teach here with a provincial pride of place, only a few would insist that San Francisco State should be the college of choice for their own children. Of the wealthy great-name families in the Bay Area who make financial contributions to the institutional life of the community, none contributes substantially to San Francisco State. They give generously, however, to the established empires, Stanford and the University of Cali-

[1] © 1967 by Esquire Incorporated. First published in *Esquire Magazine*.

fornia at Berkeley. In highway miles, San Francisco State lies almost
exactly between these two neighboring academic countries, and the
shadows they cast would have seemed large enough to keep the in-
between place forever in the shade.

But for a variety of reasons, many of them more nationally
important than the recent instant history of the college itself, SFSC
is worth looking at. It is, in fact, with peeps here and there in professional journals and even in the mass media, being looked at. There
is more to its picture than the present prominence of its ninety-four-
acre city campus as a second neighborhood for the hippies of Haight-
Ashbury who haven't yet dropped out. It might well be that SFSC's
newness, its lack of traditions, its unpredictable and generally older
streetcar students, its young faculty and its young come-and-go administrators, its compulsion to be anti-Establishment, its willingness
out of conflicting necessities to absorb and to improvise, it might be
that this unformed character is the source of its brash and eccentric
spirit. And it might be true that this spirit is peculiarly suited to a
noisy confrontation with some of the unanswered questions about the
new industry we call college education in America.

The necessities confronting SFSC are of essentially different
kinds, and they grind against each other like gears which were never
designed to mesh. In the first place, there is the monstrous bureaucracy
which presides over the state college system in California. It has so
many offices and officers, so many bureaus and boards and channels,
so many regulations and produces so many tons of mimeographed
material full of unreadable statistics and incomprehensible prose that
one has to believe there is a clerical factory here large enough to have
run the British Empire—Gilbert and Sullivan fashion—a century ago.
What is hard to believe is that all this Kafka machinery was designed
to reach the individual student who comes to class at SFSC—bearded,
long-haired, or plain—and demands nothing more complicated of his
education than that it should interest him and mean something. If it
doesn't, he may drop the particular course. If he drops enough of
them, he drops out. The clerks and computers of the college's own
huge bureaucracy will record his vanishing. The figure will be for-
warded to the higher stations of the bureaucracy off campus. Added
to other such figures, it will finally issue forth as another unreadable
document.

To expect SFSC, which is at its new campus a child of thirteen years, to emerge from the bureaucratic maze which governs the seventeen other state colleges, as well as itself, into an identifiable character and spirit is like asking of a State Department staff member that he speak in his own voice. But it has happened. It has been going on steadily for the ten years I have taught at SFSC, and it points to the other necessity which the college confronts: an intense desire to make its own destiny in its own character and by its own spirit, the bureaucrats be damned. (But when you damn them openly, the gears of the opposing necessities grind with a public noise, as they did last fall when several members of the English Department joined in a reading on campus of a published poem banned by the San Francisco police for being obscene, the reading making local headlines which prompted one member of the off-campus governing boards to suggest that proposed faculty raises had something to do, after all, with proper faculty behavior.) The character and spirit of the college cannot be tagged in a phrase, for there is no long-lasting tradition with which to associate it. But it certainly has something to do with San Francisco itself, and it is surely affected by the life-entangled histories the students bring with them to the campus.

A glance at the campus itself returns something unmistakably and unimpressively institutional. Its ninety-four acres are located on what used to be sand dunes in the southwestern corner of the city. It is not far from the zoo, the Pacific, an artificial lake, and a municipal golf course. It is bordered on two of its sides by the nests of modern housing projects. Its own twenty or so new buildings, if you are sensitive to architecture, are offensively unimagined. On the other hand, they might be regarded as unfortunately suited to the traditionless spirit of the place. They are all so ruthlessly functional, so arrogantly plain, so insistently rectangular or square, so regularly banded or punched with windows that it is easy to believe they all arrived on the same day in huge cartons marked Easy-to-Assemble New Campus. Not one of the buildings bears a personal name. They are all designated by the faculties and subjects they house—Humanities, Natural Sciences, Education, Psychology—as if that too had been stamped on the original cartons. They give off a timid quality of being subject to recall, as if the cartons might be hauled out again, the buildings recrated, and the whole campus shipped back to the manufacturer.

But if one is disposed to look at the brighter side of his own metaphors, he can pretend the buildings were designed to make the human condition prevail over the masonry which houses it.

The most telling feature of the physical arrangement doesn't belong to the college. It is the municipal streetcar marked "M" which passes one of the college's corners on a main artery of the city's north-south traffic. For SFSC—despite its two new Residence Halls on campus, which house eight hundred overprotected students—is essentially a streetcar college, As such, it shares some of the characteristics of similar institutions throughout the country: a higher average age for its students; a full program of evening courses; part-time jobs in the city for most of its students; a sense of personal connection with the college that is limited for many of its students to individual professors and a particular department; a general lack of interest in the college's sensibly modest athletic programs.

Above all, SFSC's identity as a streetcar college ignores the idea of the campus as a fortress, or a retreat. By way of that overcrowded "M" car, or the student's own auto, some of the city's living implications are brought to the college, and some part of the college is returned to the city. More than anything else, this transportation accounts for the living day working its influence upon the general academic intention.

I came to SFSC's English Department and Creative Writing Program after two years of teaching at Yale. My students there were predictably male, predictably between eighteen and twenty-four, most of them predictably bright, some eager but most of them casual, some brilliant and none stupid. None ignorant either, unless of life itself. But how could it have been otherwise at Yale, eleven and twelve years ago in the stifled yawn of the declining Eisenhower days? For me it was not good basic training for what lay ahead at SFSC in my government-issue, gray-metal office.

Students I recall from those first years come back to my mind with more associations than a teacher ordinarily has for students. They were, indeed, too stamped by life to bear the single stamp of "student."

I remember a young man in his twenties, Irish-handsome, slow, huge, expressionless. He never spoke in class. He never kept the appointments I made to speak with him about his papers, which were marked by tortured insights wandering in a confused prose. Then one day he appeared in my office to tell me he was dropping out, leaving for another state. He was a drug addict, and the stuff had become too easy for him to obtain in San Francisco. He went on to talk for a long time in a flat voice about his life, and though he occasionally smiled, it was as involuntary as eye-blinking. He told me of his boyhood, of moving with his Okie parents up and down the agricultural valleys of California. They were migrant laborers, and often, to make him steal for them, they beat him with lumber.

I remember a retired rear admiral from Virginia who had once published a book on semantics. He was back at the college to work for an M.A., and whenever I passed him in the crowded corridors— my slumped shoulders and his ramrod back—he would always brighten and call me "Suh." He had been in all the bloody sea battles of the Pacific, but he was now most intent on learning why modern poets weren't uplifting, like Longfellow and Whittier. I remember the graduate student who had his B.A. from Harvard. He was an expert sailor and had once crossed the Atlantic in a small boat with a single companion. He wanted to work out an arrangement about his grade, for he was not going to complete the semester. He was joining the crew of *Everyman*, the small boat which sailed in protest into the restricted waters of the Pacific where the United States was testing atomic devices.

There was the woman who hated cities and built her own house on a ranch she ran sixty miles from the city. She traveled that distance to classes through the two years of completing her M.A. She was an extraordinary poet. There was a woman in her thirties whose ineptness required that I discourage her from taking any more courses in writing. She begged that she be allowed to, the writing meant a great deal to her, it was a consolation. She was sick; she had cancer. I remember a young woman with an oddly passionate desire to be a kindergarten teacher. She pleaded with me for a passing grade in freshman English, which she knew she hadn't earned. "I love children," she cried. "I'd be such a good teacher for them."

I remember a former carpenter and a former policeman. They were both unhappy with the way of life provided by their work, and both of them became superior students partly because they had done that work and knew that life. And I remember housewives, so many housewives who, with their children in school, were coming back, as freshmen or graduate students, to resume their own formal educations. For many of them it was nothing more than a concealed therapy, but some of them chased after their studies with fire in their eyes. There weren't enough available hours of philosophy and English and history to make even the slightest dent in all the piled-up years of dishes and diapers.

At SFSC, then, many of my students were unpredictably more than students, and in their persons they raised some of the unanswered questions about college education in America. In a figuratively theoretical sense the questions might be said to have begun as soon as the School of Business at Harvard began enrolling more majors than its Departments of Greek and Latin. The theoretical side of the questions lives today in the millions of students attending colleges and universities, the millions upon millions who are going to attend them. What are they to be taught? If business is acceptable at Harvard, why shouldn't creative writing, for instance, be acceptable at SFSC? And don't we today know so much in our multiplied fields that we can't even begin to teach a significant part of it? What part, then, shall we teach? Should the student's sense of immediate relevance prevail over his professor's sense of history? How much history? If Shakespeare, for example, had gone to Oxford, he would not have had to study Shakespeare; but today the study of Shakespeare criticism is a career in itself. What, anyway, does scholarship hope for? Our students know the Germans were heroes at it, but they also know it finally counted for nothing.

For the individual faculty member at SFSC the theoretical nature of the questions is reviewed, assessed, and argued about in endless committees. His mailbox is stuffed every day with mimeograph jargon about where we are now. If, after years of it, he concludes "Nowhere," he learns to speed-read or ignore. His wastebasket is full a minute after he enters his office. Not so easy to discard are the daily life-entangled questions which need to be answered on the spot.

Should the earnest young woman who has always wanted to be a kindergarten teacher and who is probably marvelous with children be expelled from the college because she cannot pass her required composition courses, no matter how many times she repeats them? What does she have to write as a kindergarten teacher? Should you

stretch your sense of permissible allowance for the more than competent and mature man who felt compelled to leave in the middle of
the semester to sail into atomic test waters as his part in his own sense
of what he was being educated for? And if you do that, can you at
the same time fail the incompetent student in the same class who
faithfully attended all the meetings of the course? Can you set aside
your "academic integrity" for a more human feeling and permit the
woman who has cancer to continue in creative writing courses she
thinks she needs to have? And if you do that, can you deny your permission to an equally incompetent student who is not sick?

The questions and their implications are hard ones, and they
are not unique to SFSC alone. The faculty response, however, generally is. I know very few colleagues here who would step aside of the
entanglement with the aid of the always available opener: "The rules
of the college require. . . ." They respond rather to these new varie-
ties of academic dilemmas with an almost sloppy intuition for that
judgment which does not separate the student's human context from
his classroom predicaments.

"The faculty here is much less rigid than any other one I have
been associated with or know of," says the newly appointed president
of SFSC, John Summerskill. A clinical psychologist in his early forties
who came to the college from Cornell University, where he had been
vice-president, he was given an early opportunity to act in the spirit
he commends. Students staged a boycott against the college's dining
facilities, arguing the food was poor and the prices excessive. President
Summerskill permitted a student-hired caterer's truck to drive on campus and park before the entrance to the cafeteria.

How a faculty as large as SFSC's keeps free of academic
rigidity is difficult to determine. It certainly has something to do with
the great number of students whose lives have been and are deeply
entangled with more than their formal education. It also has something to do with the fact that the college's programs in creative work,
in music, art, film, and drama, as well as in writing, are dispropor-
tionately large and honored. The work between faculty and students
in such programs encourages informality as well as individuality.
By their nature such programs not only endorse but seek out faculty
whose professional work in the field is at least as important as its
possession of the proper academic calling cards. When Kay Boyle and

Wright Morris, for instance, shared their SFSC office, it was surely a unique event in the world's history of higher education. There was not a single college degree between them, but between them as eminent authors were the more than fifty books they have written. Mr. Morris's own work is the subject of several doctoral dissertations and a full-length book. Miss Boyle's work has been reprinted in critical editions, and serious studies of her place in American literary history are also underway.

The more conventional scholars of the faculty are at least aware of the college's creative emphasis. Of those who hold Ph.D.'s —and they constitute a significant majority of the full-time faculty— there aren't many among them who are possessed by their subject at the expense of possessing it, who have but one scholarly idea in their heads and but one string on their fiddles for sounding it. I can't imagine the most academically square of my colleagues in the English Department at SFSC introducing himself to a newcomer by saying, "I'm a Tennysonian. What are you?" A department joke is what he would be. But this is the way I was greeted by a senior member of the English Department at the midwestern university where I first began to teach.

The most contributing influence upon the college, of course, is San Francisco itself. In the most practical sense, it's as plain as bread and butter. The city has pulling power, for faculty and students alike. The professor who has recently come here hasn't chosen the college because of its inadequate salaries, its deplorable office conditions, its so-so library, or his twelve-hour teaching load. Nor has he come entirely because his particular department is a strong one and getting better or because of the college's vague but growing reputation as an exciting place. Put the college back in its cartons and transfer it to any of the other seventeen sites of the California State colleges, and the new faculty man might not come at all. So, too, for many of its students, especially those who have come from out of state. They may well have decided for San Francisco first and the college afterward. This is especially true for the student who thinks of himself as "creative." The older Beat show, transformed now into the mammoth Haight-Ashbury hippie show, has put San Francisco before the country's young as the great Bohemian grove.

The actual living relationship between the city and the college is a continuously subtle, occasionally dramatic affair. Some part of both conditions were involved in that reading on campus by faculty members of the allegedly obscene poem.

A local poet named Lenore Kandel, who has no affiliation with the college, had written a poem of about a hundred fifty lines which she entitled *The Love Book*. It was locally published and was being sold in the Psychedelic Bookshop on Haight Street. Into the store strolled two of the city's finest: plainclothesmen with the sober duties of leading San Francisco citizens toward cleaner living through cleaner reading. The Kandel poem describes the act, actions, and cosmological meanings of sexual intercourse without so much as a single traceable literary debt to Victorian circumlocutions. It is, in fact, very much in the language which the two policemen must have heard all through their adolescence. But the written word is something else again, and reading as they browsed they indignantly seized the books without further to-do. Warrants of arrest were issued to a co-owner and clerk of the bookshop for violation of the state's obscenity laws.

The story made the front pages of San Francisco's two newspapers. Immediately, voluntarily, and, as it turned out, effectively, six members of SFSC's English Department involved themselves. Four of the six have Ph.D.'s; three of them have published at least one volume of their own poetry. A spokesman for the faculty group announced to the press that they would read the entire poem on campus in the Gallery Lounge, a single-room building about the size of half a basketball court. It once housed the college bookstore but is used now for most of the campus readings of the Poetry Center and as an art gallery.

The rear admiral's Longfellow could not have drawn a fuller house. Every chair was occupied; every foot of floor space had feet in it. Not everyone who jammed his way into the building was a student or faculty member. There were San Francisco poets, there were costumed hippies, there were curious citizens, and there were newspaper reporters and TV men who came close to strangling and maiming a part of the audience as they dragged their cables and cameras. The room is windowless, and smoking is permitted. The reading, when it got under way, proceeded in smog.

Those who came for a show were not prepared, perhaps, for

the show they got. James Schevill, then director of the Poetry Center of the college, a nationally known poet, professor, and biographer of Sherwood Anderson, introduced the proceedings with a few words. Gray-haired, quiet of voice, Mr. Schevill referred to the poem as a celebration of love and to the occasion of the public reading as an academic response against the authoritarian challenge to write and to publish and to read. His colleagues thereupon shared the reading of the poem, each coming to the microphone in solemn professorial dignity, each reading about thirty lines before returning to his seat and yielding to another reader. There was an almost religious quality to so ceremonious a reading. More important than the air of grandeur, with which the poem was thus invested, was the effect, given the nature of what was being read, upon the audience. There was no self-conscious tittering; there was no embarrassed smiling. If anything, the scene, in retrospect—with its TV equipment, its male professors liturgically pronouncing the unmentionable words which express a female's work and joy in love-making, its audience of hundreds so massively and uniformly solemn—the scene recalled seems a satire against the natural, though the miracle of the natural is what the poem so pretentiously celebrates.

The event speaks of something central to the existence of the college in San Francisco. In a larger or more truly cosmopolitan city, the event, had it taken place at all, would have been less noticeable. In a smaller city or town which is organized around a large university or small college, the academic administration would have been under pressure to suppress the faculty involvement. San Francisco is unique in being a city provincial enough to have its police high-handedly seize a poem, sophisticated enough to have the chief of police know better than to interfere with the campus reading of the seized poem, provincial enough again to make a great public hoopla out of the whole scene, and finally compact enough to make the city's life a moral concern of the college and the raised voice of the campus a concern of City Hall and Nob Hill, as well as Haight-Ashbury.

Thus those connected with SFSC enjoy a richer community status than the one ordinarily reserved for an American city large enough to justify a streetcar college. A decal in the rear window of the student's car which says SFSC means more for him in San Francisco than CCNY does in New York. At the same time both students and faculty do live in an urban area here which is large enough and rich enough in its resources to shut the college out of their lives when they choose to. They can have their cake and eat it too. Free of Berkeley's overheated academic environment and of Stanford's withdrawal into lushness in proper Palo Alto, the community of SFSC is capable of willing itself into and out of local conspicuousness.

Sometimes the stage gets larger than the local one. This happened recently when a handful of the college's students decided to do something about a curriculum they found to be too often uninteresting and irrelevant. Out of a few improvisations grew a large program of courses which they themselves loosely organized and administered. It was sponsored by the Associated Students, a student organization with elected officers and in charge of a budget, collected from student fees, which is close to $450,000. The new program was called the Experimental College and at the time was studied by students and administrators throughout the country.

The students began with a simple assumption: what the college offers as courses does not exhaust the possibilities. What if the student wants to study Zen but the college insists on Plato? Surrealism in American literature instead of realism? What if the student finds the text in sociology a bore and prefers to learn by some form of work in the society itself? What if he is genuinely tired of the routine of hopping from subject to subject in fifty-minute classroom doses? What if he is tired of term papers and final exams as the only way of recording who he is and what he has achieved in relation to the studied subject?

If the assumptions of a few students about the curriculum were simple, their program of correction was equally uncomplicated. They would offer their own courses, let students enroll in them as they will. The problem of which courses and what teachers was not forbidding. The students were not out to create an establishment of their own against the establishment of the college they questioned. Anyone could teach whatever he chose to. It was all voluntary. There was neither pay for the teacher nor credit for the student. If a few interested faculty members offered their time, so much the better. (As many as forty eventually did, for what professor hasn't idly dreamed of the one course he'd *really* like to teach if he could shake loose of the restrictions of his department and college?) Students themselves taught, and people not connected with the college taught also, showing, if nothing else, that the impulse to teach is hidden in all of us. If the amateur teacher proved to be a bust or if the course he invented was a dud, the students who had "enrolled" stopped attending.

But the students who were instrumental in shaping the Experimental College immediately accomplished something more real and lasting than the educational grab bag itself. With political astuteness, they had foreseen that they would. What could have been more designed to impress an already liberal and impressionable faculty and administration than the actively expressed concern of their own students for the college's curriculum of study? Cynthia Nixon, a senior majoring in English, wife of the former president of the Associated Students, was the student principally involved in shaping the Experimental College. She makes very plain what she had in mind: "to influence the college itself so there wouldn't be any necessity for an experimental college in the form that we now have it."

As a demonstration of how well they knew what they were after, the Experimental College, in its second semester of operation, with funds supplied by the Associated Students, hired Paul Goodman to teach. He met with students in discussion workshops, he met with them in groups in their homes, he talked with them at lunch in the cafeteria, he got in arguments with Mrs. Nixon, who has a hard mind of her own and generally disagreed with him, he lectured to the college at large, he appeared on local TV programs. He raised his own Goodman furor about the absurdities of our educational traditions. The atmosphere, then, was deliberately charged for educational revision in the form of curricular changes.

By its second year of operation, the Experimental College had succeeded in enlisting formal support from the administration and the faculty. Professors teaching in the program, with the approval of their departments and deans, could now offer specific courses for which the enrolled students received credit. In the last academic year the Experimental College offered approximately seventy courses each semester, some few of which were for official college credit. Approximately twelve hundred students were enrolled, and the Associated Students allotted $23,000 to the program's operating costs. The courses offered ranged from the respectably offbeat (Job and Faust; the Kennedy assassination), to the subjectless (transcendental deep meditation; seminar in nonverbal activity), to plain fun and games

(Zen basketball). One might now fairly say of the program that it was and is a lost battle which may have gone a long way toward scoring heavily in a continuous war.

What was won has many manifestations, and if they are not all directly traceable to the Experimental College—which was, after all, made possible in the first place by the eccentric character of a college which permitted it, provided rooms for it, and then encouraged it—they all partake of that program's desire for experiment and change.

The college appointed John Sheedy of its English Department to the new office of dean of undergraduate study. He is determined, through college channels, to change the curriculum required of all lower classmen, which for so many years now has remained fundamentally unaltered. For so many students who have been stuck with it, it is the same old high school stuff. Mr. Sheedy argues for a curriculum of required study which offers "defensible alternatives." He is aware that the key word for many students is "relevance" and that they want a primary involvement to be the basic assumption of their education. He is also sympathetic to the students who have on their own begun a work-study program which involves them in San Francisco neighborhoods as tutors, counselors, program directors, and who want an interdisciplinary major which will provide them with college credit for their field work.

President Summerskill is also bent on some changes, and he proposes the possibility of an official institute in the college for experimental studies. Last spring, stirred by student concern and activities, the college canceled classes for a two-day conference in which faculty and students exchanged views on curriculum, student participation in the machinery of academic affairs, and the relationship of the college to community and national issues.

What was most importantly won by the handful of students who were most active in making the Experimental College was the demonstrated evidence that students can be instrumental in effecting changes in matters over which they have no official control.

What was lost was the Experimental College itself, at least as it currently operates. Cynthia Nixon flatly acknowledges this defeat. "Too much was tried for too soon. The program of study lacked intellectual discipline. The hippies took it over. Though they aren't antiintellectual, they're antiacademic." She believes the program needs to be cut back in order to improve its teaching and intellectual content. It needs, most of all, to appeal to the "straight" student, the one not affiliated with the hippies or the activists, the one merely committed to the college department in which he studies.

Hippie, activist, and straight: those are the tags which identify the commitments and styles of the students at SFSC. The difference between the hippie and the activist is more than a matter of clothes, hair length, beards, and drugs. A long-haired and bearded male who smokes pot and has had a few trips with LSD is an activist and not a hippie as long as he believes and participates in student political action for the purpose of effecting change. The hippie at SFSC, on the other hand, will ordinarily have had some experience with drugs, but he needn't, though he often does, make a uniform of his hair and clothes. The essential difference between him and the activist is that he disdains political action, which can only end by emulating the establishment itself. He eschews group power, prefers feeling to knowing, emphasizes the verb *be,* arguing from it that he already is what he wants to become. Turning his back on campus politics and action, he identifies himself with the unifying principles of art and the esthetic. If he is not himself endowed with the gift to create, he will at least make an artful creation of his life. Our ordinary associations with ideas of success and failure are meaningless to him.

The straight students, who by far constitute the majority at the college, are most simply understood as being neither hippie nor activist. They take what the college dishes out, and though they may grumble about it, they go on with their work, get their grades, their degrees, and begin their careers. But even the straight student at SFSC ordinarily comes to the campus with more to his life and intentions than the word *student* implies. The demands he may make upon his individual professors, though they do not issue from party platforms, often partake of the spirit of those platforms. They too speak for more continuity between the living day and the academic intention.

When the straights turned their backs on the Experimental College, they left it clear for the hippies to contend with the activists in what the program of courses was to be and how the courses themselves were to be conducted. From the assumptions by which the Experimental College was created by a few activists, the doors had to

be left open to any possible course taught by any volunteering instructor. But a seminar in silence, for instance, taught by a hippie and
well attended by his followers, was far from what Cynthia Nixon and
others must have had in mind when they wanted the students themselves to hurl the challenge at what they considered the antiintellectual
prejudices of some of the college's own departments of study. But any
rigorous attempts by those who had loosely organized the Experimental
College toward a firmer structure would have left them open to the
charge of creating an establishment of their own.

The characterizing will up and down the college is toward
anti-Establishment behavior. The college administration tangles with
the bureaucracy above it, in the offices of the government in Sacramento, or in those of the state college system in Los Angeles. The
faculty, through its Academic Senate and its individual professors,
tangles with its own administration. The students, at least a significantly vociferous number, are happy to take on the administration, or
the faculty, or both.

The question raised by this spirit to the point of dilemma is
obvious: to be merely against the Establishment makes for consoling
noises and self-congratulation; to have nothing clearly in mind that
would substitute for the Establishment's pills and doses merely certifies
the incurable nature of everyone's confusion. It can even exalt confusion to a form of significant excitement and then mistake mere
excitement as a form of meaningful education.

After all that is obvious is seen and said, one can say about
SFSC—as about so much else in the California version of American
life, even San Francisco style—that those very noises and colors by
which it makes itself a national item are also the very qualities by
which it ought to be suspect, at least unto itself. Improvisation can be
curative and restoring. It can be lamentable too. How many degrees
are there, after all, on the scale of differences among such monumental
improvisations as a mediocre actor and soft-sell TV salesman as
governor, a song-and-dance man as senator, and the little thing of a
so-called college class in which students are only required to contem-
plate each other silently through the gaze of love and ignorance?

No one but the stuffiest traditionalist can believe today that he
has the final answers for what ought to be taught at a college, and
how. After the concentration camps, after atom bombs, during Viet-

nam and our reasonable fears of instant annihilation, humanism itself, the source of all we teach, appears bankrupt. It is, therefore, to the point for a college to create a furor about what it teaches and how. It is especially accurate when the college, out of its streetcar habit of life entanglement, concedes to the students themselves a significant hearing in the expectation of a sensible voice. But that, too, needs a second look, for it is easy to confuse respect for students with the finally disrespectful wish to be "with it," to escape the student accusation of being square or straight or hooked, to score points with the younger generation for immediate satisfactions.

There is, for example, the chain of events which followed upon the dramatic campus reading of *The Love Book*. It brought a few of the college professors in more intimate touch with hippies who had nothing to do with the college. Through the naturalness of fellow-feeling on the part of those involved in a shared cause, some of the profs and some of the hippies were able to keep alive for some days afterward what we have taken to calling a "dialogue." Out of this context something emerged that was to be called the Happening House. Its main intention was to sponsor dialogue in the most informal of ways between professors of the college and "leaders" among the hippies, and just ordinary hippies, and any other interested and potentially contributing citizen. The sessions were to take place off campus. About forty faculty members volunteered their time; President Summerskill endorsed it with his blessings, though SFSC had no money to give.

Because this, too, is such a loosely structured arrangement, it is not easy for an outsider to tell what it is all about. Perhaps it assumes that in a dialogue between sympathetic professors who cannot finally keep themselves from being learned, and hippies who cannot keep from being coolly resistant and lovingly rebellious, something meaningful to the visions and experience of both styles would "happen." But surely some of the hippies must have more slyly interpreted the encounters: when you drop out, the profs will chase you. Some of them are parental and some of them want in with our establishment as well as their own.

Tenuous as it is, Happening House is nevertheless an attempt at a more formal connection between Haight-Ashbury and the campus than has heretofore existed. It takes cognizance of that connecting streetcar between the two neighborhoods. It elaborates upon what was already there between the college and the hippies in the biweekly readings of poetry and fiction at the I and Thou coffee shop on Haight Street. The owner of the shop was a former student and part-time instructor at the college, the manager of the readings was a senior in the Creative Writing Program, and some of the college's students and faculty were among the readers.

Nothing could come more generously from the academic world to the world of Haight-Ashbury than Happening House. It gives away the time and energy of professors who teach, write, and raise families. But the generosity itself commits the two worlds to mutually held condescensions. Even if the prof sees himself as hippie, even if he takes LSD trips, votes for or practices whatever is meant by free love, at the end of the month he draws a state paycheck. Most of the hippies and the profs are thus bound to the same old speculations of the poor and the rich about who are the truly poor and who the truly rich. It is also sadly true today that the outsider cannot touch anything in Haight-Ashbury but that he touches a national product as well as people. The neighborhood is overrun not only with gaping tourists, and not only with reporters and photographers, but with graduate students working on theses in sociology, psychology, anthropology. Add now the SFSC professors who believe in the happening of a dialogue.

The student activists are also worth a second look. They disdain the hippie passivity implicit in dropout; and they, by contrast, labor like revolutionists at bringing off the changes they want. Mr. James Nixon estimated that he gave between seventy to eighty hours a week to his job as president of the Associated Students. He admitted ruefully that it had been a long while since he had the time to study from books, but then he would have you understand that books and library are but one of the roads to educational experience. At some universities there is great concern about football players who may not be attending classes. At SFSC one needs to be concerned that the students most heatedly and seriously concerned with education haven't the time for their own education, at least not the book and library and classroom end of it.

No one who has been at SFSC for the past ten years can truly expect of the place that it will settle for the quiet shade between Stanford and Berkeley. Sometimes, in exhaustion, in an impulse for resolution and order, a faculty member begins to long for it: a class, a library, and just plain students. At optimistic moments one even thinks it might finally come to pass. The growing reputation of the college has attracted new faculty, many of whom come four-square with Ivy League Ph.D.'s. They are already beginning to raise their voice for the more conventional possibilities. But then I, at least, find myself trapped into arguing against what I long for. I tell myself that it is in the nature of things for the beast to be the kind of beast it is. Who would argue neck surgery for the giraffe? Within tolerable limits, then, better a first-rate and original eccentricity at San Francisco State than a third-rate imitation of one of its traditional neighbors at Berkeley and Stanford.

Of course, in a resignation to final exhaustion, a faculty member today can fold his arms across his chest and wait. The Grade-B governor's movie started by Ronnie Reagan—with its on-again and off-again budget cuts, its tuition proposals for the state colleges as well as the university, its unbearable air of Grade-B sincerity disguising cynical political intentions—this old movie rerun may finally quiet the college. For the first time, despite the pulling power of San Francisco, there is difficulty in recruiting faculty. Perhaps, by the time Reagan is done, the buildings of the campus will really be put back into their cartons and returned to the manufacturer. One can then stand at the corner where the streetcar stops and point to the place where the strange college used to be that was once worth a look.

CHAPTER 2

Going Radical

Rachel Kahn-Hut

𝄢𝄢𝄢𝄢𝄢𝄢𝄢𝄢𝄢𝄢𝄢𝄢𝄢𝄢𝄢𝄢𝄢𝄢𝄢𝄢

The alarm rang at 6:30 A.M. In the past that ring meant that I must go to campus to teach my eight o'clock class. This time it meant going to campus to stop others from teaching their classes. In between these two events I had come to define striking and picketing as professional behavior. And I had learned what Max Weber meant when he said: "In a sense, successful political action is always the 'art of the possible.' Nonetheless, the possible is often reached only by striving to attain the impossible that lies beyond it."[1]

I arrived at State after studying for ten years in "elite" colleges which were often regarded as intellectual oases in the midst of their

---

[1] M. Weber, *The Methodology of the Social Sciences* (New York: Free Press, 1949), pp. 23–24.

33

surroundings. State was my first experience in a community-centered commuter college. At that time I accepted without question the ivory-tower image of the university where education and the development of knowledge were free of political influence. In this perspective the university provides a setting where undergraduate years offer a moratorium from the pressures of the practical world, where one is allowed to explore new ideas, meet new people, and undertake new experiences.

The comparison of State with the elite schools I knew was a disappointment. The silent majority who set the tone of the classes seemed either dull or lazy. But in time I realized that this evaluation was not necessarily just; rather, these students were not interested in the kind of education I prized. Traditional liberal education requires time, energy, and security, advantages which San Francisco State students generally do not have. College for them is not a moratorium from life; it is the time to develop the tools and techniques required for an occupation, the time to develop the basis for social mobility. What happens in these four years can determine their future life styles. It is not surprising that such students do not give a very high priority to the notion of four years of intellectual development for its own sake.

But even for their purposes, the students clearly showed deficiencies in training. I was horrified to discover that juniors and seniors had no idea what it meant to discipline their thinking. One day a student said, after reading some works of Freud and G. H. Mead, "Mead wouldn't like Freud." He then relaxed with the sigh of a job well done and the pleasure of a real sense of accomplishment shining on his face. I allowed that he was probably right but asked him why he thought so. As a response I received a look of pure fury. "Dirty pool," it seemed to say. "I had an insight and you say 'not enough'; that's unfair." I understood such limitations better when I discovered that many students had never written an essay exam or a term paper during their college career. Inevitably, poor training is a fact of life in a system where a professor teaches four classes per semester, where he may have fifty students in a class, and where he must read all student assignments without assistance. In these circumstances the teachers have neither the time nor the facilities to provide a well-supervised education. I began to think that the problem was not that students were unwilling to learn but rather that they were short-changed by the system of education we offered them.

While the students may have been unresponsive to theoretical questions raised in class, they were alert to issues concerning the effect of the larger society on the college. One of the most familiar features near the center of the campus was the Free Speech Platform, where a variety of speakers addressed ever-changing crowds. The speakers rarely addressed matters which concerned me, but rather they demanded ROTC off campus, no recruiters from the military-industrial complex, no more racism. The complaints were presented very emotionally and often seemed quite juvenile; the speakers were very determined to force their views upon others. I had little sympathy; I felt that living in the world which might result from their assumption of power would be little better than living under the current establishment.

When I heard that there was to be a student strike on November 6, I assumed it would not differ from previous strikes and rallies and paid scant attention. I cannot remember exactly what my intentions were about honoring the strike, but as it happened, my intentions were irrelevant. My class did not meet because the campus was closed by administrative edict. A closed campus, in this case, meant that all academic business came to a halt when the doors to buildings were chained shut, locked, or blocked by policemen. I was irritated by this disruption of campus life. I blamed both the administration and the students, but primarily the latter.

The student demands (see the Appendix)', especially the one for an open enrollment policy, seemed to attack the basis of a system which I thought valuable. How could a college take in every applicant, no matter how ill qualified? Even those demands which seemed potentially reasonable, such as the establishment of an ethnic studies department, were unreasonable when associated with the demand for immediate implementation. When such immediate action was not forthcoming, the students were willing to turn to disruptive tactics which did not fit my definition of a proper strike. I had no interest in participating.

But I had no control over the matter. Before long our days fell into a pattern in which the mornings were spent waiting for the daily confrontation, and the afternoons were spent trying to calm our nerves in order to return to work. Never before had I watched

a battle between citizens and police. Nor had I ever heard crowds
scream in fear and hatred or heard the "thonk" of clubs against
bodies. At this time I even developed a previously unneeded talent; I
could pick out the numerous plainclothes policemen infiltrating the
campus.

The campus was so unsettled that I could not meet my class
again until after Thanksgiving, three weeks after the disruption began. At that time I was teaching in a neighborhood church—the first
of a variety of off-campus locations used during the next two months.
An informal group on campus contacted the nearby churches, and
many of them allowed us to hold classes on their premises. But the
requests from professors for classrooms were greater than anticipated,
and one by one the churches, unable to cope with the influx, asked
us to leave. (My class moved so often in the following months that
one student referred to it as "the oldest reliable traveling educational
crap game.") I cannot speak for the other instructors, but I made
these first arrangements less for political reasons than to reestablish
some regular pattern of educational activity in a situation which was
continually and unexpectedly changing.

One general response to the unsettled conditions on campus
was the attempt to solve problems through discussion in a series of
formal and informal meetings among and between faculty and student
organizations. The first general faculty meeting was announced for
November 12, a week after the student strike began. There was no sign
at that time that the momentum of the strike would abate. Therefore,
some positive action to resolve the conflict was required of either the
faculty or the administration. For a week the faculty remained in almost continuous session, but it soon became clear that answers and
solutions would not come from this body. Leaders with answers are
hard to find among people who are usually contemplative and analytic rather than decisive. Practiced in the appreciation of various
points of view, we were swayed by a good speech and applauded almost any well-presented position. The only consistency shown by the
collective faculty was their resistance to those few who were calling
for a strike.

These meetings often included more than five hundred participants, too large a group to organize effectively. And so we broke into
departmental caucuses in the hope that concrete proposals would

emerge from these smaller groups. But these meetings produced only very general resolutions affirming the mood of crisis on the campus and demanding that someone find positive solutions. A few resolutions did present clear suggestions, but these were so broad—calling for a radical redefinition of the entire enterprise through a campus constitutional convention, for example—that they would take a long time to implement. Thus they provided no solution to the immediate problems. (At that time, few of us imagined the disruption of the school would become so serious that we would come to consider just such fundamental changes in the organization as essential.)

Our general faculty and departmental meetings were supplemented by informal, schoolwide meetings with students. Under constantly changing circumstances meetings were often planned on such short notice that they had to be announced through the mass media. Faculty and even departmental meeting schedules were broadcast by radio and television stations, and the city newspapers noted the resumption of classes. The cooperation of the media was one sign of the tie between campus and community, of the involvement of the whole Bay Area in what was happening on the campus. The students came to these meetings to find out what they assumed the faculty meetings had accomplished; I and other faculty went to find out what the students were doing and what position the nonactivist majority was developing, and to ask what any of the student groups considered the appropriate faculty role in their strike. "Just follow the black students and accept their demands as legitimate" was the dominant response. I was looking for leadership, but I was certainly unwilling to follow without question or to trust the students whom I saw as so intransigent.

We recessed all meetings on November 18, the day the state college Board of Trustees met in Los Angeles. Members of our Academic Senate and student representatives from several of the state colleges attended that meeting. The next day our representatives presented reports to the faculty. The speakers agreed that the trustees had shown no intention of recognizing the mass of dissatisfied students —or faculty—as responsible individuals whose point of view should be considered when making decisions for the campus.

I finally began to develop an appreciation for the students' perspective on their problems in facing the established authorities.

The trustees treated both the faculty and the student representatives in the same manner—autocratically. At their meetings the trustees passed a resolution forbidding any negotiations between themselves and the faculty. By that act, they obliterated any political distinction between us and the students. In that case disagreements between us could only be bickerings among the dispossessed. And so the groundwork for a coalition between students and faculty was laid.

Later that same day, the college president, Robert Smith, addressed us and requested that we accept the trustees' ultimatum and return to our regular teaching schedule. For many of us it seemed impossible to acquiesce. As a practical problem, we could expect continued resistance from a large group of students, so that any attempt to reestablish normal schedules would only create the context for more violence. By asking us to ignore this fact, the only legitimate authority, Smith, seemed to have abdicated his position of leadership. We were left facing a threatened acceleration of violence from the students and complete indifference from the trustees. If solutions were to be found, we would have to find them ourselves.

At this crucial moment a faculty member suggested that we hold a convocation of administrators, faculty, and students. The convocation was to provide an arena in which we could speak together and reestablish some trust and understanding. It was a slim chance, given the frustrations of earlier attempts at dialogue. But by a quick and enthusiastic acceptance of the motion, the faculty voted to reaffirm its familiar pattern of dealing with problems. There was to be more talking.

I hoped that the convocation would provide the opportunity to educate the students. Maybe they would learn to accept the necessary limitations of bureaucracy and the slowness of all social change. The students saw the convocation as an opportunity to educate the faculty. They wanted us to understand the legitimacy and necessity of their demands. And in fact, I soon discovered that the students were not making impossible and unrealistic demands. For instance, they had already developed course titles and a prospectus for their academic programs in ethnic studies. However, the convocation never addressed the issue of whether a department or school should be established to study the problem of minorities in America.

The representatives of the administration and faculty seemed to say, "We agree with you in principle about the value of ethnic studies, but we can do nothing about it." When the students argued for the legitimacy of such a department, they were answered with discussions of the various bureaucratic arrangements which would have to come first. Both the administrative and faculty representatives were unwilling to respond to the question that I heard clearly, though obfuscated by layers of obscenities: "If you don't like the system either, why don't you devote your intelligence, experience, and position of responsibility to trying to change it? Why are you using your powers to try to convince me that the system must remain as it is?" I heard the students asking for what we all hope to find—men who have enough knowledge of an organization and enough power within it to bring about needed change rather than to enforce acceptance of the status quo. We wanted administrators who see themselves as creative men rather than as helpless bureaucrats.

Nevertheless, I still asked: "Don't the students realize that bureaucracy always moves slowly?" The answer came from a colleague: "You and I understand that, but the only experience many of them have had with bureaucratic authority was when it was used to tell them 'no.' " And I began to realize then that these students and the faculty may live in different worlds. It is easier for us to accept the acknowledged inequalities of the society than it is for them to do so. We already possess enough rewards to allow us to wait patiently; but to go slowly for the students means to see their futures sacrificed to sustain the order which benefits us more than it benefits them.

Lesson 1: Evolution continues—today's university will not be the same tomorrow. I began to watch the events at State from the perspective of things I already knew. We tend to forget that there is no absolute definition of the university. The definitions have changed over time, and even now, not all institutions of higher education are alike. Where once there were a small number of faculties, now there are dozens; and the range of possible faculties differs radically from one university to another. Many academicians argue that business administration, nursing, recreation—or even, perhaps, general semantics —do not belong in a university. But these subjects exist as part of the curricula because interested parties argued successfully that they should. Once the argument was won, it was accepted that these fields contain knowledge which should be elaborated in the academic setting. There is little reason to assume that the evolution of the university will stop. A study of the history of minorities in America, a program to teach students how to work effectively in ghettos, and courses in which students learn how to direct social change, all these topics can be demonstrated to be important modern studies. They would consider issues which most academics admit are not adequately covered in contemporary universities. The refusal to establish such new departments suggests that the present faculties insist on monopolizing the definition of what it is valuable to know.

Those thoughts began developing during the convocation, which came to a sudden end the week of Thanksgiving. There was no opportunity for further rumination. One president resigned, an acting president was appointed, and official faculty meetings were arbitrarily suspended. We entered another period of departmental and informal faculty meetings—meetings which frequently were disrupted by the daily forays of the police on campus. During this period more teachers began meeting classes off campus; also, the demand for a faculty strike began to grow. As other alternatives disappeared, this demand no longer sounded as preposterous as it had a month earlier.

Lesson 2: The self-fulfilling prophecy: to think oneself powerless is to be powerless. At this point the only official meetings possible for faculty were departmental. In such meetings I heard variations of this theme: "There goes the ball game. The acting president has made a brilliant move. He has shown us that we have no power; the students can organize and the trustees can enforce ultimatums, but we have no base from which to do either." I suddenly wondered how my colleagues could say that. It seemed to me that the major difference between the faculty and the students was that the students believed in their right to organize and acted on that belief. If any change was to occur, it would come at their instigation. Conversely, the faculty, who saw themselves as powerless, succumbed to every threat. By their own actions they made their definition of powerlessness come true. Nothing could be expected from them.

Lesson 3: The "real" world requires "real" action. The picture was becoming clear to me, but I had no idea what to do. Then, a few days before Christmas vacation, the AFT local on campus gathered membership support for a strike and began negotiations for strike sanction from the San Francisco Labor Council. I knew nothing about this, but I did see the AFT informational pickets at entrances to the campus. Among the picketing faculty were many whose statements I had applauded during our faculty meetings. I was pleased to see that they had not given up. I began to think that maybe the activists were speaking the truth. Ideas and values are meaningful to the degree that they lead to action. Otherwise they have little social importance, no matter how virtuous they make one feel. So when friends asked me if I were interested in joining the union, I was now ready to say "yes." It was becoming a matter of principle. Yet I still hesitated to join the picketers—I looked to my departmental colleagues for some alternative. During our departmental meetings various members were willing to say, "We support the right of our colleagues to teach off campus or to strike." But such support stopped short of "putting my job on the line." At one of the last meetings before the faculty strike, a prospective striker said, "I do not ask you to strike with us, but I do ask you to commit yourselves to rehiring anyone who might be fired for strike activity." The silence which followed was painful. Those who remained silent were men who called themselves liberals, men who wanted to retain the traditional university— that marvelous marketplace of ideas. But they could not see that allowing people with dissenting views to speak is not sufficient. Sometimes it is also necessary to defend those who might be penalized for speaking. If one does not protect the rights of those with whom one disagrees, then there is little meaning in the statement that one is interested in and tolerant of opposing ideas. I finally saw that the university which I valued would never be protected by these inactive men. The next day I joined the picket line.

CHAPTER 3

From Lecture Hall
to Picket Line

Arlene Kaplan Daniels

ʃ♦ʃ♦ʃ♦ʃ♦ʃ♦ʃ♦ʃ♦ʃ♦ʃ♦ʃ♦ʃ♦ʃ♦ʃ♦ʃ♦ʃ♦ʃ♦ʃ♦ʃ♦ʃ♦ʃ

W hen the San Francisco
State campus began to show ominous signs of disturbance at the opening of the student strike on November 6, most of us were caught unprepared. It is easy to say now that we should have seen what was
coming; hindsight is a great help. But at that time the student strike
did not reach most of us. Some faculty supported the strike—and the
demands of the black and Third World students—by canceling
classes. But the majority did not participate. They either offered sympathy—while continuing to hold classes—or ignored the strike entirely. I fell into the medium-liberal category, which has since been
castigated as wishy-washy. I looked around my classes, saw attendance

42

was down, and muttered that nonstrikers should tell their absent colleagues to borrow class notes and assignments in order to make up the work. But my attempt at tolerance showed that I had missed the point completely; the student strike was not just an educational experience for young radicals. It was a serious protest over long-standing grievances. And it required every one of us on the faculty to take a stand.

The entire campus community first became involved in the controversy because of the growing problem of how to manage the strike. The tactics of the strikers and countertactics of the antistrikers were disrupting the campus. Classes were invaded; fist fights erupted in and around the buildings. There were also reports of intimidation and destruction of property. Many students and faculty were enraged by these tactics; but they were also opposed to the presence on campus of the police, who were daily secreted away in various obscure locations as a stand-by, protective force. The accumulated outrage over all these occurrences drew the faculty together in a rather unusual series of meetings convened to consider the issues. Up to this point, relatively few in the college had been touched by the disruptive events. My classes certainly had not been invaded, and I rather imagined that some of my colleagues were exaggerating both the dangers they faced and the necessity for a severe response to the strikers. I, like many others, was only relatively interested in the issues; since some of my friends were going to the faculty meeting, I went too.

It soon became clear—even to those of us who had never attended a faculty meeting before—that it would be extremely difficult to use this body to set policy or develop plans for action; this traditionally deliberative body was virtually incapable of any decisive action. Some faculty extremists argued for a teachers' strike in support of the striking students, others argued that disruptive student strikers should be punished. The middle weighed all the possibilities at exhausting length. The faculty muttered restively and members began drifting away before the lunch recess officially began.

The faculty meeting might have dissipated if it had not been for the appearance on campus of a special division of the San Francisco police—the Tactical Squad. They marched onto campus in what is now the classic manner: military formation, special helmets and visors gleaming, long truncheons hoisted like bayonets. The students fled screaming in all directions. Later, reports of the innocent or unprepared who were clubbed and arrested in the melee circulated freely. One incident seemed especially prepared for the faculty. Members of the Tactical Squad chased some students out to the edge of the campus. Pausing outside the auditorium where faculty meetings are held, a group of teachers returning from the lunch recess had a full view of the capture of one student who was thrown to the ground and repeatedly beaten by a group of police.

When we resumed the meeting, those who had witnessed this brutality were in a decidedly agitated and militant mood. Word of their report spread, convincing many laggards to return to the meeting quickly. Clearly, many felt the need to take a firm stand immediately before the situation deteriorated further. Again, the radicals wanted to strike, while the conservatives were ready to debate the issue indefinitely. But instead a suitable alternative was proposed and accepted. The faculty voted to continue in deliberative session (without resuming normal class activities)' until a satisfactory solution to the current difficulties was reached by either ourselves or the other parties involved. We hoped that by this maneuver we would prod the local administration into positive activity. After all, what else could we do?

The hours spent in faculty meetings indicated that the size and diffuseness of the group were suited more to random monologues than to concerted action. The only effective organization seemed to be the departmental caucus. The principle became: repair instantly during the recess from the full faculty meeting to departmental meetings and there hammer out a series of resolutions for action to present at the next session of the faculty meeting. After agreement among the department members on these resolutions, a dedicated committee typed proposals and duplicated them on the office hectograph for distribution to the rest of the faculty. Soon the auditorium was flooded at each meeting with resolutions from departments, student organizations, and individuals. Working coalitions within departments began to make contacts with other departments where similar coalitions were forming. Faculty members on the campus were beginning to become political.

Before this incipient politicization could result in action, the school was plunged in successive waves of catastrophe under which the full faculty meetings disintegrated. The students became more actively rebellious, leading to increasingly frequent confrontations with the police. The trustees put pressure on President Robert Smith to fire George Murray. (Murray was a part-time instructor in the English department and a member of the Black Panther Party who was alleged to have urged black students to carry guns on campus. See Chapter Seven for further discussion of this incident.) And the trustees pressured the president to force the faculty back to classes, even though no solutions to campus problems were yet in sight. But Smith could not convince a rebellious and agitated faculty to agree to reopen the school. They proposed a campuswide convocation as an alternative. The convocation was expected to provide the arena for dialogue between dissenting groups and to permit participation by all concerned members of the campus community. At the time, we were also desperate for some alternative to constant, violent confrontation.

Instead we experienced three dreadful, punishing days of public conflict between administration and student leaders, while most of the faculty abandoned any willingness to assume responsibility. At one point Smith was left to face a panel of antagonistic students alone. He represented both the administration and the faculty, for few members of the faculty were willing to participate; most members of the teaching staff did not even attend the convocation after the first morning session. Their places in the auditorium were taken by a variety of screaming student extremists. Smith showed incredible grit and pluck in facing such an audience; he never lost his temper, even under the most extreme and trying provocation. A few teachers loyally remained to watch this awful spectacle. I, among them, cursed many of my colleagues, particularly the majority who had voted for the convocation but who nevertheless had taken advantage of a holiday.

In general, few honors remain to be distributed. As the students say, Smith did not know how to rap. And the student leaders on the panel, already in a frenzy of disbelief and suspicion, seemed to think the president was deliberately taunting them with his guarded statements in bureaucratic language. But he could hardly speak otherwise since the trustees had forbidden any negotiations. Nor could it be expected that either side would make public concessions under the eyes of its constituents. The lackluster administrative explanations pitted against the radical rhetoric of the militants hardened

the opposition between the conflicting sides and contributed greatly
to the polarization of the onlookers. The meeting became a lengthy
catastrophe.

Sitting in the audience was a hair-raising experience designed
to make one strongly appreciative of conventional order. From one
minute to another, one did not know what to expect. All the usual assumptions about proper behavior in colleges were in abeyance. The
most extraordinary indication of this state of affairs was the per-
missiveness shown the militants in their use of outrageous language. I
thought I would jump out of my skin if one more student said "bull-
shit" or "fuck you" to the president. Partly I was outraged at such a
terrible show of public impropriety; but I was also worried what the
consequences might be—how the militants might be held accountable,
ultimately, for their lapses into disrespect.

The end of these meetings, the resignation of the president,
and the nightmare weeks of "police protection" on campus began with
the walkout from the convocation by student leaders who felt they had
been betrayed. They had received notices of suspension from the administration during the convocation, although they had supposed
that they were discussing campus problems as equals and that questions of punishment would not be decided until the conclusion of the
convocation. And so these misunderstandings marked the end of all
attempts at campuswide discussion. For some of us, the real catastrophe
was Smith's resignation and S. I. Hayakawa's appointment to the
presidency. To the faculty, the selection of Hayakawa was a clear
sign that the trustees meant to run our college without campus consent. They appointed Hayakawa without consultation with the faculty
selection committee, which ordinarily advises in the choice of a new
president, perhaps because the selection of Hayakawa violated the
agreement of the committee that none of its members (Hayakawa
was one) would be eligible for the post. The committee members made
the agreement in order to avoid the possibility that one of them would
use his opportunity to communicate with the board of trustees and the
chancellor to further his own candidacy. And, as a matter of fact,
that is exactly what Hayakawa is suspected of having done.

Perhaps Hayakawa's chief claim to fame in the eyes of the
trustees was his public espousal of this hard-line conservative position:
Campus order must be maintained at any cost. Education is a privilege

not a right. Faculty and administration constitute the elite which decides what education will include; students may advise, but they can have no power in the decision. The blacks and others in the Third World ought to be more appreciative of what we are doing for them. Rudeness and intemperate militance in and of themselves, even in a just cause, deserve considerable punishment.

Even moderates were inclined to appreciate how that position drives the militants in black and Third World groups into ever more aggressive postures. One main tactic involved provoking confrontations with the police. The continued presence of police on campus and the regular clashes between them and the students reduced ordinary campus life to a shambles. Each day saw new disturbances; and police helicopters roared overhead, making lecturing extremely difficult for those determined to follow Hayakawa's instructions to maintain the regular classroom schedules. The campus became a no man's land of battling students and police. The terrain was scarred and trampled by police movements, student sorties, the tracks of paddy wagons and horses, broken tree branches, foliage and litter—obliterating any possible impression that a college existed there.

Watching the moral and physical destruction of our campus was a horrifying experience. And there seemed to be absolutely nothing the faculty could do about it. Many of us who felt that something had to be done to stop the escalating carnage looked in vain for any faculty body willing or able to assume responsibility. No clear faculty leadership developed during this period because Hayakawa arbitrarily and unilaterally adjourned our continuing faculty meeting as soon as he came to office. The president of the local chapter of the American Association of University Professors publicly supported the new administration; the president of the chapter of the Association of California State College Professors (another teachers' organization on campus) came out against it; the president of the Academic Senate publicly repudiated Hayakawa and questioned the legality and propriety of his appointment. However, neither of these latter two persons spoke for an organization prepared to take action.

Despite this increasingly serious stalemate, I and many of my friends were still separate from the strike-oriented faculty during the first week of Hayakawa's incumbency. We simply felt unsafe on campus and felt we would be criminally and morally liable if we encouraged students to attend classes there in accordance with Hayakawa's ruling. And so we found havens for our classes in nearby churches, youth centers, and private homes. But we perceived the situation on campus to be ever more serious and more desperate, with the growing possibility not only of greater and greater property destruction but also of serious injury and even fatalities if the daily clashes continued.

Two views predominated among the faculty. The defeatists saw the established forces on campus as too powerful to resist. And those with a plague-on-both-your-houses view found both sides so guilty and ill-advised that they could not intervene for either. Some of us could not accept these alternatives. If we were really so powerless, we had to change that situation. And it was by no means clear that both sides were equally wrong. We felt that the difficulties facing the campus were real problems of long standing. The militant students, despite their outrageous style, made some telling points. They deserved a fair hearing in the deliberations on policy decisions. The issues simply could not be solved by a show of force from the Establishment and a dismissal of the protest as inspired by a radical minority or by irresponsible children.

But if we were to act to affect the conditions on the campus, what were we to do? The remaining faculty groups were the Faculty Renaissance (an extremely conservative body organized by Hayakawa a year or so earlier) and the American Federation of Teachers, Local 1352 (a small group which included some of the "radical" teachers on the campus). The appointment of Hayakawa (in disregard of proper procedure) and his immediate proclamation (see the Appendix) of a state of emergency (without consulting any faculty bodies) were regarded as signs of extreme danger. We feared that the leadership of the college had been transferred to an autocrat only responsive to the trustees rather than to a college president who would be representative of the academic community. And so about two hundred of us joined the union in late November and early December—bringing the membership to approximately four hundred. During this period, we maintained informational picket lines. Sometimes we were asked to position our lines between students and police, and we often heard the rhythmic cry "A-F-T! A-F-T!" when the students called for help. The task was a rather nerve-wracking one, for sometimes we found

ourselves marching between closely monitoring lines of policemen—
none of whom were wearing their identification badges.

Something had to be done; we were determined to forge a
workable faculty organization which could mobilize and articulate
faculty opinion in the college. Early in December the union voted to
strike to close the campus and to try to force negotiations to improve
campus conditions. By this time, moderate, wishy-washy liberals like
me were in agreement with the old-time radicals. A strike began to
seem the only tactic available to us.

Perhaps with this threat of a union strike in mind, Hayakawa
announced (at noon on Friday, December 13) that Christmas vacation would begin at the end of that school day, a week before schedule.
The reason given was fear that when high school vacation began on
December 16, high school students from the city would swell the already massive crowds meeting in daily confrontations with police. The
administration and the trustees may also have felt that the crisis
atmosphere at State would evaporate if a sufficiently long cooling off
period were provided—or even that some settlement would be
achieved.

One fortunate consequence of the decision to expand the usual
two week Christmas vacation was the chance it provided our AFT
local to prepare to strike if necessary. The old-time union members
closed ranks with the new recruits who flocked in. A hard core of
about twenty or thirty abandoned all holiday plans and devoted
themselves to preparations for the opening of school on January 6.
This group, with the negotiating committee at its center, continued
meeting through the vacation with administration representatives,
student representatives, union lawyers, and concerned community
leaders to try to defuse the explosive situation on campus and to avert
the teachers' strike. At the same time, others began to prepare for the
conflict we all feared had been postponed rather than averted.

The union executive officers and their helpers opened a store-
front office near the college. Picket captains were chosen and their
organizational strategies were developed. A system for rapid communication with all union members was established. Such strike
necessities as soup kitchens, legal aid, and volunteer help were planned
during this period. Workers hauled junk and equipment away from
the new office, an abandoned cleaning establishment, to produce

tidiness and order. Old furniture materialized; carpentry buffs made desks and work counters. Because a strong faculty organization seemed to be the only way to convince the trustees that faculty must have a voice in setting the policy of the college, the union worked to create a structure which would demonstrate that we could and would strike if necessary.

But most of us still hoped we would not have to, that all parties would work together to find a resolution. I, for example, contributed my portion of used furniture and continued my usual Christmas holiday commitments in the wan hope that professional responsibilities to teach and do research might continue without interruption. But the trustees thus far had shown no willingness to participate in any negotiation.

January 5—the night before the strike would begin—the union held a final meeting to decide whether to take the plunge. Our negotiators reported that during the three week reprieve no progress had been made toward the solution of any of the most pressing problems on campus. The representatives of the trustees were not empowered to negotiate but only to report back to the full board on the events which transpired.

That night the meeting was gloomy and tense in many ways, we were in a terrible quandary over what action to take; no decision seemed without its dangers and limitations. I was quite distressed and shaky at what I felt might be the end of my world. What would happen to us all if we struck? Would we be fired? Would we be in physical danger on the line? Despite these fears, there were some deeply moving moments. The union president called for the vote to strike and we all roared "AYE." It was the first time in my life I heard a large group of professors (more than three hundred)' agree with one voice. We were so impressed with our unanimity after weeks of debate and indecision that we rose and gave ourselves a standing ovation. We all pounded one another on the back in euphoria; the die was cast—we would take action, fight for our principles, and maintain our self-respect.

The first day of picketing was the hardest. We were instructed to be at our stations from 7:30 A.M. to 7:30 P.M. that day for a show of strength, with five hour shifts each weekday thereafter. But aside from the length of the day, the real worry was what would happen if

Hayakawa insisted on having all those cops, who had inundated our campus before the vacation, out in force again? If violence erupted, would teachers be spared from attacks by the police? When my husband said he would take a day of vacation to accompany me on the line (though in his employment he is "management"), I became absolutely terrified. If he saw the situation as potentially dangerous, it might well be so.

When we arrived that morning, the prospects were not promising for a successful picket line. Very few picketers had arrived on time. Those of us who had were desperately cold and worried about the size of the turnout and the possibility that it portended little faculty solidarity for the strike. But as the morning wore on, more and more people joined the line. And our optimism about the usefulness of this tactic returned. The late morning was very exciting and noisy, for the picket lines became immense and turned into a solid crowd ringing the main entrances of the campus. Then as the day wore on, faculty and students began dropping away as the unaccustomed exercise took its toll.

As the picket line thinned, the police seemed to become more menacing. There was something decidedly unpleasant about the way they fondled their great truncheons. And they seemed to surge toward our lines as we walked past them, as though straining at an invisible leash. Since it was invisible, I had no idea how strong it might be; this doubt added to my uneasiness. Also the police began arresting key student leaders whom they spotted in the crowds. After seeing a few little Peace and Freedom girls led off in handcuffs for shouting obscenities and other harassment, I became quite depressed. They looked extremely frail for such heavy guard and stiff punishment. At the same time, on the line we were harassed by a strange, wild-eyed lady who tore up our literature and threw it about while she screamed that we were filthy, European, Communist pigs. She also shrieked, periodically, "Why don't you go back where you came from!" Since she spoke with a thick European accent, I found the whole bit mystifying as well as depressing. I hardly had the energy to hiss back "litter bug" as she made her rounds of our lines. The police paid no attention to her whatsoever.

By the end of the day, although I was terribly weary, I felt confident that we could survive these inequities and sustain a strike if

we must. We could and would put up with much unfamiliar and un-
comfortable physical activity in order to work for an end we believed
important. We could also congratulate ourselves for showing more
solidarity and determination than are usually found among faculty.
Most academics are happier analyzing social movements than out on
the line participating in them. Furthermore, the consequences of our
commitment had not been so dangerous after all. The professors had
appeared to man their picket stations. The police had not arrested
any faculty. Most important, I felt we could close the school by our
tactics and avert the violence which had been escalating prior to the
strike, for we had already accomplished this aim throughout our first
day.

From that day we began to develop our picketing style. Later,
when we picketed at the Administration Building entrance, a colleague
and I between us almost nagged the strike breakers to death. She
snarled: "That's right, go, go. If you really think you need to go, I
don't mind. Don't think of me. I'm dying of cold on this picket line.
But I enjoy it." At the same time I called in self-righteous stentorian
tones: "Consider what you are doing! The unexamined life is not
worth living! Do you think Henry David Thoreau would approve of
your actions?" And we two harpies flapped and croaked up and down
the line, impressing even our fellow picketers. A picket captain said
to us one day: "Ladies, I'm glad I'm on your side, otherwise I simply
couldn't stand this."

But most days were cold, damp, and lonely. The San Francisco
area seemed afflicted with perversely antistrike weather all through
the winter. Constant storms, low temperature, hail, and even occasional
snow greeted us sunshine lovers as we came on the line. As the excitement and novelty of the strike wore thin, so did the length of the picket
lines. It was not so simple for the professors, librarians, teaching assistants, and office workers to maintain pickets at each entrance to the
college throughout a twelve hour day and to picket the delivery entrances for the entire twenty-four hours. We were often very pressed
to produce sufficient numbers; some picketers remained on duty as
many as twelve hours a day to pick up the slack.

Yet we felt we had to stick it out. Only by remaining unified
in strike activity could we protect ourselves. It did not seem possible
that the administration or the trustees would fire all of us—even

though they might be happy to make deals with some and fire the rest. We also felt that the strike was a last ditch stand against an administration unwilling to negotiate the grievances of a large and growing number of its students and faculty. We feared for the future of the college if we did not continue.

I drew the 7:30 A.M. to 12:30 P.M. shift as my regular assignment. Since I live a suburban commuter's distance from the school, this meant arising all winter between five and six, depending upon the desire for breakfast and newspaper. Anyone who works at his best in the late evening can imagine the wrench this entailed. But friendships developed between the regular picketers at various stations; and it soon became a matter of honor to show up and not let the others down.

The union organization responded gallantly with mobile canteens serving hot coffee and doughnuts in the morning, hearty lunches and dinners in the afternoons. Black student organizations varied our diet by bringing us soul food. We were much cheered by all these attentions. Soon middle-aged weightwatchers in our midst were bemoaning the fact that healthful exercise does not completely offset the ingestion of many carbohydrates. In the main, however, those of us who became accustomed to the daily hours of walking reported a state of vigor unusual in our normally sedentary lives. Jokes circulated on the campus about the way to distinguish strikers from nonstrikers: the strikers looked healthy.

One problem facing the union was how to publicize our view of the strike as widely as possible. The popular press was not particularly favorable to our cause, and so we resolved to manage our own publicity. We wanted to explain to as many people as would listen why we were striking. The community of the Bay Area was concerned and involved enough to help us in this endeavor. Interested organizations, on an impromptu basis, provided arenas for speakers with differing views on the issues surrounding the strike. Soon speakers were in constant demand. In the gradually developing union code of honor, speaking engagements entitled one to a relatively commensurate amount of time away from the line. Those of us with early morning shifts were among the most eager volunteers for these assignments. As a consequence, I addressed a Christian women's sewing circle, a Democratic club, a high school class, several college and university

clubs and classes, and the Junior League. One day I even found myself at a businessman's luncheon club where women were not permitted to enter the main dining room. The club members departed to
choose their lunch at a buffet. But I was supposed to tell the hostess
what I wanted and then let her get it for me. (That day I wondered
if I might not really be happier getting up early and going back on the
line.)

As the strike wore on, it became hard to imagine any other
life. A new daily routine developed in which one picketed, addressed
the public, or helped with union office work. Many union members
also continued to meet their classes off campus so that when the fall
semester closed, any student who had wished to struggle on under
these adverse conditions might gain credit for his work. Our professional sense of responsibility put many of us in the aggravating
position of having our pay docked for work we continued to do off
campus.

Sunday evenings were reserved for union meetings. At this time
the leadership reported on the progress of the negotiating committee
and gave any other news they had collected, while we asked questions
which had arisen during the week. Also during these meetings we
gained information about various forms of survival during a strike.
The hardier professors signed up for laboring jobs offered by sympathetic unions. Other teachers' unions made loans available at no
interest. Strike funds collected from donations formed the basis of a
minimum subsistence weekly check for the needy.

The sense of unity and the loyalty to one another which developed kept us cheerful during the weeks and then months of the
strike. Traditionally, departmental lines tend to keep academics
separate and isolated from one another in their individual research or
teaching spheres. After three years on the campus, for example, I
knew very few professors outside my own department. My acquaint-
ances within that department increased through participation in
monthly meetings and some limited social contacts on semiformal occasions. But even this exposure was slight; most of my social and professional time was spent with friends and colleagues from other settings, except for one or two in my department who had been my
friends before I came to the campus.

For many of us, the strike disrupted this pattern. Interdisciplinary friendships developed in the wake of union meetings and tasks. Feelings of warmest camaraderie and even affection could not help but arise among those who picketed together, voted together, argued tactics together, and were frightened together during the weeks of crisis and the strike. One colleague remarked, for example, that he had rarely seen so many spontaneous gestures of affection—hugs, kisses, comrades' arms around each other's shoulders, sharing of food— among a normally "tight-assed, puritanical, reserved bunch of professors."

The various symbolic and dramatic events in which we participated reaffirmed and heightened these expressions of solidarity. For example, in the first days of strike, the union members decided to continue picketing despite an injunction against this activity. We felt there might be some danger of arrest but resolved to disregard the injunction anyway. And we expressed our resolution by marching back in mass to the picketing area around the campus. All lustily sang "Solidarity Forever" the entire distance of that mile march, undeterred by the fact that most of us knew only the few words of the chorus.

Union perspective and solidarity did not evaporate after the eventual strike settlement. When we attended faculty meetings after returning to campus, camaraderie and general friendship with fellow union members broke the cliques formed by departmental lines. One might greet nonstriking colleagues from one's own department with reserve or cautious amiability and even join them in the traditional seating patterns. But the great cries of friendship and the feeling of ease and warmth which generally follow the meeting with a crony or a comrade were reserved for figures here and there in the cluster of professors from such fields as English, art, philosophy, creative writing, psychology, and even a stray or two from engineering and science. Looking over the gradually filling auditorium at that first formal meeting after the strike, one could see the difference from former meetings. Prior to the strike, professors characteristically looked in, located their departmental colleagues, and then scurried quickly down the aisle to join them. But this time, hands waved from various corners of the auditorium as individuals entered. Laughter and joking and calls of greeting from across the room accompanied union members as they found their seats. Often their way was impeded by friends and brothers who wished to speak on social, professional, or union matters.

The air of the gathering, at least for the union members, was quite cheerful and excited, like that when old school friends return from holiday and catch up on news of mutual interest.

Even though difficulties in the academic life at the college continued and some of us have now been refused tenure for our political activities, most of us do not regret the opportunity we had to break through the traditional academic division and to work collectively with professors, staff, and students from all over the college. We felt that we had taken the first steps in forging a more useful and practical form of academic organization than any before. After all, we had become members of a new campus community that could organize and even fight for what it believed.

PART II

After the fact it is very easy to see those sharp contradictions inherent in higher education which have been avoided for a long time rather than directly addressed. Generally these contradictions, which reflect political and ethical issues, derive from differing experiences in life. In San Francisco, as elsewhere, blacks and other minorities were no longer willing to wait until all formal bureaucratic requirements—which slow the redress of injustice—were fulfilled. Decades of watching the manipulation of the legal system to oppose their interests had left them with little confidence in the objectivity of justice. Their arguments about the appropriate responsibility of the college to its students and to the nation were vigorous and fierce. The intensity of these concerns was pitched against the intensity of the public concern for local stability and re-

58

EDUCATIONAL ISSUES
IN TIMES OF CRISIS

ᗡ❋ᗡ❋ᗡ❋ᗡ❋ᗡ❋ᗡ❋ᗡ❋ᗡ❋ᗡ❋ᗡ❋ᗡ❋ᗡ❋ᗡ❋ᗡ❋ᗡ❋ᗡ❋ᗡ

duction of ever-increasing taxes. This hierarchy of priorities did not lead to interest in the grievances of minorities. Yet the pressures from both groups were inexorable. The Board of Trustees of the state colleges, with grossly inadequate resources to meet any of these concerns, was caught between politicians, general public, and minority and campus communities. The board members proved unequal to the situation. The following chapters consider the general educational issues highlighted by the strike at State.

In "Master Plan, Master Failure," Larson presents an overview of higher education in California, with the focus on the problems of the state colleges. In 1960 the Master Plan delineated the attempt to provide higher education to all who desired it while maintaining traditional standards of educational excellence. The implementation of the plan resulted in the organization of all public cam-

puses into one system with a hierarchy of tracks. The goals may have been well intentioned, but inherent problems in this structure provided the basis for the ensuing conflict. Perhaps the chief difficulty was that such a structure could not allow the flexibility and independence required to meet unique situations as they arose. Nor did it provide for much public participation in a public institution.

In "Ivory Tower or Modern Building?" Rothbart enlarges upon the contradictions between the elitism inherent in the university and the egalitarian values of our society—contradictions which point to some of the difficulties of the Master Plan. Many who define the appropriate role of the university as one isolated from the pressures of the practical, immediate world have refused to recognize the consequent elitism of higher education. They do not see that the tracking system, which does—and does not—encourage students to enter the university, is one aspect of an invidious social stratification continued and perpetuated by the university system itself.

In "Who Owns Social Science?" Biblarz discusses the consequence of the political context for the work of the academician. The social scientist can no longer claim independence through an assertion of and a belief in objectivity, for the myth of value free research does not apply in a world with political conflicts. Academicians must now recognize the inevitable political consequences of their professional work and take these consequences into account when planning the research they undertake.

Benét, in his discussion of how and why reporters get the inside story, provides examples of the problems which arose for newsmen during the strike at State. He considers the nature of objective knowledge from the perspective of a reporter assigned to cover a controversial story. Because the reporter becomes an influential person through his access to the channels of communication, he must weigh carefully the circumstances in which he collects facts, evaluates them, and presents them to the public. Benét asks whether long ties to the campus and strong personal opinions about the issues should qualify a reporter for or disqualify him from describing the events of the strike to his audience. He concludes—and this conclusion may be applicable to other researchers worried about objectivity—that his knowledge and deep concerns contributed to his qualifications. He argues that the understandings and methods governing accuracy and fairness in professional journalism are sufficient safeguards against bias and partisanship in presentation.

The final chapter in this section, "Confronting Irreconcilable Issues," suggests that despite a natural dislike for facing situations of open conflict, at times the rights of some are necessarily gained at the cost of the rights of others. And so a compromise mutually satisfactory to all parties is not an available alternative. Kroeber specifies exactly where the two value systems—that of the ivory tower university and that egalitarian idea of educational opportunities for all—came into conflict at San Francisco State. Is the first responsibility of the university to the problems of theoretical and timeless knowledge or is it to the solution of current social problems? Is the university primarily committed to its traditional standards of scholarship or to the issues which currently concern students? When resources like money, time, and social commitment are limited, priorities have to be set; and these questions have to be answered. At this point conflicts and demands become nonnegotiable, for both sides realize that the opportunity to pursue their goals will either be won or be lost.

CHAPTER 4

Master Plan, Master Failure

Magali Sarfatti Larson

ʃ❊ʃ

San Francisco State College, with eighteen thousand students, is one of the eighteen units in the middle segment of a vast system of public higher education organized in 1960 under the California Master Plan. It is distinguished from the others as the scene of the longest student and faculty strike in America. This chapter shows how that crisis and the continuing difficulties at San Francisco State can be traced to the problems and contradictions implicit in the structure of the state college system. Much of what is described is well known. Yet it is not idle to review this plan, for it provides the background against which the remainder of this volume may be viewed.

The Master Plan attempted to order the diverse institutions of higher education that had developed in California into a single, rational, stratified scheme for the division of educational labor. The aim was to meet the postwar boom in college enrollment by adjusting educational needs and resources. A tripartite structure was designed to maximize efficiency at all levels. "Each segment of public education," the general provision of the plan stated, "shall strive for excellence in its sphere, as assigned by this division." The three public segments—junior colleges, state colleges, and the university—are separate and distinct, are coordinated at the top, and are dependent for much of their funding upon the state legislature. All three were, until 1970, tuition free, although a graduated scale of incidental fees was imposed, and the allotments of public funds per full-time student differed widely among the three segments. According to the Master Plan, projected net capital outlay per student averaged $2833 in junior colleges, $4026 in state colleges, and $7043 in the university.

The junior colleges are two-year institutions open to every student with a high school diploma; they provide technical and vocational training as well as the opportunity for late-blooming students to transfer to higher levels. They are funded mainly by local sources and thus are responsive primarily to local interests. Most of these colleges—in their curriculum and relation to students—are more closely allied to high school than to the university or college. Perhaps their most important function in the system is that of "cooling out" ambitious students—encouraging them to take a terminal degree—while admitting them to what is, presumably, a transfer station toward higher educational levels.[1] However, their functions do not concern us here.

The distinction made by the Master Plan between the university and the state colleges, however, is an important factor in the background of the crisis at San Francisco State. In the California system of higher education, the university is king by many educational criteria. It enjoys virtually exclusive jurisdiction over traditional professional training and—in spite of a few joint doctoral programs—over the awarding of Ph.D. degrees. In addition, the university is the primary agency of research in the state, and most of its privileges stem

[1] B. R. Clark, "The Cooling-Out Function in Higher Education," *The American Journal of Sociology*, May 1960, 65, 569–576.

from this fact. The prestige of research bestows cumulative benefits on the academic community. The presence of academic stars, who win their status through research, attracts other stars. In order for the institution to retain prestigious scholars, university professors are better paid than their state college counterparts, and their teaching loads are smaller—tailored to their primary concern with research. Also, the academic stars attract large numbers of graduate students who, as teaching assistants, further alleviate the professorial teaching chores.

The specialization of the university justifies, in the view of the Master Plan, the superior endowment provided. In addition, the researchers at the university are often awarded large grants from Federal agencies or foundations to supplement these funds. These considerable economic advantages benefit all the students, however, not only the elite faculty and graduate population for whom they are primarily intended. One consequence is that the university campus facilities are strikingly superior to those of the state colleges. The libraries and labs at the university are excellent. And buildings, offices, recreational equipment, lounges, dining commons, art displays, and gardens all have an air of solid affluence, even lavishness, which is absent from the most luxurious state college campuses.

Because of a variety of screening factors, the opportunity to enjoy these university benefits is reserved to the academic and economic elite. Only the top eighth of the graduating high school class in California is admitted to the university as freshmen, while the top third has access to the state colleges. In addition to academic scores, a major screening factor is the expense of college. The highest incidental fees and the highest tuitions are charged at this level. Out-of-state students pay 50 per cent more tuition and incidental fees at the university than at the state colleges. As a consequence, about half of the university students come from families with annual incomes above $12,000; in the state colleges, the proportion is less than one third.

The state colleges are subordinate to the university educationally as well as financially. They are expected to excel in upper division instruction—their excess of freshmen and sophomores is funneled to the junior colleges, while their best graduates are directed to doctoral programs in the university. Their own master's degree programs have developed slowly because of the priorities given to undergraduate education. One reason the best students are directed to the university is that the state colleges are understood by their students and faculty to provide essentially a terminal bachelor's degree. Officially, there is no difference between the bachelor's degree offered by the state college and that offered by the university. What difference there is derives from the stratification which the educational system both reflects and reinforces. Children from the higher socioeconomic strata, from which the majority of university undergraduates are recruited, hold higher career expectations than do those from lower strata. These views are reinforced in the university environment, which stresses scholarship and the notion of an academic career. In that context the bachelor's degree is the entrance requirement for higher education in graduate and professional schools. At the college level, on the other hand, both students and faculty see the bachelor's degree as an end in itself, a practical prelude to a technical or semiprofessional career in the middle echelons of some civil bureaucracy.

A very large proportion of state college students—about 75 per cent—work part- or full-time to finance their education. Their average age is twenty-four to twenty-five, and a large number are married and have children. For these students, a terminal degree should meet primarily utilitarian requirements. Its main function is to open opportunities outside academia since a much smaller proportion than at the university continues into professional or graduate schools after receiving the baccalaureate. The degree, then, is a market commodity, a means of maximizing chances of promotion in the occupational structure to which students may already belong. The middle segment of the higher education system is, thus, the mass provider of manpower for the now mature industrial economy. The growth of the state colleges is tied to major shifts in the labor market; they are the main providers of middle-level white-collar workers in government, education, trade, finance, and insurance—areas which, in coming years, will be the major source of labor demand.

Under these circumstances, a practical, job-oriented approach to education is much more compatible with the existing institutional structure and the expectations of both students and parents than is a more diffuse or liberal arts approach. Given its recruitment and its pragmatic aspirations, the student body appears to be, as a whole, relatively homogeneous, moderately capable, and rather uninspired. Depending in part on the strictness and the demands of the field they have chosen, students work hard or try to rush through as fast and as effortlessly as possible.

In their evolution, the state colleges have expanded their capacities to meet this trend. First as normal schools, then as teachers' colleges, and finally as state colleges, these institutions have grown tremendously. Their expansion was most rapid after the war, when they absorbed the largest part of the expanding college population. From 1958 to 1975, the period covered by projections in the Master Plan, this rate of growth was expected to continue. It was estimated at 350 per cent for the whole period—twice that of the junior colleges (176 per cent)' and 60 per cent higher than that of the university (216 per cent). Thus, it is by virtue both of their assigned function and of the size and interests of their student enrollment that the state colleges are, in fact, the choice ground for mass higher education. They are not limited to vocational training or minor certification as are the junior colleges. And they are bound neither by the self-conscious elitism of graduate and professional schools nor by the traditions of independent scholarship and research of the university.

The atmosphere of the state college campus stresses practicality. The lack of amenities and the streetcar character of many of these campuses are taken for granted by the students and faculty and are additional symbols of the predominant goal of efficiency. To handle this mass instructional process the faculty work load is twelve hours a week—one of the highest in the country—and faculty have little, if any, teaching assistance. They can give scant individual attention to students—sometimes as many as two hundred a semester— or to their own research or scholarship interests. Thus, in these large-scale bureaucratized organizations, the rationalization of the educational process in terms of productivity has been realized most completely.

The problems and contradictions that appear at this level pertain directly to mass higher education as such. Except in the most technical and practical fields, which are also those most directly linked to the occupational structure, the usefulness of a general B.A. now appears dubious. As a mass-produced commodity, it is subject to increasing devaluation, and its holders are faced with growing competition. Most students in general fields are painfully aware that their degrees will not guarantee them the meaningful jobs or promotions they perhaps had expected and that few of them will make it into graduate school. This awareness is at the root of both their pervasive cynicism about their education and their cries for relevance. The students are caught in the perpetuation of a mobility myth in which they do not believe. The Master Plan is not, of course, responsible for all the problems. It merely perpetuates and intensifies them.

One view is that these problems derive primarily from an unresolved duality of goals. Even though undergraduate teaching and terminal baccalaureates are clearly the most important part and the major product of the instructional process, we find conflicting and often incompatible models in this sphere. The practical democratic orientation, which has developed since the nineteenth century in American colleges, stands in contrast to a simultaneous insistence on the liberal arts as an end in themselves—a goal derived from the elitist, "preindustrial" model of European universities. In this situation the Master Plan provided only a structural framework, not a unifying definition of goals—it offered a scheme for the efficient processing and channeling of students rather than a definition of higher education. In the formative years of the Master Plan, attempts to resolve the duality of goals in our state colleges might have been expected from three main sources: the administration and the trustees, the students, and the faculty.

The perspectives and possibilities of student power are not the subject of this paper, and we shall return later to the role the trustees play in the educational bureaucracy. The faculty, however, are of direct concern here, for the Master Plan specifically envisaged the faculty as a link between the university and the colleges. It was expected, in effect, that the university would funnel its crop of doctoral candidates into the academic staff of the lower-level institutions. However, their apprenticeship as graduate students gave the state college faculty the frame of reference that derives from a university model. According to this model, success in the academic marketplace is formally and informally determined by a network of colleagues in the same field who prize detachment from the immediate sociopolitical context and the search for "objective truth." In addition, a successful career often requires switching academic posts in order to maximize personal gains. In this situation, status is determined by the acclaim one's publications receive among one's peers. The individual faculty member thus becomes detached from the community in which he works—including his students—and becomes tightly connected to his discipline at large.

As a result of this value and status system, the universities have become congeries of departments, each independently related to the outside world by its research output and by the connections of its faculty with national guilds of scholars and scientists. The only standards of excellence that the great university recognizes come from these suprainstitutional bodies of academicians. Yet, these standards have little or nothing to do with teaching. Therefore, those who are committed to education concentrate on the improvement of their own courses or, at best, their own departments, rather than on the development of general educational standards and goals for the university. Not surprisingly these compartmentalized and atomized educational centers have been unable to develop a meaningful and coherent vision of the role of higher education at the dawn of the twenty-first century. The only group concerned with the institution as a whole is the administrative management. And these men think in terms of marketable outputs, of costs and efficiency, and of the greatness of the university in a constellation of rival institutions. Thus the university has not developed any guidelines for sound undergraduate education; nor has it encouraged such a concern among its apprentice academicians. The faculty that comes to the state colleges are trained neither to be responsible for the process of bureaucratization and mass production of education nor to offer viable comprehensive alternatives.

A second issue influencing the faculty role at the state colleges is their perception of their position as second rate in the educational hierarchy. In the words of one author, "the prestige of the universities tends to draw brighter faculty and students, while the influence of the research-oriented disciplines reaches down to colleges where little research is done, shaping their curricula and the way subjects are organized. The whole world of higher education plays 'follow the leader.' "[2] This judgment is particularly fitting in California. Partly because of this view a substantial part of California state college faculties consider their jobs as early and temporary stages in their careers (the turnover rate was 10.6 per cent in 1966–1967, compared

[2] M. Ways, "The Faculty Is the Heart of the Trouble," *Fortune*, January 1969, 94ff.

with 5.75 per cent for similar schools in other states). They take this view because the secondary position of the state colleges and the career potential they thus can offer deny the expectations for high level teaching and research positions bred by academic socialization and university-geared training. At the same time, the emphasis on teaching further hampers career development, for the teaching load allows little time for research and publication—the only way to establish an academic reputation.

These conditions explain much of the frustration and disaffection expressed by members of state college faculties. But it would be both inaccurate and unfair to pretend this is the whole picture. The best state colleges also attract another faculty which represents, perhaps, a change in academic attitudes. Closer in age and sensibility to their students, they are genuinely interested in undergraduate teaching and less concerned with research and careers. They are young enough to have been participants in the student movements of the past few years. For many of them, the rebirth of social criticism in America extends to their own disciplines, to the very notion of academic detachment and the educational goals of the university. They seek involvement in campus life and tend to have an idealistic conception of teaching which makes it an integral part of their social and political philosophy. The presence of this group may be a blessing for the bureaucratized state colleges, which are still hovering between a second-rate emulation of the university and the search for an autonomous definition. However, the system offers these recruits little encouragement. Younger faculty members who see teaching as a central part of their lives and as a meaningful process of intellectual interaction may find the massive teaching load (and the prevalent orientations of the majority) disheartening. There just are not many opportunities for flexibility or intensive work with students.

The focus on one's discipline severely limits cross-departmental communication and organization, especially in an institution that provides so few amenities that many of the faculty remain on campus only a minimal number of hours. But even where communication does occur and commitment has been made to the campus, the very structure of the college blocks the possible emergence of a faculty constituency capable of pressing for systemwide goals in an organized manner. For example, the constitutional powers granted the Academic

Senate are only advisory; and the advice is usually unheeded. There is little incentive for faculty to organize to work within that structure.

The departmental structure also divides the mass of students into amorphous and unrelated bodies. Furthermore, the utilitarian bent of our state colleges reinforces the effects of ecological and structural determinants. The students, who are, for the most part, models of practicality and whose interests clearly lie outside the college, are less touched by the campus environment than are students in other institutions. But in some respects they are very like many of their peers. A recent survey of college students finds that about three-fifths are on the "practical" side of the line (as opposed to "forerunners," who are interested in intellectually challenging and socially relevant work).[3] The practical students form the silent majority, and their presence explains both the effectiveness of determined minorities and the weakness of broader student constituencies.

In the face of the difficulties presented by the departmental structure and the perspectives of the silent majority of students, faculty reformers have few alternatives. Often they find it easier to form ties with some of the already organized student action groups than to mobilize their peers or to seek to activate large numbers of independent students. The new faculty are often associated with those student groups which are not only politically sensitive but also actively concerned with educational reform and with the search for a humanistic orientation relevant to our age. The result is often an informal network of personal alliances and strong loyalties which come into the open at times of crisis. But these ties provide adequate alternatives neither for the weakness of stable faculty constituencies nor for the absence of channels for enacting reform.

Where can serious innovations come from? One way to innovate is through informal support for individual creativity. This alternative thrives on operating parallel courses and programs on a shoestring until they gain some form of recognition. In a bureaucratic and atomized context, however, major reforms cannot come about in this piecemeal way. Their necessity must be widely recognized and broad support must be mobilized in their favor before they are officially considered. At this point, the amorphous mass of the college, through its dissidents, has managed to express some countergoals and to pitch

[3] *Fortune,* January 1969, p. 68.

them directly against the accepted goals—or inertia—of the central powers on the campus. (At San Francisco State, the specific demands raised by the Third World students for an ethnic studies college were verbally supported by the administration. However, the administration was unable to mobilize the means to implement the program until the pressure of the strike.)'

All along, we have stressed the ambiguity and the lack of clear direction of mass educational institutions. One might hypothesize, therefore, that they would accommodate or entertain alternative policies more readily than do institutions with clear-cut orientations and traditions. But here the particular bureaucratic situation created by the Master Plan for the California State colleges becomes relevant in two ways. The centralization of control makes the local administration relatively powerless to institute changes while adjusting to new problems. And even the locus of authority—the chancellor and the trustees—is not able to handle them, partly because these problems were not anticipated in the Master Plan. As a consequence, the magnitude of the difficulties intensifies as they are left unresolved.

Let us examine the system of central control instituted by the Master Plan in order to understand how it both impedes change and provides the context for disruption. As mentioned before, the Master Plan did not attempt to reconcile the conflicting possible goals for the middle-level institutions. Instead, it integrated the diverse units—large and small, urban and semirural, good and bad, old and new—into a single bureaucratic unit with power vested at the top. The time of the enterprising college presidents ended with the Master Plan and so did their direct—albeit confusing—battles with the various state boards (education, finance, public works, personnel, and, of course, the state legislature)' on which each college depended. The colleges were all under the control of one new-born Board of Trustees appointed by the governor. In California, as elsewhere, these representatives of the public represent, in fact, only the most prominent and powerful business and professional groups in the state (plus some local notables in the case of the state colleges). They share the ideology and value system commonly associated with persons in that social stratum.

The Education Testing Service of Princeton, in a survey of 5,000 trustees of public and private colleges throughout the country, sketched the following portrait of the ideal-typical trustee: He is white, middle-aged, a moderate Republican who personifies success (more than half make $30,000 a year or more). His attitudes toward students and faculty are conservative (70 per cent favor screening campus speakers; 40 per cent believe that student newspapers should be censored; 53 per cent are in favor of loyalty oaths for the faculty; 27 per cent feel that the faculty members do not have the right to express opinions), and he knows little about education as such (few of the trustees ever read about educational problems and developments).[4]

What is perhaps exceptional in the case of the trustees for the California State colleges is that they headed a huge expanding system at the time it was taking its first faltering steps. Lacking experience in the affairs of higher education, the board followed the recommendations of the Master Plan as strictly as possible, emphasizing the preoccupation with expansion at low cost and the centralization of decision-making powers. They were unable—or unwilling—to enlist the help of a bold, imaginative chief executive. The chancellor was promoted from within the ranks of the central bureaucracy when the first choice of the board succumbed to the attacks of right-wing opponents. The chancellor is considered a model of bureaucratic conservatism by the statewide Academic Senate, which has repeatedly requested his resignation.

In addition to the limitations set by ideology, experience, and high-level personnel, limits are also imposed by a super board, the Coordinating Council of Higher Education, which was designed to function as an arbiter for all the strata of higher education in California, including the private colleges and universities. The Coordinating Council of Higher Education is constituted of twelve representatives, three from each of the segments of the public system of higher education, three from the private schools, and six from the "public at large." Only eight votes are required to make effective decisions about advisable policy. The impartiality of this body is dubious since the three representatives from the private schools, plus five representatives from the public—chosen in the same manner as the trustees—can in theory make decisions for the public system. The trustees have had many of their plans for the state colleges rejected or curtailed by the council,

[4] See *Newsweek,* January 20, 1969, and the *New York Times,* January 13, 1969.

which advises on budgets, capital outlay, new programs, and new facilities.

Allocation of state funds is a particularly acute problem for the state colleges, the segment most directly dependent on them. (The junior colleges are financed largely by local sources; the university has access to considerable Federal and private endowments.) The rigid fiscal regulations set by the legislature on budgetary matters affect the decisions which the trustees may make. At the local level, this financial rigidity has disastrous effects. All colleges are financed on the same per capita formula. Each campus develops a yearly budget and submits it one year in advance. After approval by all the central bodies and, ultimately, the legislature and the governor, the budget returns to the campus as specific allotments which cannot be transferred to other uses. That is, an allocation for office equipment cannot be used for faculty salaries; the opportunity to keep the old typewriters for one more year and, instead, to hire extra faculty is not open to the college. At least, such decisions cannot be made when the emergencies arise, during the academic year. The unused funds are returned to the legislature, via the Board of Trustees. (For example, various departments voluntarily contributed funds for the new department of black studies. However, when the black studies program did not materialize as hoped, these funds were simply placed in the state salary savings rather than reverting to those departments making the sacrifice.)

Centralization, therefore, quite effectively curtails the flexibility of the local administrators. The college presidents lose policy-making power, and their function becomes that of assuaging local protests against the slow and cumbersome bureaucracy. To the dissidents (and to many others as well) such presidents are experts in managing red tape rather than administrative leaders. This unwieldy structure takes its toll most particularly in the problem campuses; San Francisco State, for example, had seven presidents in nine years.

The centralized structure forces conflicts to the top because power to manage them has not been delegated at the local level. But the problems, in fact, require that solutions be formulated with an understanding of the local context. Unfortunately, the trustees neither possess this understanding nor consider it important. They are also hampered by serious limitations on their own power and by their unwillingness to adjust the bureaucratic guidelines to meet unforeseen

situations. Their favorite stratagem for coping with the unexpected is
to tighten controls. This strategy, in turn, multiplies the risks that the
original conflict will be magnified and broadcast throughout the system
because it mobilizes the forces of discontent against what is often
construed to be an abuse of power.

The problems related to the centralized structure of the state
college system are compounded by broader political problems. The
dependence on public funds immediately projects problems into the
public and political arenas. Thus, the state colleges are especially vulnerable to public opinion and the financial retaliation which may
occur when an adverse climate develops. The rise of student protest
on the California campuses has gone hand in hand with the growing
right-wing backlash. The backlash is manifested in the array of repressive legislation introduced to limit dissent and punish dissidents
and in refusals of the executive branch to grant requests for appropri-
ations in higher education (see Chapter Eighteen).

The trustees, appointed by the governor for eight years, are less
independent of external pressures than are the university regents,
whose term in office is sixteen years. This fact multiplies the power
and the influence wielded by the exofficio political members who sit
on the Board of Trustees (the governor, the lieutenant-governor, the
speaker of the assembly, the superintendent of public education). In
addition, appointees of Governor Ronald Reagan act as his uncon-
ditional spokesmen. Under Reagan's influence, educational orientations have become increasingly and openly reactionary. The central
powers of the state college system have joined the public's and the
politicians' attacks on public higher education rather than defending
the system they oversee. And the chancellor is unwilling to defend the
colleges from the dangers involved in this alliance. (For example, the
state college chancellor said he would not protest assumption by the
trustees of final decision rights over faculty tenure; but the university
president vigorously protested in a similar situation.)

Meanwhile, the discrepancies between the projections of the
Master Plan and the current educational conditions of the state become more blatant; and problems mount, reinforcing each weakness
of the system. One of the weakest assumptions of the Master Plan was
that there would be a stable rather than an inflationary economy. We
can illustrate the inadequacy of these financial projections by showing

their discrepancy with system needs, ten years later. The plan foresaw, for 1975, $648 million in state expenditures for higher education; Reagan's budget for 1969–1970 devoted roughly $781 million to this purpose. The recommendations in the Master Plan for faculty hiring recognized the necessity to provide "greatly increased salaries and expanded fringe benefits" to prevent the California-educated graduates from leaving to work in other states (or from leaving public education for private industry). In fact, however, salaries, work loads, and fringe benefits have fallen below those of other states. By 1966, the Master Plan predicted a balancing off of faculty shortages; in 1966–1967, however, 21.8 per cent of faculty positions remained unfilled in the state colleges (compared with 5.8 per cent in 1964–1965). A by-product of these working conditions is the multiplication of part-time faculty, who are paid at even lower rates and who receive fewer benefits than do the regular faculty.[5]

The financial problems of the higher education system are rooted in a tax structure which passes the most substantial part of a soaring bill on to the masses of wage earners.[6] Large sectors of the public increasingly resist paying for an educational system in which their children are, for the most part, ineligible for the most prestigious institutions. The frustation of the public, in turn, increases the possibilities of political manipulation and aggravates the financial straits of the colleges. (A bond issue for public higher education was voted down in November 1968.) The obvious scapegoats for the taxpayers'

[5] The work load for full-time faculty members is officially four courses. The departments favor the faculty members they want to keep by counting one of the courses they teach as two sections; therefore, in many cases, permanent and full-time faculty members are paid a full salary for three courses (plus administrative and counseling duties). This situation is made possible only by the exploitation of the part-time faculty, who teach two courses and get paid not half but two-fifths of the full salary. This computation ("less than half-time") eliminates all fringe benefits for this group. Furthermore, they are denied all voting rights at faculty or departmental meetings by the constitution of the faculty councils.

[6] The tax structure of California is one of the most regressive in the country. In 1969–1970, 79.9 per cent of public revenues came from taxes levied on individual taxpayers (including the income tax and the various property taxes). Among the indirect taxes, sales and use taxes—which are the most regressive contributions—represented 40.7 per cent. The contribution levied on banks and corporations stood, quite stably, at 9.5 per cent as in the preceding year.

indignation are the rebellious students (and their faculty allies)' who are now demanding expanded access at all levels of the system for the most underprivileged of the young people.

Last but not least, the Master Plan was based on erroneous assumptions regarding enrollment. Projections were based on a conservative estimate of high school retention rates—or, conversely, on a stable rate of dropouts. The overenrollment of certain campuses was not predicted. The Master Plan also did not take into account the effect the introduction of standard aptitude tests would have on minority enrollment; at San Francisco State, for instance, the percentage of blacks in the student body dropped from about 12 per cent to 3 per cent in the years of most rapid expansion. In fact, the problem that will constitute the major test of higher education in the coming years was not even glimpsed; the planners, in 1959, seemed blissfully unaware of the effects of racial discrimination and segregation on education. They did not even mention race as one of the main obstacles to the achievement of an adequate education. They stated, "Among the formidable barriers that prevent many high school graduates of real ability from furthering their education are lack of incentives, early marriage, interruption for military service, and shortage of financial resources."[7] They democratically insisted on housing, plentiful job opportunities, high school counseling, and a large scholarship program. We now know how little help this represents for minority youths, whose educational problems start much before the completion of the twelfth grade and whose difficulties are only partly economic.

A bureaucratic construction such as the Master Plan attempts to plan the future from above. It obviously cannot foresee all the situations which will arise. But perhaps the most severe limitation of the Master Plan—even if we take its intentions at face value—is that it sets rigid policy and assumes that all future problems can be managed within a framework which does not allow much initiative, not even to the governing Board of Trustees. The designers of the Master Plan could not have predicted the pace of social change, the extension of the black liberation struggle outside the South, the effects of the black power ideology, and the rise of a youth movement against the Vietnam War. In sum, the planners could not foresee that all these

[7] *Master Plan for Higher Education in California,* p. 77 (Donahoe Higher Education Act of 1960, enacted by the California legislature).

changes would result in the formation of militant student constituencies on campuses that had earlier been apathetic. Neither could they foresee that their grandiose design would help to devalue lower academic degrees without improving the situation of the underprivileged.

The basic contradictions embedded in the educational assumptions of the Master Plan were revealed at San Francisco State—forcefully and dramatically—by a determined minority of black and Third World students. In furthering both democratic and elitist education within the same institutional structure, the plan provided tuition-free access to higher education, and at the same time it built upon the socially determined selective tendencies in earlier schooling. The advantages of the already privileged were thus reinforced, while the myth of universal opportunity was maintained. The plan attempted to reconcile the two irreconcilable aspects of education in a capitalist industrial society: the manifest function of promoting equality of opportunity and the silent function of perpetuating the socioeconomic structure. The requirements for admission and the costs of education in the three-tiered system perpetuated the class and race-biased selection which had already made its discriminations at the grade school and high school levels. Admission to the best colleges and universities was reserved for the survivors of the educational hurdle race.

The fundamental contradiction built into the grand design became evident in the most vulnerable centers, where the centralized bureaucratic structure magnified the contradictions. Specific conflicts that could not be resolved at the local levels rose to the top and spread throughout the system, kindling, as they went, the various forces of discontent which had accumulated and which entered in dialectical interaction with the original challenge. The explosion of this discontent focused attention on the fact that, from its very inception, the bureaucratic organization of higher education had excluded any democratic participation. At the same time, the bureaucracy proved incapable of either meeting or recognizing legitimate and pressing demands from new constituents. Perhaps part of the difficulty stemmed from the fact that this educational system had never really been constructed to provide such constituents with its full benefits.

The crisis taught an important lesson to many students and faculty who lived through the struggle: how power is exercised in bureaucracies and how this power is used in turn within the limits set by the dominant power structure.

CHAPTER 5

Ivory Tower or
Modern Building?

George S. Rothbart

𝄞𝄞𝄞𝄞𝄞𝄞𝄞𝄞𝄞𝄞𝄞𝄞𝄞𝄞𝄞𝄞𝄞𝄞𝄞𝄞𝄞𝄞

The crisis which began at
San Francisco State College in 1968–1969 illustrates a shift in radical
demands for change in higher education. For a long time, leftist students and faculty challenged deans, presidents, and trustees as the
men who sold out for fat government research contracts, making the
university the ally of United States imperialism in the process. But
San Francisco State has no Institute for Defense Analysis or many of
the other signs of subcontracted United States foreign policy. Here the
challenges by radicals developed along different lines. The core issues
in the strike derived from the experiences of black and other Third
World students. They focused on criticisms of higher education other
than its cooptation by the military and industrial establishment. What

78

these students wanted was the development of a system of higher education which would remove existing barriers in order to provide equality in access to education. One way to understand the rationale for their criticisms and alternative suggestions is to examine various images of the university.

When members of a social institution attempt to expand or defend their influence, they develop images of the character of the institution which they offer to potential supporters. By highlighting specific aspects of institutional life, they encourage people to assume that an unambiguous picture of that institution exists and can easily be judged.

In criticism and defense of the modern university, two contrasting images have evolved. First, the university has been defined as a factory which produces the knowledge packaged in the heads of its graduates. Important research activities within the ivy-covered factory develop some of the knowledge acquired by the graduates. As a result trained technicians are integrated into the industrial system as economically productive dispensers of expertise. The second image of the university is as a knowledge establishment, an entity devoted to the production of knowledge for its own sake. Those who favor this picture often support admittedly obscure scholarly pursuits on the grounds that such activities favor the spirit of the knowledge establishment, even if what they produce has little social utility. As descriptions of the way in which universities function, the concepts of establishment and factory are not mutually exclusive. Each correctly describes an aspect of the university. The university does provide trained persons for industry and does perform industrial and defense research. It also houses many scholars who go about their nonbusiness with a serenity appropriate to the cloister.

New Left critics of the university have largely ignored the knowledge establishment image and have leveled their sharpest attacks against the factory concept. During the Free Speech Movement at Berkeley in 1964, the radical student leader Mario Savio expressed the distaste for this factory felt by many of his fellow student-products: "If this is a firm . . . then . . . the faculty are a bunch of employees and we're the raw material. . . . There's a time when the operation of the machine becomes so odious, makes you so sick at heart . . . that you can't even tacitly take part. . . . You've got to put your bodies upon the gears and upon the wheels, upon the levers, upon all the apparatus, and you've got to make it stop."[1] This criticism by the New Left fails to consider the dangers to radical goals implicit in the establishment, or ivory tower, image of the university. The ivory tower is as much in opposition to their democratic ideals as is the factory.

Politically liberal supporters of the status quo in higher education generally favor the knowledge establishment image. Taken as a picture of the way things ought to be, this concept provides a basic argument for increasing the remoteness of the university from the larger society. Proponents of this view often argue that the proper function of the university—that of social critic—is presently threatened precisely because it does not maintain sufficient distance from the larger society. Only by being independent of political and social pressures from the defense establishment can the university express its concern with objective truth. Thus, it may appear that many supporters of the knowledge establishment accept the New Left criticism of the university as factory. But the convergence of thought is short-lived. Establishment supporters also find organizations such as Students for a Democratic Society as unpleasantly preoccupied with maintaining a close and political relationship between the university and society as is the Department of Defense. In response, these establishment supporters argue that university man can develop all ideas to their fullest, regardless of their popularity, only when he is remote from all involvement whether of the left or of the right. Indeed, this idea occasionally appeals to some radicals, who know from their experience that the university functions as a relatively safe harbor for some leftist thinkers.

However, the university does much more than provide a haven for dissidents in the society. But many supporters of the university fail to see the full implications of this service. If a university did function purely as a sanctuary in which men were permitted to play—for pay— with ideas of their own choosing, it would be a social anomaly. Institutions are almost always required to demonstrate relevancy to onlookers in the surrounding society. From time to time, nevertheless, the university has been allowed to devote itself to pure knowledge, and indeed some scholars in almost all universities and colleges are given that privilege. Since pure knowledge almost invariably seems unim-

---

[1] From a speech quoted in H. Draper, *Berkeley, The New Student Revolt* (New York: Grove Press, 1965), p. 98.

portant to virtually all citizens, why do such pursuits receive support? One can, of course, sidestep this problem by arguing that an ivory tower is relevant, that scholars in educational settings develop many important ideas and much scientific knowledge. However, this answer has the quality of ad hoc argument, for, in fact, the pursuit of pure knowledge is rarely if ever seen as meaningful by either men of affairs or the general public. Thus, we must go outside the production of pure knowledge to find the reason for the existence of the university. My thesis is that the answer is found in examination of the methods available in Western society for assigning social status and prestige. The university in Western Europe and elsewhere has performed the socially relevant service of distributing prestige to selected members of the society. Membership in a university faculty has often allocated status to those children of advantaged parents who did not follow— because of predisposition, personality, or position in the gallery of sons —one of the usual careers pursued by the ruling class. In addition, the traditional university provided certification for elite or subelite professional and religious offices. Although the educational requirements for the certification were often irrelevant to the eventual position, the university provided the necessary legitimation for the assumption of positions which were not supposed to be inherited.

The modern university continues this tradition; it also serves a screening function, defining elite membership differently from other institutions, but to the same end—the exclusion of underprivileged persons. It performs this function by placing severe limits on recruitment from the bottom of the social ladder because it accepts only highly rated products of elementary and secondary educational systems. Since students with high grades come almost exclusively from middle- and upper-class families, the university confers the possibility for prestige largely on those whose parents already possess it. However, in a democracy people believe that the educational system, more than any other institution, should create opportunity. We expect that disadvantaged and lower-class children may successfully compete at the university level. Why else do we have scholarships as well as programs like Upward Bound and Outreach for the disadvantaged? Thus, the university seems to serve two masters: those who support the current order and those who question it.

This seeming paradox arises from an insufficient understanding

of the way in which a status system is maintained. Programs like
Upward Bound make little change, even in terms of numbers reached.
But they are symbols of equality. They offer the promise that the
system provides appropriate rewards to those who are proven worthy
and competent. All social systems claim validity for their own procedures of allocating citizens to invidious status positions. Conversely,
they claim that those who do occupy highly ranked offices possess the
skill for them. In our own democratically minded society, the existence
of a university system which asserts its ability to teach and evaluate
important skills supports this claim. This system is also expected to
offer opportunities to all who possess the talent to learn in it. The
operative assumption is that the skills are made available in an impersonal fashion—if students wish or have the ability to learn they
may; if not the fault is theirs. Thus the peculiar advantage of the
university as a stabilizer of social status is that its standards are not
subject to attack by outsiders. A small investment by the elites in programs for the disadvantaged validates the democratic quality of the
university and allows it to continue screening people at entrance,
moving citizens into the tracks where they "belong."

The rationale behind these claims is a faith in objectivity.
Objectivity, in the sense of reasoned demonstrable argument resting
upon clearly agreed-upon methods for deriving facts, is an idea peculiar to particular times and places. According to such social philos-
ophers as Max Weber, the result of much post-Renaissance Western
thought was acceptance of the concept of objective knowledge. As he
saw it, in that period intellectuals rediscovered the Hellenic principle

Thus, in my view, the university is not justified in presenting its
image as an ivory tower. First, historically it has performed a screening function for society. Second, in a modern democratic society it
helps legitimize the current composition of the elites. The validity of a
university in a democratic society rests upon acceptance of its intel-
lecual standards as well as upon its ability to offer opportunity to all.
In other words, it can claim to use acceptable criteria in measuring
genuine talent. It has the ability to appear to offer opportunity to all
without seriously upsetting the pattern by which the children of upper-
status persons enter upper-status occupations. Having done its work, it
has, in effect, bought and paid for the luxury of socially frivolous
thought.

that "one could put the logical screws upon somebody so that he could not come out without admitting either that he knew nothing or that this and nothing else was truth, the eternal truth that would never vanish."[2] Although individual men may not be able to grasp the truth, they believe that it is there to be discovered by dint of inspiration and logical discipline. The concrete advantages of this approach were easy to see. The scientific experiment with its magnificent payoffs in new principles and procedures exhilarated post-Renaissance men just as the earlier logical discoveries had excited the Greeks.

The users of the new knowledge produced by the hard sciences were converted to the idea of an objective truth because they found such knowledge demonstrably more effective than any knowledge previously available. And the successes of these hard sciences led to the belief that objective truth should spread to other areas—social thought, history, and art. Weber, for instance, noted Leonardo's preoccupation with science as a path to artistic achievement. Why does a scholar or an artist try to bring his field under the aegis of objectivity? Weber suggested that the claim to objectivity helps raise a field to the level of power and prestige occupied by medicine and science. Even the leaders of totalitarian societies may have to bow before scientific truth.

The natural scientist is proud, with justification, of his knowledge; and he sets high expectations for his students in the development of specific skills. The social scientist, in order to gain such satisfaction, seeks equal objectivity. Since his field is still young and cannot at this point claim much universal knowledge, he claims objectivity, not on the basis of a body of knowledge, but rather on his use of methods which appear to be scientific. The value of these methods for helping the social scientist to answer important questions—or even the questions he asks—is widely debated within the profession.[3] But they have the advantage of appearing scientific and objective to outsiders. In this way a claim to objectivity insulates the field from outsiders and makes it the province of only those who are properly trained in the methods for discovering truth. The long years required to conform to the standards and to enter a knowledge profession are likely to deter non-

[2] Max Weber, "Science as a Vocation." In *From Max Weber: Essays in Sociology* (New York: Oxford University Press, 1946), p. 141.
[3] See, for example, S. M. Rosen, "Keynes Without Gadflies." In T. Roszak (Ed.), *The Dissenting Academy* (New York: Vintage, 1968).

elites from becoming insiders. Of course, this approach ignores the possibility that objectivity—and scientific knowledge—may come to be superstitiously valued in a quite unscientific way.

In the social sciences, for example, the sharpest critics of the widespread introduction of quantitative (scientific) methods have argued against the indiscriminate application of scientific tools to problems before social theory has developed enough to indicate which tools are most useful. These critics contend that application of scientific method in this way is faddishness rather than science. It is akin to the superstitious value primitive tribes attribute to the mere possession of penicillin or fountain pens—even when they have no conception of the context which transforms these revered objects into practical, useful tools. For example, high regard for intelligence quotient scores, because they are thought to be objective, still exists despite the growing body of research which shows the cultural and class bias in the tests from which the scores are developed. Scientific methods, then, either may become irrelevant to the answering of important questions or may become instruments of protection for a social order.

The absolutism of the belief in objectivity which is built into many fields thus turns out to be advantageous to elite groups. But given the great social respect for objective knowledge, it is hard to mount any attack on the current system as illegitimate. To be against the university system is to be against knowledge. If the standards of the university are assumed to be objective, then the student's skill can be fairly measured by his incorporation of an objective body of knowledge. Thus, the knowledge establishment image of the university confers a direct benefit on the elites. It provides legitimacy for the screening process, by virtue of its great prestige as a purveyor and disseminator of objective thought. In this way the apparent paradox of the knowledge establishment as ivory tower can be explained. The university does not facilitate attacks on the status system by infusing that system with new blood; rather, it's infusions are a primary mechanism for defending the system and limiting recruitment into it.

In a special sense, then, it is in the interests of the ruling class to preserve the status of the university as a knowledge establishment. If the university is to make its most effective claim as an objective screening device, it must preserve its cloistered, truth-seeking character and remain uncorrupted by the short-run rationalities of government and industry. But whether functioning as cloister or contractor, the university serves the ruling class.

In addition, the educational system plays a role in social mobility. Industrial societies, past and present, uniformly sustain a certain amount of social mobility. Their occupational requirements are complex, changing, and expanding; and they usually cannot find all the necessary talent among the privileged classes. However, social mobility has an undesirable consequence in that it may create feelings of deprivation among those who are not able to become mobile. Students of industrial organization have observed that workers offset aspirations for occupational mobility set by the American dream of success by developing a consumption orientation. The idea seems to be: "If I can't become foreman, I will concentrate on buying a home and new furniture."[4] However, when consumption is also not possible, the disadvantaged are doubly resentful. Thus, complex, urban, industrial societies have the management of aspirations as a major problem. The right people must be motivated to aspire to the new jobs created by a changing technology, but the rest must not be left with their desires inappropriately frustrated. The educational enterprises of industrial societies deal with both these problems. They do create opportunity for a limited number of talented persons; at the same time, they are able to defeat the aspirations of the immobile. By using the ideology of objective standards, the society is able to deny the validity of the argument that the system is at fault: "You had your chance."

As a symbol of democratic opportunity, the college both fosters and defeats aspiration. It is also the last lap in a race whose outcome is almost fully determined. The college validates the end product when social mobility has already occurred in an anticipatory fashion. If the student's family is mobility oriented, if it has already acquired some middle-class standards, and if it has passed those standards on to the child, it has enabled him to participate fully in his early educational experiences. Thus the family does all it can to ensure that the child is fully accepted into the university. Many American families are able to provide the environment that prepares children for the university route to success. But very few families were able to do so in their early years in the United States. For that reason, newly arrived ethnic

---

[4] See E. Chinoy, *The Automobile Workers and The American Dream* (Boston: Beacon Press, 1965).

groups have not used the university as a means of mobility. Most persons from those groups began by acquiring skilled blue-collar jobs, by entering low-level white-collar work, by entering small business, or by going into politics (which created business opportunities without private accumulation of capital by means of graft and contract work for city government).

Traditionally the second generation went to college. The sons and daughters of those who already had moved one step up the mobility ladder could understand the importance of college, and their families could help finance the educational process. Even such ethnic groups as the Jews—with cultural interests in mobility through education—did not, by and large, try the college route in the first generation. Despite their admiration for scholarship and scholarly concerns, the barriers to education were not easily surmounted. The university forced the white ethnic groups to wait for the special kind of mobility that it promised until they had advanced along other paths.

In summary, the university has attempted to pass as an ivory tower. This image, along with that of the knowledge factory, has masked the fact that the university serves the elite of the society in ways even more complex and pervasive than many New Left critics assert. Only when we understand this historical and contemporary role of the university can we begin to understand why the current relationship between the university and the blacks is so conflictful. Unlike the white ethnic groups, the black people at San Francisco State and elsewhere fundamentally question the present role of the university as legitimator of the current order.

It has been said that the reason for all the black militance in the universities is that the faculties largely are sympathetic to the cause. Thus, the university provides a setting in which blacks can get a piece of the action. This explanation is not sufficient. For one thing, professors are concerned citizens who have a tradition of not doing anything that causes a fuss in the outside world. Their sympathies do not provide the alluring offer of a power base to the black militants.

Instead, the explanation for black militance in the university seems to be that more and more blacks have come to realize that a college diploma is a more crucial contingency for blacks than for almost anyone else. Labor statistics suggest that for urban black males receiving high school diplomas (or spending two years in a junior college) does not greatly alter their already high chance of becoming unemployed. But a black college graduate achieves something his less educated brothers cannot—an unemployment rate significantly lower than that of the average white worker (even if higher than that of the white college graduate).[5] This fact must have been apparent for some time to black people, for virtually every public opinion survey shows that an extraordinary number of black parents hope to see their children go to college. Indeed, one survey indicates that when blacks and whites of similar socioeconomic status are compared, black parents have higher educational aspirations than do parents from a number of other ethnic groups.[6] Because of discrimination, the typical black parent cannot reasonably hope that a son can use his high school diploma to attain a skilled blue-collar job or to become a foreman or even to rise to a low-level white-collar job. But if the young person has a college degree, he can become a school teacher, a welfare worker, or a federal employee. In these professions blacks have more equal opportunity than they do in others.

Thus, if black people can just get through college, their occupational future is virtually assured. But the ideology of the university, more than the ideology of big business, responds to this need by reasserting its conservative emphasis on objectivity and standards. One of the implicit standards, for example, is a high level of articulateness in "proper" English. Such a standard poses a truly enormous burden on any American group on its first step up the social ladder. The orientation of the university toward a whole series of peripheral concerns—as the marks or style of an educated man—further complicates the task of mobility through education. Black people are in the first generation of upward mobility, without the anticipatory manners to facilitate their climb, and yet they see that they must leap the college hurdle if they are to become mobile. In this move they are encouraged by black militant groups which are attempting to upset the educational ideology by denying the correctness of at least some of the prior screening standards.

The switch to new standards presents many problems. Elite

---

[5] U.S. Bureau of the Census, Census of Population, 1960, Report 5B: *Educational Attainment*, Table 4.

[6] B. C. Rosen, "Race, Ethnicity, and the Achievement Syndrome," *American Sociological Review*, 1959, *24*, 57–58.

universities make few changes in their not-so-raw material. Institutions such as Harvard have so great a degree of initial selectivity that they hardly need a faculty; a library and a collection of peers are sufficient for their already highly developed students. What happens when institutions of higher education face the problem of educating raw material—those who need help—rather than the problem of educating those who need only a little polish and certification?

Most special programs for minority students are financed by government grants for intensive experimental work with a small number of students, and some have offered clear indications of progress in their students. For example, at the College of San Mateo (a junior college located in a commuter suburb of San Francisco), the Outreach program demonstrated impressive results—and with very modest investments. Some highly talented people developed a radically new program which was strongly militant and was oriented to minority self-help. It recruited students primarily from a nearby black ghetto. (It was so successful that some of its graduates went on to their home town school, Stanford University.)

But then something happened. The black faculty said, "Let us no longer treat our program as an experiment; let us intervene on a large scale in the ghetto world." At this point the program began to generate resistance—it was no longer an experiment. It now required extensive financial and personnel resources; and it threatened to make significant changes in the surrounding community. Most of all, it threatened to change the nature of the College of San Mateo. Perhaps for these reasons, plans to expand the program were stymied by financial difficulties, and in the early weeks of 1969, the national wire services carried the news of "revolution and rioting" by black students at that San Mateo campus. Establishment opposition to the continuance of new programs, accompanied by increasingly violent protests from those who lose the most from the rejection of these programs, marks the history of the war on poverty. Even where programs are successful, they do not receive encouragement.

Apparently, then, the educational institutions, with the grumbling consent of their trustees, can accept radical programs on one condition: that they be classified within the ivory tower idiom. The programs must be experimental and scholarly (that is, constructed for a scientific evaluation). They must not establish strong ties outside the educational system because such connections raise the possibility of usurping the traditional right of the university to define the criteria of knowledge. Teachers begin to fear lowered standards of admission and pressures upon them to pass marginally acceptable students. In other words, the educational institutions have a rhetoric of openness which is the most radical of that of any societal institution, but they also have an educational ideology and structure which are most resistant in response to attacks on the current order.

American industry has responded to charges of discrimination by seeking some minority people for high-status jobs. When industry cannot find minority persons with full credentials or experience, it often promotes persons who meet lesser criteria. Thus industry indicates willingness to question the absolute nature of its own criteria of performance. The educational establishment, in contrast, has usually insisted that both its minority students and its faculty be fully certified by traditional standards, and it has refused to question the appropriateness of its standards. Its accommodation to change has been actively to recruit acceptable persons from minority groups. But this strategy is not easy to pursue as long as high standards for admission are valued. For example, the population explosion in California has resulted in the tightening of admission requirements at the university and a consequent tightening at the state college level, which now must handle its own population plus those refused at the university. One result of the increase in admission standards at SFSC was that the proportion of black students dropped from 11 per cent in 1962 to slightly over 3 per cent in 1969. The faculty and administration responded by implementing a special admissions program which permitted the recruiting of 428 underqualified students. However, this administrative concession did not indicate a new wave of change in the college. First, the figure of 428 was developed only after numerous student demonstrations, culminating in a much publicized sit-in in the administration building in the spring of 1968. Second, the college did not enroll 428 students. The administration claimed that the former president had promised only to accept that many students. When some of the 428 applicants did not enroll, no additional invitations were sent to alternates. Third, no funds were forthcoming from the state trustees to meet the special problems of educating these students. The program was free to continue as long as it could do so without modifying the procedures of the college.

This kind of official response is reflected in another educational innovation—black studies. The trustees of the California State colleges have not exactly opposed black studies and its counterparts, ethnic studies and community work-study programs. The trustees insist only on limiting these programs and controlling them. At San Francisco State, students were able to use their great commitment and limited Associated Students funds to move into the community without massive government aid. The trustees acted against this state of affairs by making changes in the administrative code to give themselves control of student organization funding.

The San Francisco State College black studies program and other similar programs represent a demand to make changes in the world of the minority poor. The proponents do not plan to transform a few minority students into symbols of democratic opportunity. The strikers of San Francisco State, both students and faculty, demanded a college that would demonstrate its relevance—but not by screening students to achieve a mirror reflection of the traditional status system. Instead, they wanted a program which would attack the present allocation of status. The greatest debate arises over the demand that the college open its doors to as many students from the urban and suburban ghettos as can be recruited. Yet this radical plan conveys the sum and substance of the new ideas. The college must have the resources to make a serious dent in the vast number of minority (and non-minority) persons who are the products of elementary and secondary educations that have prevented them from having a choice as to whether to continue their education. The SFSC faculty proposed a new standard of excellence: that they be judged not by the quality of the students they take in but by the quality of those they turn out.

These new ideas in education present a serious challenge to the structure of our status system. When an open admissions policy is introduced, the present system, by which we hide the failures of democratic opportunity, may collapse. At present, the faulty end products of our elementary and high school system remove themselves via the drop out route, or they are sidetracked into the junior colleges, where their aspirations are allowed quietly to subside. An open admissions policy forces us to look at these students and at ourselves. It forces the college to try to cope with their problems; it gives the college a great self-interest in the improvement of these students if the college is not to lose its reputation. If we were to be successful with these students, we would also undercut the rationalizations of those elementary and secondary systems which claim that these students cannot be educated. Most important, the university would no longer do the dirty work for the rest of the society. If minority communities are to be rejected in their aspirations for real power, that rejection will have to be made openly, rather than through the covert mechanism of the two-track educational system.

Finally, these programs have shown that their greatest promise is that they may feed their graduates back into the communities, where, as teachers and organizers, they can mobilize the communities to change their situations. The new programs, in this way, show their greatest contrast to the special opportunity programs of the past. Those programs provided only a way out of the continuing unpleasantness of minority ghettos for their graduates rather than a new way of life for all minority poor. The new programs are the first signs that a drastically revised educational system may soon be constructed. The architects of this new system are developing their preliminary blueprints and testing them under fire, for the societal response to them has resulted in campus turmoil.

CHAPTER 6

Who Owns
Social Science?

Arturo Biblarz

This chapter critically examines the established conception of social sciences as value-free disciplines, including some assumptions about the nature of man that underlie this conception. In the presentation of an alternative position, it is argued that both the view that social science is an endeavor that must strive to be value free and also the major criticisms of this view are incorrect. Both views mask the value commitment of most social scientists. The alternative, based on a Marxist approach to the study of society, is presented as a more adequate description of the relation of social science to value systems.

Most discussions of the moral or ethical position of scholarly

92

research in social science accept the view that the scientist should show detached curiosity, noninvolvement, and an attitude of objectivity toward the various concerns of his fellow humans. In this sense, objectivity means that the social scientist must attempt, as completely as he can, to keep himself outside the interests of his subjects. (In this paper, the term *objectivity* is generally used interchangeably with the term *value free*. It does not refer to the willingness to change a position when it is contradicted by facts or to the ability to recognize the nature of external reality.)' He should not presume to evaluate the emotions and goals of the human beings involved in the phenomena he observes. Whether he is counting people and grouping them into different age and sex categories or studying the characteristics of families suffering from starvation, he must remain value free.

For example, the social scientist who is investigating campus disorders is not to be concerned with establishing the legitimacy of radical causes or with helping the college administration to find effective methods to prevent these disturbances. Instead, without taking sides, he should try to explain how the phenomenon came about, its development, or its consequences. In this way the particular case becomes an instance in the larger, preferably universal, generalizations about social processes. Ideally, such generalizations should apply equally to campus disorders, peasant riots in medieval Europe, feuds among primitive peoples, and marital discord among upper-class American families. Once discovered, the truth about the particular cases—and its relationship to the larger generalization—cannot be disputed by any parties to the disorder regardless of their personal involvements. In this sense truth, or knowledge of reality, is seen to be value free.

This state of detachment cannot be totally achieved. Since the social scientist comes from a nonscientific community, he cannot completely abandon the habits and desires that characterize his nonscientific life. The personal background of social scientists as well as their present situation and their ambitions for the future often have a clear influence on the problems they choose to investigate and the focus of their studies. Students of religion, for example, are likely to be, or to have been in the past, very religious themselves. They may show some predisposition to focus upon the positive aspects of religion as opposed to the negative. They may study, for example, the possibilities for social cohesion provided by religion and be puzzled by—or explain away—indicators of religious oppression in society. Because of this potentiality, many consider the appropriate way to manage the encroachment of personal biases in research is in the recognition and public statement of the scientist's values. In this way others can make allowances for his values when they interpret the specific findings. Wherever possible, however, the scientist must neutralize these values so that they do not affect his research at all. This position often results in the tendency to use a methodology which permits investigations of any given problem by the collection of indisputably "objective" facts, such as age, sex, and occupation. There is a countertendency to ignore or even explicitly to reject more ambiguous dimensions (such as institutionalized racism) for these are felt to incorporate values or personal beliefs. Thus they are ignored or neglected even though they may be more socially significant than the usual demographic variables.

This point of view is related to the epistemology of British empiricism, which affirms that the only reality human beings can know is the reality transmitted to them by their sensory experiences. To understand reality, therefore, one must understand these experiences as directly as possible by overcoming the interference of human passions and of various subjective factors. These factors attempt to force the reality that is experienced through the senses into one that conforms with the desires of the observer. Scientists who are primarily concerned with a systematic understanding of reality must be the most zealous subordinators of their own subjectivity. Thus, the general attitude of sociologists toward the question of objectivity is based on assumptions which involve the nature of the relationship of human beings to their environment. In this context, one of the most important of these assumptions is that human beings are essentially passive receptors of the reality experienced through their senses. Knowledge of what we consider external reality is something that happens to us. It happens best when the only inner desire that motivates our attention is our unfettered curiosity, that is, a desire to know reality in terms that are independent of any other concern. In this manner, the social scientist is exhorted to practice what is called pure science, or the search for truth for its own sake. In this search his voluntary activity must be restricted to observing the events that concern him while he interferes with these events as little as possible.

The practical aspect of this position, that is, the insistence that social scientists strive to be value free and professionally uncommitted to moral positions, has recently been strongly criticized. Alvin Gouldner, for example, asserts that the value-free conception of social science is a myth and that such a state of affairs is neither possible nor desirable. The only justification for the myth, according to Gouldner, is that it helped social scientists to acquire a measure of autonomy from government, religion, and "the parochial prescription of the social scientist's local or native culture," allowing the pursuit of basic problems and independent theoretical implications.[1] Thus Gouldner implies that sociology has had some autonomy, meaning that a discipline developed which could consider problems and concerns that were independent of the pressures and interests of other parts of society. But if it is impossible for social science to be value free, as Gouldner asserts, such autonomy could never have existed. At best, a different set of values may have been substituted for those Gouldner refers to. David J. Gray points out:

> While sociologists may congratulate themselves on their newly attained "scientific" status, the fact is that as opposed to being truly value free, rather, they have become but professional handmaidens of the going value system. In effect, by refusing to make value judgments themselves, they have tacitly accepted the values of others . . . [and] have assumed a new role as employees, consultants, or technicians serving the present establishment, which, on the matter of values, is by no means so shy.[2]

It can be said that when social scientists assume such a professional handmaiden role and encourage their students to do the same, they too are not being shy in making value judgments, even when these judgments are cloaked in the ideology of ethical neutrality.

Both Gray and Gouldner conclude that social scientists should investigate important and relevant issues and that they should not refrain from making judgments about these issues. Since they both hold the view that such judgments are inevitable, this advice amounts to a plea that value judgments be consciously and openly made,

[1] A. Gouldner, "Anti-Minotaur: The Myth of a Value-Free Sociology," *Social Problems*, 1962, 9 (3), 199–213.
[2] D. J. Gray, "Value-Free Sociology: A Doctrine of Hypocrisy and Irresponsibility," *Sociological Quarterly*, 1968, 9, 184.

rather than remaining unconscious or disguised. But it does little good to urge sociologists to become "relevant" as Weber and Durkheim were while the issues involved remain clear and unresolved. Furthermore, social scientists are and have been involved in studies that are relevant and which usually involve a value judgment, even if it is unstated. What else are we to make of all the studies on crime, delinquency, race relations, the family, industrial sociology, suicide, urban problems, political behavior, problems of Third World countries, and so on? Many claim that the issues involved are relevant, and that most of the social scientists involved are against crime, delinquency, and suicide and are concerned with understanding these phenomena in order to help in their prevention and control. In fact, these judgments are often explicitly stated. In recent years, higher education has become an area in which these problems of value commitment are particularly salient. The continuing occurrence of student rebellions in universities across the country and the increasing radicalization of students and, to a lesser degree, of faculty members have resulted in a growing body of literature by social scientists on the "problems" of higher education. Whether or not authors claim to present value-free analysis or research, the information offered can be used to support or attack any one of the value-committed sides in this arena.

If we can assume, given these considerations, that the major part of the work done by social scientists is indeed value relevant and value laden and if no other alternative is possible, then the implications of this situation should be explored in terms of these very points. The issue would then no longer be should sociologists keep trying to be value free, even if this is an impossible aim, or should they become relevant and make value judgments consciously? Rather, the issue becomes, given that value judgments and relevance are inevitable, what choice does the sociologist have, if any? What are the bases for the judgments he makes, and what alternatives are available?

These questions cannot be answered within the framework of British empiricism. However, a different conception of human beings and of the manner in which they learn can serve as a context for a concrete examination of the situation of social scientists and professors in this society. On the basis of this other perspective, a Marxist approach, it is possible to understand the actual and possible bases of value judgments made by social scientists. This alternative view sees that humans exist in an environment with which they continuously interact, so that they are never passive receptors of experience. Reality is then discovered or created in the process of interacting with the environment in a purposeful manner. The struggle for survival is such a process of interaction. In this manner, human beings learn about the world by changing it or failing to change it; and in that process they also shape and change themselves. Thus men are not merely passive receptors of experience; they invent new tools and discover properties of nature by the use of these tools. A microscope, for instance, suggests exploration into structures and life forms never before known. And so men use this knowledge to change the conditions of their existence, inventing tools and procedures to change the course of human life. Sterilization, for example, becomes a possibility when problems caused by unwanted children arise. At the same time, the problems of giving birth to children become less serious. The real world now contains fewer mothers who die in childbirth than it did previously. Men have created a new reality. And this reality in turn changes the risks and expectations which shape the character of present and future generations. Fear of childbirth is a less common psychological experience; and the death of one's mother is a less typical experience of childhood.

Thus, there are no static aspects in the relationship between human beings and reality. Knowledge is acquired through practical experience, which depends on the activity of men, not on their passivity. And this relationship between experience and reality occurs throughout the society even in the educational institutions. At San Francisco State College, as in many other institutions of higher education, most of the faculty believed, before the strike, that they had a significant voice in managing the affairs of the campus. Against the background of the strike many demands for change were proposed by the Academic Senate, where they were often passed by large faculty majorities including many nonstriking members. Since the Academic Senate is recognized by the administration as the legitimate, organized voice of the faculty, the ease with which that same administration rejected these proposals forced many faculty members to realize that their power was much inferior to that of the administration. (See Chapters Ten and Thirteen.) In 1970 it was even possible for the chairman of the Academic Senate to assert, while defending the actions of the administration, that the college is an administered organization where those in power are not required to be fair; they have the power to do as they please. Thus people acting upon their environs discovered the nature of academic reality, including new aspects of social reality. Only when opponents tried to buck the system did they clearly see where the power was in that system and how it was used. Some chose to accept this reality; others chose to fight against it. In this manner, success or failure not only teaches us about reality but changes us as well, as a result of the new knowledge we acquire in the process. People can become objective, in the sense that they become aware of the character of the real world, by participating in struggles. But this does not mean that they become value free.

Like any other participant in human activity, the social scientist is not and cannot be value free and any attempt to achieve or increase the likelihood of value-free science is doomed to failure. From this perspective, it is not surprising to find that in the practice of science, values are involved in a variety of ways and that scientists, instead of being passive, are very active in their pursuits. They produce results that are judged by their ability to predict and control human relations with the environment, which then may be consciously altered or maintained. The choice for social scientists, then, is not whether they should strive to be value free. It becomes, instead, a question of what values are being pursued, what alternatives exist, and whose interests are promoted. As social scientists are generally aware, values do not exist in the abstract; they develop out of the activities and experiences of groups. Values always exist in the context of associations of human beings, pursuing interests together or in conflict with each other. Thus, for social scientists the choice becomes whose interests should be served by their work. The strike at SFSC was a clear conflict between the administration (and its supporters) and the striking faculty and students. The struggle was in part an attempt to establish which set of values would prevail. The social scientist becomes part of that struggle when he formulates his research questions. Will studies of higher education help administrations maintain order on the campus? Will they help militant faculty keep their jobs? Will they show students how to get more power or how to develop closer links with campus or noncampus workers and poor people?

Social scientists have generally chosen to put their skills at the service of the Establishment, groups wielding considerable economic and political power in the society.[3] These groups attract this loyalty from social scientists because general power can be translated into specific consequences for academics. This power is seen in the ability to influence and participate in legislatures and in boards of trustees and regents and to control the funds from public and private sources which are used for research and teaching.[4] To the extent that the interests of those powerful groups exist in contradiction to, and at the expense of, the interests of other groups, there are value-laden consequences in the efforts of social scientists who put their skills at the service of those in power and who train others to serve them. Consciously or unconsciously, the social scientist expresses by his choice the values that he supports and the relevance of his scientific endeavors.

The question then is not only knowledge for what but also knowledge for whom. The ideology of ethical neutrality once again masks a real and practical commitment. Thus, social scientists who claim to be value free often attack as biased anyone who uses concepts like exploitation or imperialism. Although these terms can be defined as clearly as most other social science concepts, they do point to undesirable aspects of these economic activities from the point of view of workers and Third World people. On the other hand, these social scientists may be perfectly content to use concepts like productivity and counterinsurgency, which can refer to the same economic activities but which connote the concerns and values of those whose powers and privileges are protected and extended.

The alternatives available to social scientists, then, are to continue to service groups in power, thus using social science for the maintenance and expansion of that power, or to alter their commitments, individually and collectively, and to use their skills to serve

---

[3] For a description of these groups as well as of the manner and the extent to which they wield power and their existence as a class, see G. W. Domhoff, *Who Rules America?* (Englewood Cliffs, N.J.: Prentice-Hall, 1967).

[4] See J. Ridgeway, *The Closed Corporation: American Universities in Crisis* (New York: Random House, 1968).

the interests of groups without power.[5] Because of the sharp conflicts in the United States today, an increasing number of social scientists are beginning to adopt the alternative which involves the use of social science to discover and improve methods for altering power relationships in effective and relatively permanent ways. The choice of this alternative requires the study of the problems of the powerless, of the causes of these problems, and of the institutions and structures that perpetuate them. More important, it involves the study of how to solve these problems. To accomplish this end, the social scientist must develop methods for altering or changing institutions and structures which oppress the politically weak and keep them powerless. As a consequence, a commitment to this alternative involves the study of reform, and it involves the study of revolution.

Social science disciplines, as they have evolved in academic circles, have claimed an independence which was never real. Social sciences have always been applied, rather than pure, and their application has consistently been used in the defense of established power. The alternative tradition, that of Marxism, has been practiced outside universities, by revolutionary intellectuals like Lenin and Mao Tse-Tung. They put theory into practice and helped transform the societies in which they lived.

Today, struggles at home and abroad are becoming intense and violent. Because the issues and their supporters are more and more polarized, it is increasingly impossible for social scientists to ignore these problems. For these reasons, social scientists should understand that they must make choices and make them consciously since their consequences are sometimes unpleasant. For example, faculty who participate in union struggles, black people's struggles, or in other segments of the radical movement are less likely to be offered jobs or tenure if their activities are known. For the social scientist who wishes to apply the Marxist perspective suggested in this paper, the implications are serious. Sometimes radical social scientists can obtain funds to do their research if their intentions are somewhat disguised. But a clear involvement with radical movements, whether in or out of the university, frequently results in dismissal.

Therefore, once a social scientist makes a commitment against

[5] Some possibilities in this direction are suggested in T. Roszak (Ed.), *The Dissenting Academy* (New York: Random House, 1968).

the status quo, he must be prepared for a difficult career and sometimes even a short one. But, as we have argued above, men can and do change the reality of the world through struggle. So the initiative need not always be left to the other side, which has established its version of reality. Radical social scientists can and should build support for their political-intellectual position and thus to some extent for themselves, both inside and outside the university. A critical group in this respect is the university faculty. Radical social scientists must join with other radical faculty, and a substantial part of their energy must be devoted to attempting to persuade other colleagues of the validity and importance of their perspective. In this manner it would be possible to increase the participation of the discipline and then the participation of the university in the process of change that is beginning to occur in American society.

The growing strength of the union movement in institutions of higher education provides another possibility—the alliance of intellectuals and workers. In spite of all their problems, unions are more likely to fight for radical faculty brothers than are most other organized groups in the university. Thus radical faculty have significant sections of the labor movement as potential allies. When principled alliances of these kinds are formed and maintained, there will be an increase in the ability of radical faculty and scholars to become significant forces for progressive change in the United States.

CHAPTER 7

Interpretation and Objectivity in Journalism

James Benét

Reporters are often asked for the inside story by those who believe that news work enables them to know more—especially about politically charged happenings—than they are able or would dare to tell publicly. They are often thought to have acquired this story through acquaintance and involvement with the people about whom they report. The unexpressed assumption is that the inside story is valuable and so the means of obtaining it are implicitly approved. But how far inside is the reporter to go? Is it desirable for him to be a participant in the world he reports? The question arose for me during the crisis of 1968–1969 at San Francisco State College since I was both a part-time faculty

member in the teachers' union and a full-time reporter assigned to
the story for *Newsroom*, a nightly television news program. In retrospect, I conclude that fairness and involvement are not contradictory
concerns but, in fact, are complementary. Perhaps the explanation of
how I came to this conclusion may have some significance for other
professionals, like academics, whose work is also believed to require
a certain degree of detachment. Let me begin my explanation with
an analysis of the events.

What happened at the college seems to me, in blunt summary,
to have been repression by Governor Ronald Reagan and his administration—aided by some faculty—of a student movement that had
genuine and important grievances and that sought desirable reforms.
The seriousness of the student demands of recent years first became
clear to me—as it did to many others—during the Free Speech Movement at Berkeley. I remember discussing with students at that time
their insistence that the regulations against political activity on the
campus were wrong. They argued that students were entitled, like
all Americans, to campaign and collect money for candidates and
that to bar these activities on the campus was effectively to deprive
them of such rights since the campus was where they were—their
community and their home. I began to see that the rule barring
political activity on the campus was not simply an expedient defense
against politicians' meddling. It was an unconstitutional abridgment
of the civil rights of individuals who were of voting age. This student
movement was not frivolous, like the panty raids and hell raising of
earlier years; nor was it adolescent defiance of parent surrogates. It
was not the unpolitical behavior that it was said to be. Instead it was
a principled effort to correct an injustice which denied to students the
rights and responsibilities of citizenship.

After that realization I tried to examine students' positions
with more care as they extended their opposition to the Vietnam War,
to the powerless "sandbox" student government, to the apparent disregard of the university for many community needs, and to the irrelevance of some of the curricula. Archibald MacLeish, in a Charter
Day address at Berkeley on April 24, 1969, summarized what has become the view of many:

And how can a generation of the young, born into the world of the

diminished man and in revolt against it—in revolt against its
indifference to humanity in its cities and in its wars and in the
weapons of its wars—how can a generation of the young help but
demand some teaching from the universities which will interpret all
this horror and make cause against it?

With this background of increasing thoughtfulness about the demands
made and the questions raised by the students at Berkeley, I paid
careful attention to the details of what was being demanded when I
and other reporters joined thousands of students and faculty around
the Speakers Platform on the San Francisco State campus in early
November. As the students explained the disruptive campaign that
they called a strike, I concentrated my attention on the content of
their fifteen demands rather than on the challenging style of their
presentation, as some other reporters—and many public figures—
tended to do.

The reasons for many of the demands were at first obscure to
me. The most difficult one to understand was that all black students
who wished to be admitted to the college in the fall of 1969 be accepted. I wondered how one could run a college that way. But I took
every opportunity to discuss the demands with the strike leaders and
the black administrators who supported them. Through these discussions I came to believe that in general the demands were defensible.
The admissions proposal, it turned out, was an effort to sweep aside
the usual procedures for one experimental year. As an education reporter, I knew that many educators agree that requirements for excellent high school grades and high scores on scholastic aptitude tests
favor conventional middle-class students and unjustly block poor
minority groups. And I knew of the successes at Berkeley of special-
admission students who, though not qualified by the usual standards,
were nevertheless able to earn good grades—another in the growing
number of demonstrations that high school grades are not, in all cases,
the best predictors of college success.

I was also well aware that the administration of the state college system could be infuriatingly frustrating. I learned this not only
from sitting through many long, wordy meetings of the college
trustees—where student and faculty views were hardly considered—
but from some involvement with the bureaucracy as a reporter. As
one example, a graduate student called me for help in obtaining his

student loan money. In this preposterous situation a bank had granted the loan, and the student had been admitted to the college. But until he was registered, an obstructive bureaucrat refused to release the check, without which the student was unable to pay his registration fees. The bureaucrat explained that Federal policy forbade it. However, the appropriate Federal official speedily and forcefully overruled the obstruction once he was informed of the situation. I could understand how such treatment might appear to young, unsophisticated, and justifiably suspicious black men, not adroit enough to find a reporter as an ombudsman. They might feel that the treatment was based on racial prejudice and that it called for more than a polite protest. I knew, too, that the proposed black studies program, accepted long ago in principle by the college, had encountered just this sort of obstruction.

In addition to objecting to bureaucratic obstructions, the students were protesting actions by the chief executive of the state. Before the student strike began, the governor called for the dismissal of George Murray, an instructor and graduate student and one of the leaders of the Black Students Union, for allegedly having told students to bring guns onto the campus. The report was based on the statement of a single student reporter about a rally which no college official attended. Mayor Joseph Alioto asked the district attorney to find legal grounds for prosecuting Murray, but the district attorney could find none. And Murray denied the charge, insisting that he had only repeated a familiar piece of the black militants' rhetoric: that blacks are entitled to carry arms in self-defense. Yet the governor exaggerated this report into grounds for insisting on Murray's immediate ouster, contrary to college process and in a way that could not fail to inflame the already aggrieved black students. Later, in support of his viewpoint, the governor said publicly that a group of students had obtained admission to the college by threatening an admissions officer. College President Robert Smith had told him about it, he said. Smith denied saying anything like that, and the admissions officer denied that any such incident had occurred or that he had ever admitted anyone under threat. Yet the governor never retracted his statement. These are only two of many provoking actions by the governor in response to alleged acts of violence by students. In all this, a harsh inhumanity was shown to both students and faculty by the governor and—later on—by his chosen president at San Francisco State, S. I. Hayakawa. The governor derided "wishy-washy" administrators who hesitate to use police force against students; and he charged that the faculty had incited student misbehavior. Hayakawa called a day when police beat numerous students the most exciting day of his life since his tenth birthday, when he first rode a roller coaster.

It was, therefore, not surprising that polite requests and efforts to work through legitimate channels were giving way to vehement demands and actual destruction of property. The demands would be obtained "by any means necessary," the leaders of the Black Students Union and the Third World Liberation Front said, in a phrase repeated again and again. A student leader told a faculty and student convocation, "Either you recognize that we have a right to decide what our education is going to be about, or your school won't go on." Through a variety of means—not all of them violent—the students did try to shut the college down. But it was the violence which made the news and brought swarms of reporters to the campus. All of us were kept busy collecting details of the physical disruption at State. The students invaded classrooms and heckled instructors, even intimidating them, though I know of no physical attacks on students or faculty. They threw rocks through windows, set stink bombs and paper fires, damaged several typewriters, overturned files, and were presumably responsible for several bomb explosions. The only serious injury was to a black student accused of attempting to set a bomb which exploded in his hands.

The tactics of the young blacks may have been wrong and misguided, as I think they were. But they do not seem to me to have been an adequate justification for what followed. In response, as the whole nation knows, first Smith and later Hayakawa called police to the campus—and their presence led to increased violence. Instead of quashing the student protest, the harsh police tactics immensely broadened student and faculty support for the original strikers. The police struck out with their clubs—even at obvious onlookers. They issued arbitrary and contradictory orders. They knocked down men and women students alike, as well as some shocked faculty members. All this activity put the issue of violence in quite a new light. Although it is extremely unpleasant to have several dozen black men shouting epithets and threats at college administrators, police violence produces an entirely different reaction. An ancient anxiety arises, *Quis custodiet ipsos custodes?*, for these are the guardians of the public peace. If they abandon law and order, the fabric of society seems visibly rent before one's eyes; all security is gone. Though in the abstract calling police to a campus when students act unlawfully has great plausibility, in practice the use of police has often proved disastrous because it has expanded the conflict and intensified the dispute.

Reporters saw numerous students whose worst offense was to be insulting, beaten into bloody helplessness. Black students were especially abused. In one unforgettable episode, however, a white student was brutally attacked when he came out of the main doors of the library carrying his books, in full daylight, and in view of a large crowd. He evidently startled a police officer standing nearby. The policeman turned and began to beat him and was quickly joined by another who beat him too, until he lay still at the top of the steps. While the student violence has been greatly exaggerated, the police violence has been condoned. The mayor and the governor, though political opponents, praised the police work. Not one policeman was ever publicly chided by any official for the many cases of obvious brutality which were witnessed daily by reporters—and which were documented on television and in newspaper photographs. However, the San Francisco courts gave the hundreds of students and nonstudents, blacks and whites, who were arrested for merely attending forbidden rallies, jail terms of several weeks. In two cases of defiant young radicals, the sentences on misdemeanor charges were six months in jail. (The general procedure of these trials is described in Chapter Seventeen.)

Under these circumstances I had to decide what to do, both as a reporter and as a teacher. I could not ignore that each of my roles had an effect on the other. Especially, I think, my view of what was best for a teacher to do in this situation was influenced by a reporter's experience. Many professional reporters in the United States are trade union members in the American Newspaper Guild, and I have belonged to this union for more than thirty years. Consequently although union membership seemed a novelty to many college faculty, it did not seem so to me. And in fact, I became convinced that the union might be the most effective force in creating a desirable outcome to the conflict. Not all unions, in my view, are useful and effective. But this union group showed energy and courage, particularly on an occasion when a group of demonstrating faculty—all, I think, union members and certainly led by prominent union leaders—marched between the police and students to try to prevent a further outbreak of violence. I admired the gesture, even though it was not wholly successful, and I joined the union a few days later.

Basically I had two reasons for joining. First, I wanted to protest police violence and try to reduce it. Second, I wanted to encourage faculty resistance to pressures that would lead to destruction of the California system of public higher education. Union leaders thought that if a sanctioned labor union strike were in progress, the police would become more orderly since that would be a familiar situation to them. This viewpoint seemed reasonable, given my observations of other labor strikes in San Francisco. Union picket lines, the police know, are lawful. San Francisco is a strong union town, and the police behave in general as peace keepers toward union lines; they ignore minor violence in order to quiet a difficult situation. I believe that the teachers' strike did help to reduce violence. And so, even for this short-run gain, a teacher could feel justified in trying to strengthen the union on campus.

My second reason for joining the union grew out of my experience in following the state educational system for more than a dozen years as a reporter. The Board of Trustees, which governs the state college system, is now dominated by Governor Ronald Reagan, who appointed most of its members. The state administration has shown, I believe, little concern for educational values, evidenced by an insistence on cutting education budgets regardless of the demonstrably invidious effects this cutting has on the institutions concerned and regardless of the inevitable necessity of turning away many thousands of students considered eligible for admittance. Moreover, I think, the governor has used the problems of higher education to make the state colleges and the University of California political scapegoats, which he lambastes vigorously in many of his speeches. In this endeavor, he has had opponents in the rebellious students, whom he could summon to battle almost at will—as he did in the Murray episode I have related—and over whom he could, in the eyes of many of the public, win famous victories to further his own political career.

Under harsh and indifferent authorities, the traditional form of faculty organization, the senate, which relies on its persuasiveness to influence the administration and trustees, appears sadly ineffective. (See Chapter Ten for a detailed illustration.) It seems to me that union organization offers a channel through which faculties may come to utilize the allied power of the local and even national labor movement. Faculties may have more chance than the present system offers to protect their rights, their livelihood, and the educational values they cherish. Perhaps unionization can strengthen the professional quality of the faculty. Certainly newspapermen tend to believe that union organization has been beneficial to the quality of their work; increased wages and job security have allowed a sense of professionalism and responsibility. Publishers long ago dropped their argument that it would produce bias in the news.

In my case, the added security of union membership was illustrated by the ready agreement of the journalism department (in contrast to many other departments at SFSC) that newspaper union members could not be expected to violate union principles by crossing a picket line. We were safe at a time when other teachers were being warned that five days' absence would automatically terminate their employment. Of course, we were not entirely safe—we lost pay for the period, and we ran the risk that in the future the department might decide that we were no longer desirable instructors.

So much for my activity as a faculty member. As a newsman, despite my efforts to divide my roles, I could not ignore a certain conflict of interest in being both reporter and teacher. Such a situation puts unusual pressures on the reporter. Before the strike prevented me from doing so, I was teaching two classes at the college, so that I spent Tuesday and Thursday mornings in a classroom building. There I met in the hallways not only fellow journalism teachers but other colleagues with whom I had become friendly in my ten years of teaching on the campus. Many, quite naturally, tried to persuade me of the greater or lesser importance of a particular bit of evidence. And some became angry at what they took to be my bias. I remember a professor of economics shouting at me from a second-story window, "How about a little objective reporting, Jim?"

But in considering the reporter's task it is important to remember that he is always involved personally to some degree. Most newsmen have their own opinions, and they hold them quite strongly, just as I do. Some newsmen at San Francisco State privately called the student leaders "troublemakers" and their demands "ridiculous." Others focused on the lack of restraint shown by the police. Reporters know that their emotions become aroused and that they have strong opinions. But their professionalism, they believe, consists of being fair in reporting despite that fact. We seek to assure fairness by applying some widely accepted rules. Regardless of individual views or emotions, professional reporters believe that they have a common interest in accuracy, and they evidence this belief when they freely consult each other in attempting to establish exact quotations or references. Similarly, a viewpoint does not prevent a reporter from questioning the accuracy of clearly interested sources. Thus at San Francisco State, the reporters, whatever views they might have held, quickly learned to ignore Hayakawa's repeated assurances that most of the students were in their classes during the strike. Reporters undertook the difficult task of checking for themselves. These counts, partial though they had to be, soon showed that many of the largest departments in the college were crippled by the strike, and some were for all practical purposes shut down. This estimate from the reporters who made the surveys was accepted by all reporters, regardless of personal preferences or of official denials. These surveys tended to corroborate my personal view that a substantial share of the students supported the protest demonstrations. But another rule is that reporters have to look for opposing evidence. Like scientists who must look for evidence to disprove as well as to prove their favorite hypothesis, reporters must guard against the wish to distort the picture. And so, like the other reporters, I was quick to investigate claims by the administration that some schools and departments in the college, such as business and physical education, were little affected by the strike. Again, regardless of our personal viewpoints, we reported that these exceptions did exist.

Also, in work of the highest professional standards a reporter guards against the semantic trap of using pejorative or laudatory terms which pass as descriptive. According to this rule, reporters did not follow Hayakawa in characterizing the protesting students and faculty groups as "anarchists"; usually reporters spoke of "demonstrators" or "strikers." And the title *silent majority*, claimed by the opponents of the strike, was generally qualified by any reporter who cared to use it by putting the phrase in quotation marks or by applying a modifier like so-called. After all, there was no evidence that these opponents were in fact a majority.

These general principles are useful for a fast-working reporter to ensure that he is at least roughly covering the ground of his story. But they are inadequate as guides to what journalists currently call interpretation or news analysis.[1] Events at San Francisco State illustrated very well the major reasons why the shift toward interpretation and away from objectivity has occurred in journalism. Complete objectivity is extraordinarily difficult, perhaps impossible, to attain in the very brief space of a news report. In addition, the rules by which journalists once supposed they could guarantee objectivity fail to do so. This failure may manifest itself in a variety of ways. An assignment may have an inherent interpretation. During the height of the conflict, for example, a *San Francisco Chronicle* reporter was sent to interview Hayakawa in his home with his family present. Without making overtly favorable comments, the reporter produced a sympathetic picture of the college president.

Whether the reporter supplies what he calls background, the context of events or circumstances, may also affect interpretation. This is a particularly difficult problem in television, where news items are typically very brief and the reporter has little opportunity to explain. Hayakawa's statements were frequently reported, particularly on television, without the additional material necessary to enable the viewer to understand the situation. For example, one day Hayakawa read before television cameras and reporters a statement that when police attempted to arrest individuals on the picket line, "the films show clearly that that mob of teachers and student pickets did everything possible to prevent legitimate arrests." Reporters who were aware that this press conference was held too soon after the picketline disorders for film to have been processed, asked Hayakawa when he had seen the film. He replied that cameramen had told him of it. Asked which cameramen, he replied that all cameramen looked alike to him. "It's a report of a report," he said. "A semantic flight of

[1] See, for example, C. D. MacDougall, *Interpretative Reporting* (5th ed.) (New York: Macmillan, 1968), a leading textbook; and B. A. Weisberger, *The American Newspaperman* (Chicago: University of Chicago Press, 1961, p. 169ff.

fantasy?" asked one reporter. According to my observation of the scene which Hayakawa reported, a group of students—but no teachers that I saw—huddled around one of the student leaders and tried to hide him or shield him with their bodies, something short of "everything possible." However on this and other occasions Hayakawa's accounts of what was happening at the college were presented without the reporters' observations, which were often contradictory. As far as the narrow rules of news objectivity went, Hayakawa's view was accurately reported. But if one may assume that his intensely participatory view of affairs was biased, then the public was simply being offered his biased picture, not an objective description of the event.

Another weakness of the rules of objectivity is that they lend themselves to exploitation by clever press agents. It is well known that the Chicago industrialist W. Clement Stone at his own expense supplied Hayakawa with a personal press agent. And soon after Hayakawa assumed the presidency the college public relations office was also increased by adding a third man. Reporters are well aware that self-serving accounts prepared by such representatives—even when their truthfulness is not in question—are likely to be unbalanced. On one occasion, with the skillful management of the public relations men, two students from the University of Hawaii, members of the Young Americans for Freedom, presented Hayakawa with a large box of orchids just outside his office door. As soon as reporters began to ask serious questions, he retreated through the door, leaving the reporters with nothing to write about except the student gift. As trivial a piece of news as this may seem—for there was no evidence that the students represented anyone but themselves—the flowers gave a fresh note to pictures. The story was, in television jargon, a visual one. Both newspapers and television used it widely, and it marked a success for the press agents. A reporter who failed to report the gift of flowers could have been called to task by his editors for suppressing news. And to suggest the artificiality of the event would violate narrow rules of objectivity. Television has its advantages—I reported the story with a smile.

These problems of fair presentation of news have convinced many reporters that pursuit of an unattainable objectivity is a mistaken enterprise. Yet interpretation has its own set of pitfalls. It must be distinguished from deliberate bias. Professional newsmen generally reject the contention made by some underground and New Left journalists that a conservative bias in much of the American press should be met with a compensating bias in the opposite direction. They also reject conservative arguments for them not to rock the boat. In the opinion of reporters the best interests of all are served by open and honest discussion of all views on any issue. In addition, even in interpretative reporting, facts—or what the scientist may call empirical data—still make up most of the content of the reporter's stories. The thoughtful reporter realizes that he cannot furnish exhaustive or irrefutable support—as a scientist might—for his general statements; his moment is too brief. He is simply signifying to his audience, as convincingly as possible, that the facts support his interpretation and that his statements are not mere bias. This signal is essential to his credibility, for, although the crusading reporter is a familiar folk hero, many laymen (including most publishers) are quick to demand objectivity when reporting conveys an interpretation of which they disapprove.

Even where the experienced reporter does take responsibility for his interpretations and does try to report all other important viewpoints as well, this effort does not always avert controversy. During the San Francisco State events, Hayakawa admonished reporters not to listen to his enemies; and readers and viewers often protested the prominence given one group or another in the conflict. The only occasion during the long dispute when my superior editor criticized my coverage was an instance of this sort. I made film interviews with several people who complained of their treatment when held overnight in the Hall of Justice after a mass arrest on the campus on January 23. But I neglected to film my interview with the police captain in charge of the jail so that he could be shown responding to these complaints. The editor correctly pointed out that since film has a much greater impact on the viewer than description of an interview does, I was in effect being unfair to the jailer. This cautionary tale should suggest the care with which newsmen try to allow all sides their hearing.

An obvious corollary is that the reporter must be fair in choosing the very small amount of contextual data he has time or space to report. For example, although much of the reporting at San Francisco State described the police violence, I and many other reporters tried, in fairness, to find episodes of correct police behavior. On one occasion, I filmed and televised a police sergeant restraining an officer who was apparently about to attack a student for taunting him. Fellow police later told me that the sergeant was "the last of the good guys," but I suppressed that in my report because I thought it would cancel the effect of what was a praiseworthy bit of behavior. On another occasion, I filmed and televised a lieutenant and his "cool" squad, who ignored taunts and obscenities. The lieutenant cheerfully clapped his hands to the rhythm of the derogatory chants and revolutionary songs of the student demonstrators.

The effort to attain impartiality or fairness in reporting often leads newspapermen to say that you should let the story tell itself. This attempt is their equivalent of the scientist's inductive method. But even the inductive method requires a theoretical focus for selecting the problem to be examined. And similarly the presentation of a news story contains an element of intuition, which also implies a theoretical focus, in grasping what the facts seem to indicate. But the intuition of the newsman, like the definition of the problem in scientific inquiry, develops from considering the facts; it cannot ignore them.

Thus, I found myself puzzling over the degree to which the black students, so impenetrable a group for a middle-aged white newsman to study, represented widespread aspirations of the black community and to what degree they might be, as some contended, merely a small number trying to blackmail the college for personal advantage. Some of their leaders spoke persuasively, some merely offensively. I was struck by a resemblance between the swagger of the young, beret-wearing black militant and the traditional swagger of the young military officer—a swagger expressing a professed readiness to die in combat that seemed to me quite pitiful in either case, but especially in the former, in view of the overwhelming force the students faced. But I withheld any judgment of the black students until the day a prominent physician and newspaper publisher, Carlton Goodlett, spoke to a strike rally and cried out that the black community would not let its best children be destroyed and that it had waited a long time for a revolutionary youth. I saw the student leaders then as he seemed to see them. They were not just dissidents or hoodlums. They were the flower of the black community, and its hope. In that sense, these students were truly representative of the aspirations of the black community. To me that view was convincing because of what I can only call an intuitive perception. But this view was also consistent with all the facts I knew then. Later it was further supported when Goodlett brought numerous prominent black people, including a city supervisor and a Berkeley city councilman, to speak in this vein at other strike rallies.

Finally, the competent newsman is not simply a technician or a hack; he makes professional judgments as he forms his own interpretation, as he comes to see the story, as he would say. An instance of this judgmental process occurred on a day when anxiety seemed to mount among the people on the campus to an almost unbearable degree. Police had dispersed with some violence and numerous arrests a very large demonstration. Several of the arrests apparently were made merely because people did not get out of the way fast enough. Both students and police seemed very angry by the end of the day, and my friends among the faculty and other campus informants were in distress that would be hard to exaggerate. Everyone seemed to be anticipating that as bad as things were, they were certain to get worse. As I was puzzling over how to present this story effectively on the air another newsman handed me a pistol bullet he had found on a campus path. That, I saw suddenly, was what everyone was afraid of. And I held the bullet before the camera that night and organized the rest of the account around this symbol of the increasing violence that everyone feared.

It may still be asked whether the personal value system I disclosed by my behavior is an appropriate one for a reporter. A reporter must consider not only his professional and ethical standards but the way in which his activities affect his credibility with his audience. When I was on the staff of the *San Francisco Chronicle,* an experienced reporter told me that he thought my impartiality as an education reporter might be questioned because I was also a teacher. But, he added, if other *Chronicle* reporters could run for public office without objection from management—as two had recently done successfully—he thought I could justify my activity. During the SFSC events, I can recall only one reporter who commented that my being a member of the teachers' union might be bad for my station. In general, other reporters were more complimentary about my coverage than otherwise. Yet I was taking a risk in this politically charged situation that my station and I might be to some degree discredited if a public issue were made of my affiliations. Fortunately this did not happen. As it was, our reporting on San Francisco State, of which I did the largest share, earned us more compliments than criticism. Even an attack by Hayakawa himself, when he appeared as our guest and sweepingly accused all the reporters on the program of being his enemies, did us little harm except perhaps with his most devoted partisans. Our mail contained abuse for a few days, but the net result was in our favor. There are other risks in involvement, but they are the sort reporters encounter everyday. For a businessman, an official, or a politician, a news story can be of great importance, and the reporter who writes it is, to that interested person, a participant in his affairs willy-nilly. Consequently he tries to win the reporter to his side. Even the most skillful reporter may sometimes be manipulated by a subtle and skillful person who is the source of information on a particular story.

These were the risks. What were the advantages of the two roles? Why did I find them more complementary than conflicting? One advantage, obviously, was my acquaintance with the faculty and students. A reporter needs informants and values sources. More important, I think, was my familiarity with what the college was like in normal times—knowledge which supplied a useful contrast to observations made during the crisis. I could appreciate the effects of the earliest demonstrations both in my own classroom and elsewhere. For example, my journalism students were not, on the whole, very supportive of the student strike. Nevertheless, they were so concerned about it that during the interim between student and faculty strikes, they needed to discuss the matter before we could undertake any class work. Perhaps because I knew how disturbances on the campus affect the educational enterprise, I became aware more quickly than some other reporters did of the profound disruption, which some of them at first tended to minimize, because I knew how disturbances on the campus affect the educational enterprise. And I saw my teacher colleagues changing their attitudes and focusing with increasing concern on the campus difficulties. As a teacher myself, I could share their emotions. That experience led me to join the union—and of course, taking that step also helped me to understand some parts of the story better. True, this understanding from within was as a teacher only, and I could not pretend to special understanding of the administrators' or the students' viewpoints. There I was little better prepared than any other reporter.

Perhaps, too, the involved reporter—whatever the basis for his involvement—is forced to take the story seriously, in a way that the detached or indifferent reporter sometimes does not do. The flippant tone and the bright gibes of sensational journalism are no temptation to him. The inside story does not receive its focus from gossip. Perception of what an event means to those involved can help the reporter to organize facts into a coherent picture.

The positive advantages of involvement by the reporter are tacitly recognized by modern news practice in the tendency toward specialization. The police reporter practices a specialty hallowed in newspaper tradition. Science, politics, and finance have long been specialist fields. Sections of the newspaper closely linked to the advertising department—churches, real estate, travel, food, theaters, and books—have also produced their specialists. More recently, education, architecture and planning, urban affairs, and military affairs have begun to acquire their specialist reporters. Not infrequently, a reporter assigned to cover the courts decides to attend law school or a political reporter takes temporary leave from his paper to participate in a political campaign. In practice it is difficult and perhaps impossible to draw the line between penetration—in depth, as some say in current journalistic cant—and participation in the affairs of the groups the specialists report.

To summarize, the shift from so-called objectivity in reporting to interpretation means that a reporter must try intensively to understand social relationships, personal motives, and other generating forces of the news. He cannot content himself with mere accurate recording of "factual" data. This concern leads to involvement, perhaps at first only through friendly associations with the individuals participating in events. But eventually, observations of events lead to the formation of a personal viewpoint and perhaps even to participation as a private citizen. In my view, this participation is an opportunity the reporter should welcome rather than reject. The reporter can accept the risks implied by involvement, relying on his professional standards to protect him, or he can renounce the opportunity to learn more about his general field and his particular story than can be discovered in official announcements, public meetings, and formal documents. But those who favor this latter alternative in the name of objectivity may relinquish part of their professional responsibility. If matters turned out badly at San Francisco State, it was not, I think, because reporters tried—as many did—to understand the feelings and ideas of students and faculty, as well as of administrators, trustees, politicians, and the general public. It was not because of the efforts of teachers who protested, at much more risk, against authoritarian college governance, ruthless political exploitation, and police brutality. Much more blame may attach to those who fearfully—or with some false notion of professional objectivity—stood aside from the painful conflict. The active participants were not the only ones who affected the college in a time of crisis. Those who were passive onlookers were equally responsible for the destructive and demoralizing aftermath to the events at State.

CHAPTER **8**

Confronting Irreconcilable Issues

Theodore Kroeber

♪✲♪✲♪✲♪✲♪✲♪✲♪✲♪✲♪✲♪✲♪✲♪✲♪✲♪✲♪

In November 1968 the president of San Francisco State College, Robert Smith, called an all-campus convocation to air the issues surrounding the student strike, which was then two weeks old. At that point, the faculty was still largely uncommitted and surprisingly uninvolved. The students directed the strike at the administration of San Francisco State and the state college system rather than at the faculty. But both faculty and students were electrified by the proposal of a convocation for the whole campus community. It seemed to provide a marvelous opportunity for communication among factions and thus an opportunity to avert the threatening violence.

119

At the first meeting of the convocation, I was asked to sit as the faculty representative on a panel held in the main college auditorium. The remainder of the panel consisted of student strike leaders, representatives of the administration, including Smith, and a moderator, Professor Jules Grossman. The auditorium was filled early by students and faculty, so the proceedings were carried by closed circuit television to other large rooms and auditoriums around the campus. The local educational television station, KQED, also carried the proceedings to anyone in the San Francisco Bay Area who cared to tune in.

By the end of the first morning session, I was aware of the reasons for the difficulties we were having in solving the problems accented by the strike. The issues raised by the student strikers (for example, a call for the end of racism on campus, the demand for an increased say in curricular matters) did not appear on the surface, at least, to be ones the faculty would be unwilling to help implement. Yet as I sat in and listened to the panel proceedings, I wondered both why we seemed bent on taking a collision course and why the convocation had ever seemed so promising a method to avert it. The answers to these questions emerged as I listened to the students talk that morning—comparing their words with my experience with our faculty. In summarizing that morning session, I selected four areas in which to contrast student and faculty positions.

The first of these was the focus on the institution. The student strikers made very clear that the source of their energy and the focus of their work were outside the college. Their concern and interest were in the community or communities from which they had come or where they were spending most of their energies. They were responsive primarily to community needs and community demands rather than to college needs and college demands. For these students, the college exists to serve the community directly. To this end, they had established and operated extensive community aid programs, including tutorial assistance for children in deprived areas, work in the city juvenile hall, a community leadership training program, a draft information service, and communication media for community public relations. Some of these programs had already been in existence for five years.

But this focus of attention is radically different from a traditional academic view of the institution. The faculty think of the college primarily as a self-contained institution with its main focus on the pursuit of knowledge. They tend to believe that the major college activities stem from their own activities, such as writing, doing research, and teaching, which are all performed on the campus, in the laboratory, or in their studies at home. Even where college projects do operate in the community, the faculty do not see their major function as helping the community but as serving educational goals—that is, developing information or training teachers. The faculty feel that once established, the college sets its own rules and defines its own concerns and that ultimately such independence best serves the community which established the college.

The two views, student and faculty, on the role of the institution seem to be incongruent. If students succeed in bringing the college into the community—and the community into the college— many faculty will feel the loss of what they see as the traditional political isolation and immunity of the campus. They foresee that they will be expected to explain their activities to an unsympathetic and naive public. At the same time, they will have to engage in a continuing fight to keep political issues from damaging the openness of their inquiry and the effectiveness of their teaching. But, on the other hand, if the college remains in isolation as an ivory tower, the students fear that whatever skills and knowledge they may gain will be irrelevant. In their view, the isolation has already gone so far that the critical problems of the time are not being faced, investigated, or attacked. Thus limited college time and resources will have been wasted (80 per cent of our students work full- or part-time), for their college education will not have prepared them for the world in which they will live. With these antithetical priorities, conflict seems inevitable. The battle for the walls had to be joined, with one side trying to defend their existence and the other trying to tear them down.

A second nexus for collision was the issue of violence. Most of us were brought up assuming that at least the college campus was a quiet and peaceful place where rationality held sway and where conflict, if it occurred, certainly would be verbal and quiet. Middle-class morality requires a sustained level of public propriety; and our traditional expectation is that college behavior will conform to these standards. We do not touch each other in anger (or in affection), and we want our classrooms to be free of invasion of any kind. In return for the freedom to teach as we want, we allow others to teach as they want. We do not expect to have to defend the value of our philosophy, our psychology, or our microbiology. This perspective has been at the base of our campus way of life; we like it that way and believe it to be productive. Perhaps most of the students at State also started out thinking this way about the general problem of public demeanor and violence. They are certainly not all of that mind now. Over and over, before and during the convocation, one could hear just how far away from that position many had come. These students told us repeatedly that poverty, racism, neglect, and complacency had become acute problems and that our peaceful solutions were ineffective. They openly said that morality required that any means necessary be used to solve these social problems. And many of the means proposed were, by traditional standards, violent. In essence the students said, "If I have to come into your classroom to bring my message to you and your class, I will come in even if I have to force my way in." For many professors no matter could be more serious. Their angry response focused upon the idea that these actions attacked academic freedom.

The third point which caught my attention that morning in the convocation concerned standards. Many faculty bring up the issue of standards of academic worth when new programs are proposed—especially if they are student initiated. As faculty, we take comfort and pride in the standards with which we were raised; they affect merit promotions and appear in principles such as "rank has its privileges." We qualified for our jobs by living up to them, and we continue to respect them. Through history they seem to have proved their value. Any new standards introduced at a college may threaten not only the personal positions of the teachers there but also the whole academic community by affecting faculty members who may wish to join, other campuses currently training future teachers, other colleges where students may continue their educations, and institutions which grant research and other financial aid. Nonetheless, students are questioning the value of these standards. They ask what it means to be qualified to teach. For example, does a Ph.D. automatically give a young, white, middle-class scholar knowledge of black ghetto people? Does it inform him of their strengths, imbue him with their culture, allow him to communicate with or for them? The students also raise questions about our admission standards. They wonder if SAT scores and high school grades are predictive of future contribution and achievement. They point out that we have restricted our way of viewing the world and of living in it to a style which is not universally accepted as valid. (See Chapter Six.) Furthermore, the students argue that unless education at colleges is relevant to the life of the student, whatever other standards that education meets are unimportant. We were faced with another example of tradition versus revolution, of the well-established versus a new wave, of the entrenched system versus a rapid and thorough reform.

The fourth and final issue I reflected on that day concerned the exclusiveness of proposed ethnic programs such as the black studies program. One of the most controversial and revolutionary aspects of the program was the proposal that the black studies department have an all-black faculty. I think this exclusiveness is one of the most interesting and one of the most complex issues involved. It is also one of the most central. Most members of our faculty come from liberal civil rights–oriented backgrounds, and many have at one time or another spent their energies in a struggle for integration. Interestingly enough, integration was also very big with the students until about 1966, and it was emphasized in the very student programs out of which the current programs have come. This focus gradually changed as experience in the community began to suggest a need for more complex answers to the ethnic problems than those offered by such powerful but simple slogans as "integration now." For example, much of the work of white tutors in black areas was undone by the simple fact that the relationship of black child to white tutor only perpetuated the image of white superiority. A shift was made in this program to put black tutors with black children. Although the success of the move is still to be assessed, it is not too early to see the success of the same principle when it is used in the college recruitment of minority high school students. Sending ethnically identified college students to do the recruiting has shown immediate results. The high school student cannot avoid the conclusion that if his "brother" is already in college, old prejudices are no longer so well entrenched as he suspected. The advisor must be wrong who told him that no one of his race should bother to apply to college because he could not possibly be admitted.

Even for those on the campus who appreciate the importance

of ethnic role models, there is a liberal tradition which reads something like this: "Ultimately we all have to learn to live together. Ultimately all people have something to contribute. So why wait? Why not get together now?" This is the integration tradition, and it comes into conflict with what we heard from the student strikers on the morning of the convocation. What they were saying about integration was more like this: "We must do it differently, at least for now. Without integrity there is no real integration. We must risk the label of reverse racism in order to foster positive identity. Once our identity is established, a true collaboration with you can and will emerge." So the issue of separatism versus integration comes up again. But now the earlier roles of black and white are reversed, and there is still another antagonism to add to the conflict.

Given the polarity of the views expressed on issues so fundamental to the system of education, collision could have been and should have been anticipated. Still there had been high expectations for the convocation. On the faculty side, hope must have arisen because it appeared that the convocation supplied a context in which a verbal solution could be achieved: where men of goodwill can speak together, they can find mutual understanding. To many striking students the convocation must have seemed a rare opportunity to reach more people than had ever listened to them before. The convocation was also official recognition of their existence and importance. At some level, we all knew that there could be no solution to these apparently irreconcilable positions unless each side listened to and understood the other. The convocation may have helped only to establish clearly the issues of conflict, but for a fleeting golden moment it seemed to offer the chance for solution.

PART III

𝑭*or many of the faculty,*
SFSC, though generally peaceful on the surface, is not the same college
it was before the strike. The faculty now understand clearly that
they have no voice in decisions about campus affairs. The strike did
not suddenly alter the process of decision-making on the campus; but
it did destroy many of the existing myths about that process.

And so it may now be more difficult for many faculty members
to maintain their professional image to their own satisfaction. Kinch's
chapter shows the importance of gentlemen's agreements in support-
ing this image. Prior to the strike these agreements enabled the pro-
fessor to maintain a picture of himself as a free professional even
though employed within an extended bureaucracy. But such agree-
ments are easily broken, and when they disappeared, it became clear

MYTH OF
FACULTY POWER

♪∗♪∗♪∗♪∗♪∗♪∗♪∗♪∗♪∗♪∗♪∗♪∗♪∗♪∗♪∗♪∗♪

that the administration does not grant any self-governance to professors greater than that given to other workers who punch a time clock. The faculty saw with discouraging clarity that if their views contradict the preferences of the trustees, their votes carry no weight. When the administrative decision makers choose not to listen, the academicians have no further recourse; letters of protest, threats of resignation, votes of no confidence have all the impact of Don Quixote tilting at windmills. The chapter "Folly of Academic Resolutions" illustrates the ineffectiveness of traditional professional tactics. But these are the tactics of men of reason; and many are still not willing to relinquish such activities despite their limited value in the political arena.

The faculty is still divided in its analysis of the events; many

127

*members, though unhappy with the state of affairs on campus, felt
that they had no alternative but to return to their teaching after the
strike and to work from the inside. Some of these people eventually
resigned their faculty or administrative positions in frustration at the
difficulties of reaching their goals through traditional means. Other
members are still committed to the existing academic hierarchy despite
bitter disappointments and frustrations with their colleagues as well
as with the administration. The next two essays present two different
analyses of the factors which led faculty members to make their varying and contradictory decisions.*

*Bartelme's chapter "Psyching Out the Strike" presents a psy-
chologically oriented impression of what may have been motivating
the individual professors who did and did not strike. It suggests that
both creative and destructive impulses are released in times of crisis,
when normal authorities are under attack, and that such forces may
be found on either side of the picket line.*

*"Which Side Are You On?" examines why faculty members
who considered themselves political liberals could be found on both
sides during the strike. One reason suggested is that the political
allegiances of these professors do not provide a clear and consistent
directive when action is required. The liberal faculty members—as
distinct from either the identified conservatives or the radicals—are
caught on the horns of a dilemma in the current campus revolution;
they have a commitment to the advancement of minority rights and
the belief in the importance of specified procedures for resolving
political disagreements. When forced into a decision, these liberals
scatter into the conservative and radical camps, depending on whether
or not they accept the current institutionalized procedures as basically
just and essentially nonpolitical. Those who are convinced that the
system is not just give priority to the advancement of minority rights.
Those who maintain their belief in the impersonal justice of the system
believe that individual injustices, though lamentable, must wait upon
the workings of institutional patterns of redress.*

*"Aristocratic Workers" provides a perspective from which to
summarize the preceding essays. Cavan presents an analysis of and an
explanation for the difficulty faculty members face in changing their
tactics to meet new situations. College professors are in the interesting
position of receiving great respect in the society at large as long as they*

have no power. As a scholar or a professional man of knowledge, a professor has the prestige usually restricted to the free professionals. However, when he recognizes his real position as a worker in a bureaucracy, the situation changes. For some, it may be an unhappy paradox that when the professor begins to unionize and to strike, he can hope to gain more control over his working conditions than he now possesses, even though he loses the prestige granted to him in his days of political innocence.

CHAPTER 9

The Failure of
Gentlemen's Agreements

John W. Kinch

Institutions of higher education very elaborately camouflage the contradictions inherent in their structure. One such hidden contradiction arises from combining an extensive and elaborate bureaucracy, dependent upon observable criteria for standards of performance, with a collegial system, where intuitive and subtle judgments about professionals are made. The contradiction remains hidden through the use of unspoken gentlemen's agreements between the administrative officials and the academicians. This chapter examines new perceptions of this contradiction—perceptions which develop through participation in an organizational crisis.

Probably no other institution in American society relies more on unspoken gentlemen's agreements than does our system of higher education. It is assumed that no rules are required when the workers are highly educated and well socialized to the professional doctrine of independence and self-discipline. A man's classroom is his castle, and any attempt by his boss (chairman or dean) to invade this domain is seen as a violation of the most sacred tenets of the institution—academic freedom and respect for professional competency. Thus the bureaucracy is requested to assume that its regulations are met.

It is understood by the authorities as well as by colleagues that a professor meets his class, teaches the subject matter described in the announcement of that class competently, and distributes grades to students according to an implied standard of fairness and equity. It is further understood that the professor spends the many hours during the week when he is not in his classroom in activities that enhance his professional standing. In most colleges and universities, the professor is formally expected to be in his classroom anywhere from four to twelve hours a week. Except for occasional faculty meetings, committee assignments, and office hours, the remainder of the time is unspecified. What the professor does with this unassigned time is judged only in the long term, when he ultimately produces some product—as an article, book, or formal report.

Compare this situation with typical work settings. The laborer punches a time clock and may be closely supervised by his foreman. The medical doctor in private practice has no supervisor, but he does have a highly structured and demanding appointment schedule. With the possible exception of the minister, only the college professor enjoys the freedom of so many hours left to his own discretion.

Of course, the system of informal agreements includes a greater range of understandings that can be described here. For example, in many colleges and universities an instructor who is sick and cannot meet his class calls a colleague or his teaching assistant, who takes over the class for him that day. Alternatively a professor may simply ask the department secretary to place a note on the classroom door saying that the class will not meet that day. The possibility of formally hiring a substitute teacher (as would be expected at lower educational levels) for a day or even a week would probably not be considered. Because the organization of the course is left up to the instructor, no one wishes to bother with the problem of finding a "credited" substitute for such specialized instruction.

Most college systems have formal regulations to cover many administrative responsibilities of the participants. Although in any institutionalized setting these formal regulations are modified through informal understandings, the difference between the college/university and other settings is the degree to which these informal arrangements predominate. In academic bureaucracies the claim of professionalism provides a powerful rationale for overriding or ignoring organizational routines. Most of the participants in the system have experienced a long period of socialization where, it is argued, they have been taught the virtues of independence and self-discipline. Supported by this professional ideology, they respond indignantly to any questions about the quality of their performance. And any specific question about the amount of time and effort spent in professional activity is taken as a challenge. This ideology of professionalism is reflected throughout the academic structure. The complexities of bureaucratic administration may dilute the vehemence with which adherence to self-discipline is expounded, but in the levels closest to the working profession it is still very strong. The importance of the ideology of professionalism is certainly clear to any department chairman reviewing colleague performance. Higher authorities may expect the chairman to supervise his colleagues, but to maintain their allegiance he is careful to avoid any appearance of supervising.

Another unspoken agreement involves the selection of department chairmen. The faculty often elect their chairmen following some democratic procedure. Yet the formal rules of the organization say that the chairman of the department is named by the president of the college on the recommendation of the dean. The gentlemen's agreement is that the dean and the president rubber stamp the departmental choice. Thus the combination of formal and informal procedures permits the administration the ritual choice of its own representatives. The chairman thus fills a position in which "management" assumes that he is one of them, while the workers expect him to share their perspectives and priorities. If he is lucky, the contradictions never become apparent. If he is not, he may share some of the woes of the foreman in industry.

With these problems in mind, many chairmen go through a

face-saving ritual even before they accept the position to imply affiliation with their colleagues. They disavow any interest in the position
when nominated. They tell their colleagues that they are not administrators; they are educators. Once elected they announce that since
someone has to do the dirty work they will take their turn, but for
only a limited time—for certainly they have no aspirations to move
higher in the academic bureaucracy.

As they often have no previous administrative experience or
interest, many do look forward to returning to teaching and research.
Yet the chairmanship has some attractions, particularly in lesser schools
where other types of prestige—from the rewards of research and
publication—are lacking. While denouncing bureaucratic paper work
—and the essential meaninglessness of his position—the chairman may
want the recognition provided by the position and fight to keep it.
The chairmanship brings prestige, which comes with leadership and
representation of an august body, and power, which comes from participating in the bureaucratic policy-making and decision-making
process.

The higher administration expects the chairman to solve the
complex problems of coordination and management within the bureaucracy. Yet membership and advancement in professional circles—
from which chairmen are recruited—come not from administrative
skill but from a reputation in scholarship and teaching. And so the
dependence of the bureaucracy upon the election of a chairman from
a collegial body restricts the possibilities of finding leaders with demonstrated administrative ability. Thus, the bureaucratic system is impeded
in its functioning by its own personnel problems. Goals of efficiency
are in conflict with principles of departmental autonomy. The men
elected to manipulate the bureaucracy and carry out its requirements
are trained neither to do so nor to value the skills involved. Yet an
extremely complex bureaucracy requires skillful management and re-
sponsiveness to technical requirements from each department head.

These requirements are particularly acute in the California
State college system. Consider the following example of the paradox.
No one would dare question what Professor Y is teaching in his long-
established class in American social problems, for an extremely wide
latitude is permitted within the classroom. The bureaucracy has no
knowledge, much less control, in this area. But the bureaucracy may

supply insuperable barriers to teaching plans which go beyond traditional course titles. When Professor Y suggests a new course in deviant
behavior, it may take two years to establish it (assuming no one op-
poses it). Professor Y must take his proposal to the members of the
curriculum committee of his department. After they review it and
append a justification for it, it is presented to the department. On their
approval, it goes to the dean, who presents it to his council to see that
it does not overlap with offerings from other departments or conflict
with notions of propriety and jurisdiction held in other departments.
Thus a course recommendation moves through the bureaucratic
machinery—from the undergraduate curriculum committee of the
college to the vice-president of academic affairs to the president and
finally to the chancellor's office, far from the campus. The request for
the course may even require approval—beyond the chancellor—of
the Board of Trustees at their monthly meeting. Finally, Professor Y
is informed that his new course has been approved. However, one
final barrier still remains. Before a course can be offered it must appear
in the college bulletin, and the bulletin for next year has already gone
to press. Therefore, the earliest date to offer Professor Y's course is the
year after next.

    These are the problems which emerge on a day-to-day basis
when professional responsibility must be reconciled with bureaucratic
restraints. Let us consider what happens in these institutions when they
are confronted with a major crisis. What occurs to acceptance of the
value premise that academicians are self-accountable when a college
is confronted with a major student revolt? The contention here is that
one of the major problems in an institutional structure like the one
described in this paper is its vulnerability to disruption and its inflexi-
bility in responding to demands for change. When disruptions come,
they immediately bring into question many of the agreements that
have long remained unquestioned by revealing where the real sources
of power lie.

    For example, during a crisis what happens to the routine of
reporting that faculty responsibilities have been met? Under ordinary
conditions the deans routinely sign attendance reports. These reports
then go to the payroll office where the monthly payroll is prepared and
then sent to the state capital. Here the monthly checks are issued and
returned to the college for distribution. The formal agreement requires

that a professor submit a sick leave form when ill so that the dean may note his absence and take the appropriate portion of salary for the month from accumulated sick leave. But informally, except for prolonged illness, the whole thing is easier forgotten and not reported. In ordinary times, the state auditor occasionally noted how very few sick leaves were used in the college and suggested that no group could be that healthy. To avoid further admonition the administration distributed a memo asking faculty not to forget to fill out sick leave forms when missing classes because of illness.

Then came the disruption and strike at SFSC. The November payroll came due before many of the faculty were involved in the student strike. Although some faculty were clearly not holding classes, most of the deans signed the attendance reports for their jurisdictions without comment. But when these reports were inspected by the Department of Finance in the state capital, the question arose whether some faculty were being paid while on strike. This question placed the deans in a quandary about the management of the report for the next month. According to the gentlemen's agreement between themselves and the faculty, they should not ask who was absent but rather wait until the absent member reported himself. However, evidence indicated that some of the faculty had forgotten their side of the agreement and had not reported their absences. And so, at the end of December, most of the deans abandoned their gentlemanly posture and asked department chairmen to report any faculty who were not meeting their classes. But many chairmen, seeing themselves as part of the faculty and not the administration, did not wish to comply. They sent statements to their deans saying to the best of their knowledge the members of their departments were fulfilling their professional obligations; but these chairmen did not consider it their duty to make an inquiry on the matter. However, some chairmen did comply by reporting absences, and some faculty did voluntarily report to their dean that they were on strike. As a consequence of these more-or-less voluntary responses, the attendance reports showed enough absences to pacify the state officials for another month. The deans however were forced to consider how to develop a better recording system for the following month.

Two additional matters soon complicated the attendance issue. First, on January 6 (the first day after Christmas vacation) the local teachers' union called a formal strike and began picketing the campus. The union formally requested all faculty and students to respect the picket lines by not entering the campus. Attendance in classes on campus dropped (by various estimates) to approximately 20 per cent of normal. Therefore it was publicly clear that many professors and students were not meeting their assigned responsibilities. The second complication arose when the Board of Trustees (and particularly the governor—an ex-officio member of the board), interested in quelling the strike, pointed to a provision in the state education code which states that any faculty member who is absent without leave for five consecutive working days has automatically tendered his resignation. The rule, said to be designed for administrative management of payroll problems in cases of death and unauthorized departure, was now claimed as being applicable to striking faculty members. This rule made the attendance reports for the January pay period a particularly keen focus of attention. Both the acting president of the college and the governor publicly announced that they would have no choice but to assume that anyone who remained on strike for five consecutive days had resigned.

As a matter of internal management within the college, the acting president asked his deans to obtain a daily attendance report on all faculty from the department chairmen. Such a plan would appear to be a practical bureaucratic solution to a relatively straightforward problem of record-keeping. However, at this point most chairmen were struggling to keep departments from complete disruption and to avoid open hostilities over the issues of the strike. The request to meet administrative directives and the necessity to conciliate faculty members who, irrespective of their stand in the current conflict, held strong notions about independence and self-determination, brought the conflicts inherent in the chairman's position clearly into focus. Chairmen reacted to the attendance directive in varying ways. Some sided with the administration and complied with the directive. One group of thirty-five chairmen (from a total of fifty-seven in the various departments of the college) formulated a joint statement which they signed and sent to their deans. Their statement reflected their commitment to their faculty:

The current situation demands the utmost ingenuity from each of us to protect the academic interest and moral integrity of the faculty and students. The system of daily attendance reporting recently imposed upon us tends to debase the faculty because it designates mere classroom presence as the only acceptable professional behavior. Furthermore, it tends to foster distrust and disintegration within each department, distort our function as department chairmen, and ultimately set fellow teachers against each other. We therefore cannot in good conscience comply with your directives.

Confronted with this statement by a substantial majority of "middle-level management," the administration had no alternative but to abandon this first attempt to develop a system of reporting.

When the chairmen refused this bureaucratic responsibility, the next highest administrative level—the deans—were pressured to assume it. They had been told the previous month that they would be criminally liable if they were detected signing false attendance reports. Yet, if they were not to sign, no one under their jurisdiction would receive payment for that month. Again, as with the chairmen, the conflict between bureaucratic responsibility and faculty loyalty appeared in sharp focus. In the past no one questioned the reports of the deans. Now the entire country knew that at least some of the faculty at San Francisco State College were on strike and thus absent without leave. Striking teachers, on the advice of their union attorney, refused to inform anyone in the administration about their activities during the strike. So the old gentlemen's agreement, which assumed a loyalty to the system, collapsed.

In order to sidestep the protesting chairmen and still avert the threats from the state, the deans developed a Weekly Performance Report. Here the notion of the gentlemen's agreement was refashioned to the advantage of the administration. This form, sent directly to each faculty member, requested that all teachers report their presence; anyone not signing the form was presumed absent. The form read:

I hereby certify that I have performed my regularly assigned instructional duties and my other regularly assigned duties at San Francisco State College during the period. . . .

These forms were to be signed each Tuesday to cover the previous week. The claim was that this system would preserve the faculty members' right to self-accountability but would not require that the strikers incriminate themselves. However, this procedure was repudiated by many of the faculty even before it went into effect. Many nonstrikers referred to the forms as the weekly loyalty oath and said that they would refuse to sign. They contended that as professionals it was in violation of their position to require them to sign an affidavit affirming their performance each week. Department chairmen complained that it was one more thing that divided their departments since the reports of one segment of the department were to be used to punish another segment. Very few seriously argued that striking faculty should be paid, but a good number objected to this new accounting system because, though taken for granted in other institutions, it was seen as an infringement of their professional status.

In order to avoid the collapse of their latest system, most of the deans indicated that they would accept verbal statements in lieu of the signed performance reports. One dean stated in a memo:

> Although I personally regard this process as undesirable, it might head off some sort of "time clock" or affidavit system, both of which have been threatened. If the signing of these documents present any of you with major difficulty, I am willing to attempt to arrange verification by any alternative method you propose.

As the end of the month came near, the deans sent out personal letters to all who had not yet reported to them, stating a willingness to accept almost any kind of report. (One dean was reported to be accepting as a sign of fulfillment of duties the verbal statements by faculty that they refused to sign.) At the end of the first month under this system, most deans returned attendance reports to the administration showing all those who had reported (by whatever means) as present and allowing to the best of their knowledge that the remaining faculty were absent during that period.

The crisis made nakedly clear that the complex bureaucracy required restriction of professional independence. This requirement had been obscured for a long time by the gentlemen's agreements. At one end of the hierarchy the governor (and the people of the state) had always operated on the assumption that there was a system for accounting for attendance. Many people in the state could not believe that it would not be possible to ascertain who was on strike the first week. "What do you mean, you don't know who was absent last week?" The governor found himself in a very embarrassing position when he had to back down on his threats to fire all teachers who were on strike for five consecutive days. He had had no idea that there would be any problem identifying who was at work and who was not. At the other end of the hierarchy there existed a similar disillusionment. Many of the faculty were completely unaware of the existence of the attendance reports that were being signed by deans for years. They were shocked to find that they had been treated all along as paid employees on an accountable time schedule.

What is so apparent now is that the middle management, particularly the deans, had for years been playing the role of guardians against disillusion. They had regularly signed and submitted attendance reports, allowing top management the security of feeling that there was complete control within their enterprise. At the same time, by not publicizing to the workers the existence of the attendance reports, they had enabled the faculty to operate under the illusion of complete self-discipline.

The unspoken gentlemen's agreements have an important function in allowing the participants to do their thing in the way they feel most appropriate. Without such agreements the institution must stand on its rigid rules and regulations. But the viability of these rules and regulations has never been tested, for the gentlemen's agreements were always there, obscuring the actual situation. These agreements have been the glue that has held together a flimsy structure built on contradictory assumptions. When these agreements fail in times of crises, the structure wavers.

Now that the crisis has left each side deprived of its vital misunderstanding, the institution appears to be a badly patched facsimile of what it was once thought to be. The drift toward stronger bureaucratic control and greater regulation and investigation of the academic's activity, which began during the crisis, seems unalterable. But without further crises, over time each side may again become blinded to the patchwork accommodations and regain former illusions. At present there seems little hope that the current enlightenment will be used in California for constructive innovation.

CHAPTER 10

Folly of
Academic Resolutions

Patrick J. McGillivray, Worth S. Summers

Pʀₒfₑₛₛₒᵣₛ — Professors expect to have a say
in governing the academy. In fulfilling this expectation, they rely on
the intellectual force of reasonable persuasion rather than on the tactics of power. They assume that policies are modified by the use of
evidence and logic and by consideration of ethical standards. Thus,
faculties have formed senates to reflect their collective opinion. The
senates accomplish this end by making statements which are generally
indicative of feelings in the faculty. These statements usually take the
form of resolutions to inspire, inform, or instruct those bodies or persons to whom they are addressed. The statements also purport to report
the opinions and feelings of the academic body accurately. What do

senates hope to accomplish by passing these resolutions? Because of their august and respected position, senators imagine that their opinions carry particular weight and, therefore, that they persuade as well as instruct or inspire by statements of their convictions. This chapter considers the validity of that assumption by examining the effectiveness of passing resolutions in times of crisis.

Crises in higher education have become almost commonplace. Perhaps they are merely symptomatic of underlying problems: the depersonalization, irrelevance, and unresponsiveness of educational bureaucracies, and the political interference in and the impairment of an already inadequate educational process. These problems and issues have produced considerable debate, discussion, and analysis in the media and on virtually every campus. It is hard to imagine a reasonably informed professor who is not alarmed and concerned about the current status and prospects of higher education. On California State college campuses the crisis at San Francisco State in 1968 generated a very intense concern which led many professors and students to seek some program of action designed to help effect a solution. One inescapable fact explains much of this concern: they live in the same system with San Francisco State. What Chancellor Glenn Dumke can do at San Francisco State, he can do at Sacramento State or at Chico; what S. I. Hayakawa can do at San Francisco, a new president imposed by the chancellor can do at Pomona or San Fernando.

Traditionally, academics have responded to serious crises by passing resolutions that deplore and condemn. However, the idea that a resolution is effective in persuading the powerful is a myth; and though some state college professors may still tenaciously cling to it, the myth is becoming clearly untenable in the light of political events in California, which have forced many faculty members to recognize the futility of passing their thoroughly debated and well-reasoned resolutions. While such resolutions may give professors a sense of accomplishment, they have been proven ineffective simply because the men in power ignore them.

Yet this myth of the power of the resolution persists for reasons deeply rooted in the traditional role of the professor. Generally professors are reluctant to engage in any collective action which threatens to submerge their characteristic independence and individuality. Passing a resolution, however, is entirely consistent with cherished norms of reason and persuasion. Professors believe, moreover, that colleagues and students change their beliefs and actions largely on the basis of factual or moral evidence. A resolution, then, inasmuch as it does present facts or intellectual or moral judgments, is an exercise in academic persuasion. The academic man does not see the resolution as a wordy, empty gesture; rather it is an act in complete conformity with his theory of power. The implicit assumption underlying the academic theory of power is that those with the capacity to act in a situation will do so when they are presented with evidence that such action is either reasonable or moral. Such an assumption explains why the resolution is taken seriously by the academic community and why much time and care and debate go into the formulation of such statements.

The experience at Sacramento State in response to the crisis at SFSC illustrates this process. The initial response on the Sacramento State campus to the chancellor's peremptory suspension of George Murray was to send telegrams. On November 1, 1968, the Association of California State College Professors (ACSCP) and the American Federation of Teachers (AFT) local sent telegrams to President Robert Smith at San Francisco State congratulating him on his "courageous" stand in defying Dumke's efforts to fire Murray. Unfortunately, Smith capitulated and fired Murray twenty-four hours later. Various interested educational groups then began to marshal additional forces. On November 4 the AFT local sponsored a meeting of all interested faculty and students, and there was wide-ranging discussion of the issues. An AFT-sponsored rally on November 13 drew several hundred people to listen to a series of speeches attacking Dumke and Governor Ronald Reagan and expressing sympathy for the student strike at San Francisco. These meetings were the preparation for bolstering faculty determination to formulate a resolution.

At a meeting called by the AFT and the ACSCP on November 19, the decision was made to take a bold and unprecedented step: to demand an emergency meeting of the Academic Senate or, failing this, to demand a general faculty meeting. The executive committee of the senate would not call a special session of the senate but was willing to put the issue of San Francisco on its agenda sometime in December. The executive committee also refused to call a general faculty meeting. Their reasoning was that the cause of San Francisco State would be hurt by a poor turnout of professors. The AFT leadership decided to bypass the senate and to go through the necessary procedures to call a general faculty meeting.

Convening such a meeting involved considerable effort. The faculty manual specified that a meeting had to be called if 20 per cent of the faculty requested it. Petitions were prepared and circulated, and with some effort signatures were gathered from 25 per cent of the faculty within thirty-six hours. At this point even the most militant faculty thought in terms of resolutions. At a series of AFT Steering Committee meetings resolutions were prepared and strategies for countering anticipated opposition were developed. Priority was given to a resolution condemning Dumke and the trustees for their interference at San Francisco and expressing support for the efforts of the faculty there to settle the issues. Other resolutions expressed alarm over police violence, called for a convocation every Friday to discuss the crises in the state colleges, and, finally, demanded an investigation of the accreditation status of the state colleges.

On November 25, the meeting was called to order when about 300 faculty members (out of a total of 580) and 150 students had assembled. The first hour was devoted to a panel discussion of the problems of the state colleges; and the second hour was devoted to the introduction of resolutions. The first priority resolution contained the following statements:

> The faculty of Sacramento State College commend the Academic Senate and faculty of San Francisco State College for their continuing efforts to restore a normal academic environment and to cope with the complex problems facing San Francisco State College and the state college system. . . . The faculty . . . expresses its profound regret and resentment of Mr. Dumke's precipitous interference in the local affairs of San Francisco State College, [and it] . . . expresses its similar profound regret and resentment of the Board of Trustees' precipitous interference in the local affairs of San Francisco State College. . . . The faculty of Sacramento State College condemns the call by the governor and other public officials for the use of police and/or military in order to maintain classes at San Francisco State College and also condemns the threats of violence and use of violence by some individuals at San Francisco State College; the democratic educational processes cannot exist in either situation.

After a lengthy debate on a number of extraneous matters and on whether the passage of the resolution might anger people in the State House, the resolution was passed.

This victory aroused in the initiators of the resolution an honest feeling of pride in the effectiveness and boldness of the action. The students expressed some cynicism and contempt, but the liberal, agitating faculty interpreted these expressions as an indication that the students did not fully understand academic politics or the moral force such a resolution would carry with the trustees and the chancellor. However, within a week of this triumph, Smith had resigned (under pressure), Hayakawa was peremptorily appointed as acting president by the trustees without consultation with any academic body, and the general faculty meeting at San Francisco was dissolved. The new president began his rule—and continued it—by substantially ignoring the Academic Senate and any resolutions it produced.

Professors at both schools, San Francisco and Sacramento, should have known from experience how absurd the passage of resolutions can be when a body has no power. The most prestigious faculty body, the statewide Academic Senate, in May 1968 had called for Dumke's resignation. This resolution was far more radical than most in that it contained a call for action and a threat—the senate would resign. Even with the threat, the trustees ignored the resolution, explaining that they, not the faculty, had hired Dumke. The statewide senate did not resign, but even had it made the threat good, its demise would hardly have created a power vacuum.

But the passage of academic resolutions is not always ineffective. A crucial consideration is whether additional pressure groups develop to support and activate the resolutions. For example, the statewide Academic Senate and the Sacramento State Academic Senate both had passed resolutions urging the faculty to participate in a one day work stoppage if any professor were fired for striking. As a result the AFT local at Sacramento State called for a one day work stoppage on January 22 to protest the firing of strikers at San Jose State. Sympathetic non-AFT teachers were contacted, and union members and students who had already committed themselves to this policy established picket lines. The AFT reported that at least half of the faculty did not teach that day. Similar work stoppages occurred at Sonoma, Hayward, and Pomona, and, in each instance, it was the AFT local that carried out the call of the senate for action. On those campuses where, for one reason or another, the union did not organize a work stoppage, the resolution had no effect; there simply were no work stoppages.

These cases indicate that the ineffectiveness of resolutions results from various deficiences which most faculty have not been willing to recognize. First, the resolutions, once passed, often fail to reach even the audience for which they are intended. Most resolution-passing is not carried out within a well-established communication network of all interested and relevant parties; as a result, the audience for academic resolutions consists, in the main, of the same people who passed them. Second, only those who pass the resolution consider them important, for academic resolutions typically have little or no legitimacy in the bureaucratic authority system. No one is obliged to abide by them. Thus, even when a resolution does reach its intended audience, it lacks the necessary authority to force officials to act. The resolution must rely upon a far less compelling force—its power to persuade by its expression of moral concern or by its reason. But without any political leverage, moral pressure is usually ineffective. And so, even when a faculty body passes a resolution calling for action and reaches the intended audience, it still lacks the organizational means to implement action in the face of opposition or indifference.

An awareness of political realities has caused increasingly more professors in the state colleges to lose faith in the existing institutional links to the statewide college administration. And so they are cut off from the only available bureaucratic means for exercising control through reason and persuasion. Meanwhile, the authorities with real power—chancellor, trustees, and presidents acting at their direction—are unimpeded by carefully worded resolutions from the faculty. Resolutions, no matter how forceful in expression of moral outrage or how reasoned in argument, do not affect the outcome of a crisis. The faculty has become increasingly aware that it is powerless to effect changes or even to protect itself from reprisals by the traditional means of passing moral resolutions. A new form of organization is required which will permit the initiation and development of new strategies by which to express interests. Such a possibility is found in a union organization.

The AFT on most campuses has begun to organize to reach the public, to engage in informational picketing, to raise funds, and to prepare for the possibility of future strikes—the ultimate weapon in attempting to bring peaceful change. The strike tactic rests upon a rather different theory of power than that which makes the passage of resolutions seem reasonable. It assumes that those in authority act and surrender some control, not on the basis of reason or moral suasion alone, but by calculating the social and economic costs of not agreeing to do so. A strike, by generating such costs, adds leverage to faculty attempts to negotiate and to bargain over grievances with administration and trustees—to require "management" to share power with and thereby relinquish some power to the faculty. The development of the union movement in academia suggests that everywhere professors are coming to realize the folly of pursuing their old ways, the folly of academic resolutions.

CHAPTER 11

Psyching Out
the Strike

Kenwood Bartelme

This chapter speculates about
the psychological impetus for action characterizing many of the faculty
before and during the strike at State. Some understanding of psychological processes can be gained from the issues on which the strikers
focused their attention. For example, while most faculty, regardless
of political ideology, expressed moral outrage over the presence of
large numbers of police on campus, they divided on their explanations
of how this outrage had occurred. Conservatives believed that the
necessity for police had been created by the intransigent and outrageous behavior of students; in their view, this behavior had no
rational goal and was at variance with the principles of democracy

and the academy. The issues for these conservatives were clear: their outrage was directed at those who assaulted authority.

Others found it difficult to hold students responsible. They were equally angry at the seemingly arbitrary suspension of faculty and students and the threats of reprisals against the entire college from the Board of Trustees. However, even sympathetic faculty found it difficult to associate themselves with the students. Many of them were baffled by the professed tactics (nonnegotiation) and the rhetoric (ear-splitting) of the militants. Certainly the faculty and administration had never before been referred to as lackeys, pigs, and motherfuckers in public—sometimes televised—meetings.

In this confusion morality and political considerations became indistinguishable; and they also were influenced by personality tendencies. Even within a relatively similar political stance—that is, opposed to the conservative forces in the state—faculty were divided. Those sympathetic to student demands could be found all along the familiar political continuum of gradualism-activism. The justification for gradualism often developed around a pessimistic view of how successful a rebellion against the establishment could be. The gradualists pointed to the reality of the power structure as a restraint on rash collective action; salaries and other advantages might be withheld from rebellious faculties. Besides, as they pointed out, the governor, who seemed to have little sympathy with the students, was enormously popular with the people. And the college trustees, with support and leadership provided by the governor, were equipped with legal machinery for crushing any confrontation. This segment of the faculty felt vulnerable to what they saw as the impulsiveness of the students on one hand and the repressiveness of the state authority on the other. They felt they had little power and saw scant possibility for generating enough to influence the authority structure. And so they found their only comfort in the belief that the pendulum would return to a position of liberalism and moderation. As a correlate, they believed that the kind of opposition that a strike implied might delay that swing. Patience, a sense of history, and a steady, reasonable pressure on authority characterized the outlook and tactics of this group. Their focus was on practical issues.

On the other hand, the activists were predictably impatient

and antihistorical. Their identification with the student rebels stemmed from what they believed to be legitimate outrage. For members of this group, self-esteem depended in good part on open opposition to the use of police on campus and other repressive legal maneuvers. Perhaps because the moral issues were so clear to them, they were inclined to be optimistic about gaining support for their position not only from organized labor but also from the whole community. In any case, their optimism and their view of the moral issues involved outweighed practical considerations about possible adverse political consequences.

Another moral issue involved in creating these amorphous groups of gradualists-activists concerned various dimensions of responsibility. Was the first responsibility to oneself, was it to the student, or was it to society? Was it to one's scholarly work or to working with students, to social progress or to the traditional values of the academy? The gradualist saw his colleagues agonizing over these alternatives and making courageous, even though often personally repugnant—or even unpolitical—decisions. Some of the more rebellious dissenters saw the agonizing over these choices as self-interested. They were not willing to give credit, as the gradualists were, to intellectual doubts. Instead, they saw such questioning as a road to personal safety or a way of avoiding the legitimate moral issues. However, it would be misleading to accept pejorative evaluations and to assume that members of either group were weak in morality.

A psychological perspective suggests that people have individual ways of utilizing guilt in relating to social reality. Occasionally embittered critics of the college disturbances dismissed dissenters as psychopaths, that is, as people with defective moral sensibility. But the dissenting faculty and students hardly showed a want of moral idealism. In fact, they formulated their objectives specifically in terms of moral obligations and sentiments. On the other hand, neither could one easily question the moral concern of the gradualists. Many of them made exhausting efforts to secure a settlement of the conflict. They often worked without any tangible reward or support; and when they refused to join with their radical colleagues in the final showdown, they were vilified as if they had done nothing. Ways of protecting one's self-esteem seemed to separate the two groups, rather than inequalities in moral fiber. Rules embedded in conscience and attitudes toward the role of authority kept gradualists within the context of the traditional academic processes of accommodation while rules also propelled activists toward the revolt of the strike.

One way to interpret these divergent responses is to see them as consequences of an individual's relationship to the existing authority structure. Only in such times as these—when academic working life is disrupted—does the traditional authority structure come into question. At other times, academics do not perceive that structure or consider it confining. Instead, they see themselves with a charge to investigate ideas in a sanctuary, or a preserve, set apart from the world. For this purpose, they are protected by a structure which is itself supported by the legal machinery of the state. Because they are beneficiaries of the system, they are unlikely to support or sustain a movement which challenges the political distribution of power. The introversion and withdrawal permitted by a college—and often mirrored in the personal traits of college teachers—are deeply satisfying to many academics. Their preserve offers them status, peace, and security. Of course, these working conditions have traditionally been protected by a system of controls that is strongly paternalistic rather than democratic or egalitarian. The administration has defined the ground rules by which this academic preserve is conducted for so long that faculty accept them as necessary restrictions; indeed they often approve of them.

The protection which the preserve affords has traditionally been associated with a removal from the faculty of the power to make decisions considered time-consuming and petty. But the boundaries between petty and crucial decisions are often hard to draw; and the decision-making body can assume the power to make all administrative decisions any time it chooses to do so. This body is seen as paternalistic when decisions are agreeable, that is, when they support academic views of proper order. But it is seen as harsh or authoritarian when the decisions become disagreeable. And many of the faculty thought the paternalistic superstructure had turned on them in alarming ways during the strife at State. They were angry at the seemingly arbitrary suspension of faculty and students, at the threats of reprisals from the quasipolitical body that controlled the college system, and at what seemed the cynical exploitation of their chaos and anguish by larger political forces. Thus, some began to view the authority structure represented by college administration and trustees as an intolerable oppression. But not everyone wanted to relinguish allegiance to the old pattern or to consider the paternalism that outrageous. These differences indicate basic psychological responses to authority.

Authority is the main avenue through which moral behavior is internalized. Children are socialized by their superiors in the primary group, that is, by their parents. Children internalize the demands of authority in the development of a conscience, which commits them to an acceptance of rules, procedures, and roles set by the external authority. Because these principles are gradually internalized, their origins seem to the individual to be deeply personal. And for many well-trained individuals even the thought of transgression causes great discomfort. Thus appearing on the picket line aroused uneasiness in many people who were otherwise disposed to protest the encroachment of the power of the state on the college community. They were too well bred (or up tight in the student vernacular) to accept such a flouting of expectation—such unconventional behavior. The verbal behavior of many gradualists was militant, but they were unable to perform the act that would visibly align them against authority. They gave economic and ideological reasons for refusing to take this final step, and very likely in many cases these were important factors. But possibly anxiety over the visible act of rebellion was enough of a threat to their sense of self to immobilize them.

However not all faculty were immobilized. How can their responses to authority in this situation be explained? Perhaps an examination of psychological theory about the relationship between identifications within the family and authority can provide this explanation. In his analysis of children's play, Jean Piaget observed that "the conflict between obedience and individual liberty is . . . the affliction of childhood. . . . In real life the only solutions to this conflict are submission, revolt, or cooperation, which involves some measure of compromise."[1] The choice that one makes in resolving this conflict depends, no doubt, on motives hidden from awareness because the authority problem that anyone experiences in everyday life mirrors the anxieties of early childhood. In psychoanalytic terms, the trump card of authority is the superego, representing, as it does, the voice of

[1] J. Piaget, *Play, Dreams and Imitation in Childhood* (New York: Norton, 1962), p. 149ff.

conscience. This voice, which punishes transgressions upon the moral preserves of society, develops out of the suppression of willful and angry impulses common to children in their dealings with parents. Children learn to give way to parents whether or not they entirely understand why; and the superego grows from the internalization of the interdicts and values that parents believe to be important.

In theory this situation creates an ambivalence toward authority which in times of personal or social stress may be resolved in regressive actions. Three alternatives are available: Regression by antagonistic or rebellious behavior against authority on the grounds that the directives are unjust; regression by withdrawal and immobilization; and regression by violent activity supporting authority—through either direct participation or vicarious observation of assaults upon critics of the established order. All of these resolutions have a moral or valuative quality that satisfies the conscience and alleviates the distress of the ambivalence toward authority. The betrayal by what had been regarded in politically sunnier times as a relatively benign and reasonable paternalism induced in the faculty a variety of social and psychological regressions which followed the alternative responses to ambivalence about authority.

In an academic community, where concepts of status and the influence of tradition play so important a role in molding behavior, the act of striking takes on a regressive quality as a retreat from a mature style of living. The gradualists could argue that in striking, activists were indulging in an impulsive and irrational mode of behavior. For those who did engage in this behavior, the risks became very real: the possibility of losing not only one's social niche and economic livelihood but also a firm sense of who one is and what one represents. For those in the strike and on the picket line, regression appeared in exhibitionistic and impractical rebellion.

However, not striking did not provide protection either. There were risks in maintaining reason in the face of mounting social conflict and the capricious behavior of the constituted authority. Early in the crisis, for example, the militant faculty attacked the gradualists as faint-hearted and indifferent to their professed ideals and standards of freedom. Later in the crisis and from the other side, Acting President S. I. Hayakawa also attacked them. He continually denigrated the college and the faculty in his public statements. His attempts to redefine the threat of striking faculty by redefining the academic role of everyone at the college involved a devastating rhetoric: the college was second-rate, and the faculty could easily be replaced by high school teachers or by laymen from the community. Such an argument is intolerable to the psychic well-being of the ordinary professor. Some expressed the fear that the destructive forces on both sides would collide and a bloodbath would ensue. Their thinking seemed dominated by the specter of a society aggressively out of control. They maintained their security by persisting in familiar patterns of activity, even in unusual circumstances. The increasing breakdown of communication and control within the institution led some members of this group to withdraw from the zone of conflict and to carry on instruction in their home or in places remote from the turmoil. The drain in self-esteem often reflected itself in fantasies of greater withdrawal. (They would take other academic jobs, or they would remain aloof and maintain a cynical attitude toward all these social aberrations.)

Other gradualists worked doggedly through the channels of the college system to persuade a by now deaf bureaucratic structure to make flexible responses to students' demands. Their self-esteem seemed to require ignoring what the crisis had highlighted—the powerlessness of conventional faculty groups to influence the destiny of the college through conventional means. Perhaps the avoidance of confrontation and the pursuit of a conventional solution protected them from expressing primitive feelings of fear and outrage. Their regression may be called intellectual, taking the form of compartmentalization and denial of the meaning of the social and political events occurring around them.

Those who agreed to support authority wholeheartedly were free, if they wished, to embed whatever sadistic impulses they might have had in mechanisms that compelled obedience. For example, they could view with approval the use of police and other stern disciplinary activities. They could then wash their hands of any guilt arising from the strains of punitive action. Hayakawa's analogy of one of the bloodiest police-student confrontations to his first roller coaster ride is a classic description of a regressive emotion, though natural enough in the circumstances. Certain of the public, judging from radio talk show comments and newspaper letters, enjoyed the spectacle of authority punishing, maiming, and scattering the disobedient rebel "hordes." In the vicarious glow of the television screen, individual impulses could have a field day free from the chill of internal disapproval. For this group, the aggressions that one might ordinarily have, and own up to, appeared to be projected on to the activist students. Thus, some persons were conscientiously able to recommend imprisonment and even physical beatings for their capricious faculty brothers and the rebel students. Clearly there is little threat to self-esteem in a conscience that uses externalization to solve problems. For those supporting the administration and the status quo, regression was exhibited in identifying with the punitive behavior of the authorities.

All these responses to paternalism—withdrawal, denial, or acceptance of authority—involve patterns of regression. But responses to paternalism can also be quite creative and innovative. New patterns for the management of authority may evolve in experimentation or play. In most psychological theory, play in childhood (and no doubt, throughout life) is an important experience for learning to manage authority because it offers a period of trial-and-error learning while permitting an escape from the problems of authority, and it provides an opportunity to develop techniques of cooperation and arbitration. In fact, it has been argued that rules of games provide the precedents for parliaments and courts. Laws and regulations are extensions of the morality of childhood play, a morality that is itself a product of accommodating impulsive life to the requirements of reality. One way to accommodate is to accept authority as benign or paternal, as representing one's own best interests.

Paternalism represents a perennial paradox for individuality. Potentially it offers an umbrella under which the person can pursue his own interests, free—at least in the academy—from the necessity for time-consuming wrestling with social and political realities. The academy, in its ideal form, was developed as a preserve for the unfettered use of intellectual energy either for instruction or for original thought. The only requirement from the paternalistic structure of the academy, in return, is a compliance with the legal and social forms of the society. However, no private or public educational stewardship condones the use of the academy as a base for revolutionary action or for the aggressive dissemination of ideas that clash with the current morality. Precisely in periods of social crisis do these limitations on critical or dissenting behavior come into urgent question and, in some instances, are felt to be intolerable. At these points, the protective features of the system can be felt as weights that suppress the direct defense of principle and the expression of deep convictions. (See Chapter Six.)

The decision to strike, to defy the institution in so explicit a way, was a departure from ordinary academic behavior that surely reflected important values. Where gradualists were willing to compromise with the new administration while they waited for a fresh hand of political cards, cooperation with such punitive paternal symbols as Hayakawa or Ronald Reagan—and their attendant troops of police—became an impossible concession to many activists. There were moral commitments to students to serve as spurs, and there was a pervasive sense of outrage at the political assault on the college; but these were sentiments shared by many outside the striking community. The key to striking behavior seemed to be personality—the sense of having to challenge the demands and strictures of the now highly visible paternalistic structure of the state college system.

The strikers had a special range of academic interests and a rather unconventional history. Supporters of the strike were chiefly from the division of liberal arts and the behavioral sciences—except for history and political science—with a scattering from the natural sciences. There was one striker from the department of physical education and one from the school of business. There is no objective basis for forming a profile of the strikers; but their academic affiliations suggest that their interests inclined toward the philosophical, the social, and the artistic. Nevitt Sanford and his associates have thrown some light on this pattern in their researches relating the personalities of individuals to particular vocational interests.[2] They found that undergraduates with academic interests similar to those of faculty strikers tend to be impulsive, unconventional, and strongly antiauthoritarian. And their finding is supported by informal observations of the activist faculty. In their preacademic careers union members included a golden gloves champion, a merchant marine, a convict, famous authors and poets, a railroad man, a California state assemblyman, and persons who had already been punished for their political beliefs.

Activists mobilized around such people for resistance to the

[2] N. Sanford, *Where Colleges Fail* (San Francisco: Jossey-Bass, 1967).

institutional authorities. When the threatened hard line of those
authorities became a reality, a cadre of faculty formed a committee
pledged to resist the police presence on the campus. This campus, after
November 6, had taken on the atmosphere of an ominous carnival
where the political vignettes and improvisations of the revolutionary
students found their counterpoise in the disciplined and ruthless behavior of the city police. The silences of the police, the rhythmic
cadence of their comings and goings, the quick and intense surges of
violence that left their adversaries senseless and subdued, the uni-
formity of their costumes with the bizarre plastic masks and the guns
and clubs, their seeming indifference to politics and philosophy—all
stood in eerie contrast to the motley students. The students were
dressed in their own costumes of alienation, carrying black and red
banners that seemed to symbolize the death and rebirth of the society.
They were armed with rocks, bottles, and pine cones; they were noisy
and insulting toward any representative of authority; and they reacted
variably to their own capture with rage, grief, and stoicism.

The daily campus scene became a contrast between the pro-
methean images of restraint, self-mastery, obligation, necessary suffering, and repressive brutality, and the orphic images of the release of
exuberant and sometimes violent passions in the liberation of the
senses. (The striking students were represented by a troubadour, and
pretty girls from their ranks passed out exotic foods and flowers.) In
this polarized atmosphere, the pull either to tighten one's self-controls
or to regress somewhat became quite compelling for faculty observer/
participants. One measure of faculty members' involvement was the
emotional distance they maintained from the daily skirmishes. Some
opposing the repressions on campus lost all restraint. For instance,
a female faculty member, ordinarily a model of self-control, broke into
tears and slapped a student from the athletic department who was
urging the police to kill the striking marchers. Others wept openly
when the police struck students and dragged them away.

At certain points during the early weeks of the crisis, some
members of the faculty were willing to risk their heads and perhaps
their lives merely to restore peace to the campus. As their identifications with the students strengthened, they became increasingly ambitious about attaining student goals. A growing number were willing,
at least temporarily, to consider as a possibility the revolutionary aim

of the radical redistribution of power in the academic community. This attitude was not so much grandiosity or sedition as it was a genuine loosening of the bonds and allegiances to that paternalistic structure that had served the faculty so well in the past but which was offering them little succor in the present. The dangerous rather than the benevolent father became the dominant image. The archaic images of betrayal and castration were reified for academics as the threats and posturing of the governor and his administrative servants grew more alarming. Academic professionals were clearly regarded as crackbrained and disloyal employees (bad children) by the movie matinee idol of yesteryear. As the faculty came under heavier and heavier attack, the activists saw their position becoming increasingly perilous. And they became antagonistic to their conservative or gradualist colleagues who did not see these dangers in the same light. After the strike began, the disdain that activists expressed for their nonstriking colleagues reflected the extent of their emotional alienation from the traditional sources of faculty power. They saw themselves as participants in a historic revolt that would, if successful, permit them to climb over and around the paternalistic structure. They felt they were asserting their own individuality and integrity through the strike, which was a startling departure from the tactics of the faculty meeting with its usual pleas and resolutions sent to the bureaucratic hierarchy for relief or redress.

There is no evidence that the regressive feelings and fantasies of activists were different in kind from those of the gradualists. Members of both groups apparently experienced fear, withdrawal, outrage, and panic, and had fantasies of revenge; these similar attitudes were presumably integrated with the perceptions and values of the individual faculty person. However, one group within the faculty—whatever the motive—acted in a more forceful and rebellious way than did the other group. And this behavior was described as radical; the strikers were more radical than the others. From this point of view, radicalization is a particular way of responding to regressive feelings. But what does more radical mean?

Emotional and behavioral rejection of an important authority leads to alienation from conventional values. This alienation may result in a radical cynicism—a form of despair—in which political and social forms are seen as corrupt beyond redemption, and nihilism becomes the only recourse. Alternatively, alienation may result in a radical political vision—a form of hope—in which such concepts as truth, justice, and freedom will really emerge. An increase in self-esteem comes with the novelty and excitement of participating in a reevaluation of both self and society. And such deeply felt personal changes were expressed by many of the strikers in such commonplace phrases as "I've been politicized" or "I've been radicalized." Thus the explosive feeling that induced the regressive refusal to help or to serve the traditional authority was sublimated in the social vision of change; and thus it served as justification for radical action.

CHAPTER 12

Which Side Are You On?

Rachel Kahn-Hut

♪☀♫♪☀♫♪☀♫♪☀♫♪☀♫♪☀♫♪☀♫♪☀♫♪☀♫♪☀♫

The conflict at State in 1968–1969 turned administrators, students, and faculty into warring factions. The conflict occurred not only among the three groups, but also, and perhaps most bitterly, within the groups. This chapter examines one aspect of the conflict within the faculty—the difficulties of defining the liberal position when faced with pressures for social change in a context of confrontation and violence.

For the faculty, the confrontation occurred when the picket lines were established, for it then became necessary to display personal values by crossing or honoring the line. At that point, many faculty became confused by—or aghast at—the decisions of their friends and colleagues. The already announced conservatives and radicals behaved in predictable ways; but the liberals surprised one another. On both sides of the line they said of their opponents, "I just can't understand why he is doing that. I never would have expected it of him." The

159

explanations offered were usually variations of "He let his emotions gain control of his reason" or "That shows that he never really was a liberal in the first place." But such statements provide little clarification. Greater understanding may follow from examining the two major assumptions on which the liberal position is based: the value of freedom of expression and the necessity to maintain the institutions which traditionally have protected that freedom. Ordinarily these goals are compatible; yet under certain conditions the inherent contradictions become clear. Such conditions were created by the campus disruptions at SFSC.

The predominant characteristic of the academic life is its independence. Professors have more freedom than most workers in a bureaucracy to delimit their responsibilities to the employer. They account quite casually for their time; and their only tangible product at the end of a work period is a list of letters on an official document. (See Chapter Thirteen.) The professor also has the freedom to define quite arbitrarily what his client should want to achieve. Thus, the definition of appropriate academic endeavor varies from classroom to classroom. The student can be asked to demonstrate a familiarity with basic data, an ability to manipulate these data in a logical manner, or an ability to use them as the basis for new and creative ideas. (With such a variety of standards before them, it is not surprising that students constantly irritate their teachers with the question "What are the requirements for this course?") Furthermore, once tenure is awarded, the academic is the final judge of his professional performance. He is not required to develop a product with demonstrable usefulness for society, for even the eventual performances of his students are of no particular importance in his evaluation. As a consequence of these understandings, life outside the academy may change rapidly while on the inside the professor continues to explore a single idea of traditional or classical appeal.

Professors maintain this independence—despite political and professional differences among themselves—because of their commitment to the principle of the academy and to the development of knowledge. (See Chapter Five.) Since it is believed that the development of knowledge often results from exploration of new directions, it is argued that to restrict the activities of a colleague by delimiting his subject is to restrict this development of knowledge. Thus, professional independence has been secured from colleagues largely by asserting its fundamental importance in the mutual intellectual endeavor. The principle is valued so highly that even colleagues suspected of gross incompetence are rarely challenged. But there is no such clear independence from the other two interest groups of the university: the direct client—the students—and the employer—the Board of Trustees and the local administration. The degree of pressure they place on the academics varies according to circumstances in each institution. But the power of the administration is always strongest, whatever the circumstances, in public institutions.[1]

This absence of faculty autonomy became obvious at SFSC in the fall of 1968. The clearest sign that professors had no control of the campus and no independence within it was the presence of the police, who symbolized the current physical and political attack on the academy. The faculty protested their presence but had no power in the matter. The struggle to control the college occurred between the students and the trustees, who fought to define—among other things— the appropriate role of the faculty. The students would no longer accept the definition of their role as being subordinate to the faculty. They wished to become partners and even leaders on the campus. They demonstrated both their importance and their independence in their ability to mobilize the campus community and to focus its attention on their concerns. But for many faculty this new-found student power was a direct threat to the myth of their own authority. If they did not have the power to organize the college around their traditional theoretical or analytic concerns, they preferred the pragmatic definition of the college advanced by the trustees to the revolutionary definition of the students. At least the trustees might be expected to offer token acceptance of the honorific status of faculty.

Yet during the troubles at State the trustees refused even token support to the notion of the independent self-governing academic community. First, they suspended a faculty member, George Murray, without considering the principles of due process by which the faculty supposedly are governed. Next, the trustees made it perfectly clear that they saw no necessity to accept duly elected faculty representatives

[1] C. Jencks and D. Riesman, *The Academic Revolution* (Garden City, N.Y.: Doubleday, 1968). Interestingly enough, however, they see the power of public officials declining.

as participants in the decision-making process; they refused even to negotiate. Thus, the trustees presented their definition of the faculty as a group with no legitimate role in determining the future of the campus. And so the faculty view of its position was attacked by the students and denied by the trustees. Although this conflict was always latent in faculty relations with the trustees, the full implications were newly revealed to many. (See Chapter Nine.) For example, at a general faculty meeting after the conclusion of the strike, the faculty voted to prohibit the continuation of the current student disciplinary procedures. The President of the Academic Senate, who chaired the meeting, was asked to explain the meaning of the decision. He noted that according to the faculty rulings the decision became the law of the campus, but according to administrative regulations the president of the college had only to take the vote under consideration. And so the faculty vote had no effect; the prohibited disciplinary procedures were continued.

The lack of faculty power revealed in this crisis was used by some members to explain the apparent contradiction between their statement of liberal values and their unwillingness to go out on a limb. They acceded to the administrative authorities because they saw no benefit in fighting a doomed battle. Many hoped that if they acted "responsibly," the faculty would eventually earn a voice in decisions affecting the campus. They felt no compunction about crossing the picket line in order to carry out their responsibilities. They saw labor union strategies not only as nonprofessional but also as the final attack upon professional status and authority. But in this same situation, others of the faculty came to feel, paradoxically perhaps, that only by use of labor union tactics could their professional voice be introduced into policy discussions about the campus. These professors manned the picket lines and forced their wavering colleagues to make some decisions. Not crossing the picket line—either out of fear of potential violence or from a general opposition to crossing picket lines—was counted in the daily census in support of the striking students and faculty and also in opposition to the policies of the trustees and the acting president, who demanded that the campus remain open. Crossing the line from a feeling of responsibility to currently enrolled students or from an overriding need to earn a paycheck was counted in support of the trustees and in opposition to the dissident students and faculty. There was no way to remain neutral or to demonstrate partial agreement on either side.

The majority of the faculty on the campus were in this ambivalent position. This group included many who regarded themselves as liberals; they joined neither the AFT local (on the left) nor the Faculty Renaissance (on the right). Forced even against their will to take sides, they often found it necessary to explain their choices—both to themselves and to their colleagues. At first, opponents tried to talk about issues, perhaps to convince each other to change position. But the major obstacle was that there was very often agreement between debaters on everything except the conclusion to be drawn from their common experiences.

Because liberals could find power used illegitimately by both the dissident students and the administrators, the rationale for one's actions developed primarily by noting the crimes of one side. The radical view, deploring the repression of the trustees, was accepted by the liberals who joined the picket lines. The conservative view, deploring student violence, was persuasive for liberals who crossed the line.

The radicals enumerated the failure of the trustees and their administrators to resolve the educational problems of the campus. Proponents of this view focused upon the trustees' attack on the college, which was implicit in their refusal to abide by due process in the suspension of Murray. (The faculty committee with jurisdiction in the case found so many violations of procedure in their collection and evaluation of evidence that they advised the reinstatement of Murray. Their recommendation was ignored.)

The trustees further demonstrated their indifference to the faculty by ignoring the faculty representatives sent to confer with them —not only about Murray but about long-standing problems of the college. When the trustees refused to negotiate with the faculty, they demonstrated that they felt they could develop an educational system while ignoring the concerns of those involved in the implementation of that system. It appeared that to retain their professional authority, the faculty had to demonstrate their political power. Thus, in the radical view, the trustees, through their own insistence that the faculty were employees, forced that faculty to adopt trade union tactics in order to get a hearing.

The radicals were also seriously concerned about the presence of the police on campus. The hatred or fear the police created in many members of the campus community led to violence which responsible individuals could not control. The radicals felt that the police were brought in because the trustees were unwilling to use the traditional academic method of resolving disagreements. The trustees defined participation in the convocation—a campuswide discussion of the issues—as support of the striking students. The radicals decried this view of the situation as well as the willingness of the trustees to use police to inhibit disagreement in the constituency. Many liberals also protested what they saw as an arbitrary use of bureaucratic power to settle problems and a reluctance to admit other parties to the decision-making process. These persons joined the picket line. They acted not from a change in their traditional commitment to liberal values but in an attempt to protect them.

On the other side, those liberals who accepted the conservative definition of the crisis also reacted against restrictions on the independence of the academy. However, they saw the students rather than the trustees as the cause of the restrictions. Some felt that the school of ethnic studies desired by the minority students had no place in an academic environment, that the intellectual life of a college must be separated from the political life of the world outside. If one were to define the university as a place to foment revolution, they argued, one would bring into disrepute the credentials of objective knowledge—the credentials by which the university is able to attain its independence from the practical, political world. In this view, the hesitation of the administration to permit change was a proper use of power and thus cause for neither protest nor rebellion.

Other conservatives paid less attention to the substantive matter of the demands than to the tactics used by the students to implement them. First, the students presented demands rather than requests open to negotiation. Then, they invaded classrooms, where they intimidated those not in agreement with the strike. Many conservatives were outraged by these events because they believed that such disreputable tactics had no place in academia. The use of reason and logic is the accepted tactic for all purposes; changes must be effected by persuasion not force. In this view, even legitimate claims should not be supported if they are pursued improperly. The conservatives

also deplored the presence of the police; but they saw them as necessary buffers against marauding students. The police were the lesser
evil; they were present to protect the rights of the majority, the
property of the state, and the lives of innocent bystanders. As the
legitimate agents of authority, they had the right to use force against
those who disturbed the peace.

Some who took this view did recognize a danger to the college
in the actions of the trustees. But they saw these increased restrictions
resulting from a right-wing backlash among the electorate and the
legislature, which controls college finances. This backlash was brought
about by the students themselves. So although many faculty distrusted
the new college president and disliked the arbitrary way in which he
was appointed, they acknowledged that legally the trustees had the
right to do what they wished. In consequence, these faculty members
felt the president should be supported and given every opportunity to
succeed. If he could not quell the disturbances, they feared even
greater repressions in the future. And if he could quell the disturbances, he would then gain the respect of the trustees and the legislature
and be in a stronger position to bring home rule to the campus. In any
case, as long as students were marauding, the faculty had not demonstrated their ability to run the campus. And so some liberals joined
the conservatives in an attempt to protect traditional values; they resisted the notion that physical disruption was the way to argue for
needed social changes.

Participants on both sides argued, of course, that their opponents ignored the basic premise of the liberal position. But actually,
each side articulated one issue inherent within that position. This ambivalence can be seen in the definition of liberalism given in the *En-
cyclopedia of the Social Sciences:* "Liberalism is the belief in and the
commitment to a set of methods and policies that have as their common aim greater freedom for the individual man."[2] This position contains two issues. The first is the value placed on the free expression of
individual personality. The second emphasizes the importance of up-
holding those institutions and policies which protect and foster both
free expression and confidence in that freedom. The first concern pro-

    [2] D. Smith, "Liberalism." In the *International Encyclopedia of the
Social Sciences,* Vol. 9 (New York: Macmillan and Free Press, 1968), pp.
276–282.

vides a focus on the goals—the free expression of individual personality. The second provides a focus on the means—those institutions and policies intended to protect the individual from arbitrary use of authority by the state.

In more familiar language, these two issues have been discussed as "freedom to" and "freedom from." These two concerns often, but not always, are associated in complementary fashion. "Freedom from" covers the aspect of noninterference. It includes an emphasis on the authority of reason, the desirability of impersonal social and political controls, the rule of law, and the use of methods of consent and persuasion. This focus has been the concern of what has come to be called the old left, or the new conservatives. "Freedom to" covers the aspect of enfranchisement. It includes an emphasis on the opportunity and capacity for free expression of the individual. This aspect of liberalism attacks the basis of privilege by encouraging state intervention if necessary to equalize opportunity for all. Currently, members of the New Left are the champions of this view. The history of liberalism can be seen as the history of the attempt to reconcile these two concerns.

Thus it can be argued that the notorious wishy-washy attitude of the liberal is due not so much to his inability or unwillingness to act as to his perception of the complex implications of his action. One dramatic example of this perceptiveness can be found in a recent interpretation of Hamlet, which sees him not as a weak man unable to participate in the real world by committing a concrete act but rather as a committed intellectual tormented by his perception of the danger inherent in either of his choices. The crisis at San Francisco State was much like this modern interpretation of Hamlet's torment. When the independence of the faculty position was attacked clearly, some liberals acted in terms of freedom to and joined, or at least honored, the strike. In doing so they supported the principle that the university should benefit a broader segment of society than it currently does. These liberals emphasized the classic goals of the liberal position and partially ignored the classic means of attaining them. Others acted in terms of the more familiar freedom from interpretation and decided to cross the picket line in opposition to the tactics of the students. These liberals were emphasizing the classic means for protection and were partially ignoring the classic goals. Neither group can be criticized for not adhering, at least in part, to its liberal tradition.

This experience of the faculty at SFSC is just one example from a growing list of political dilemmas involving the conflicts between liberal goals and liberal means. The dilemmas arise because mechanisms developed to protect the rights of one group may eventually be used in restricting the rights of others. Max Weber considered this quandary in his analysis of bureaucratic institutions, for he saw that bureaucracy established to extend equal treatment to all citizens might in time become discriminatory because a bureaucracy is organized as a rational and efficient system.[3] The rationality of bureaucratic organization is expressed in an ability to solve problems efficiently. The essence of the system is represented by the elaborate but standardized form, which can be processed rapidly once completed; though a problem may be unique to the individual, to an official it is one of a familiar category and thus can be managed routinely. Individualized consideration of each problem could never be so efficient. But the weakness of the system is that it cannot process data or people presenting problems outside the existing categories—that is, problems for which no forms have been prepared. Noncategorizable problems are not recognized as appropriate issues for the bureaucracy to solve. They tend to disappear and are soon forgotten because the success of the bureaucracy is determined by its continual management of already defined problems. No new mechanisms of management develop until the noncategorizable ones are recognized not as aberrant and minor in importance or number but as pervasive in the social context; because of this system real and valid grievances may continue unredressed for a long time.

Today increasing attention has been focused upon such issues. Examples of the problem are found in the obstacles which the poor face in obtaining justice given the existing legal concepts and procedures. Many daily problems of the poor—such as exploitation by merchants or neglect by public authorities—are not subject to legal redress. Thus some think that revision in the letter of the law—new criteria for defining legal problems—is required to meet the spirit

[3] H. Gerth and C. Mills, *From Max Weber* (Oxford: Oxford University Press, 1946), pp. 240–242.

of justice.[4] From this viewpoint, the value of a technically legal contract should not be permitted to outweigh unethical business practice
when the unsuspecting are tricked into binding contractual relations
against their own interests. Similarly those who recognize the political
implications of various channels of protest know that the right to distinguish between legitimate and illegitimate forms of protest rests with
the state. A danger inherent in the exercise of this right is that the distinction between legal and illegal dissent is not based upon the performance of specific actions but upon the way in which they are
viewed. Violence as a tactic is neither automatically considered illegal
nor rejected by traditional liberals, for they accept violence by authorities as legitimate and even necessary to maintain society. But violence
aimed against a system defined as adequate by these liberals is not
readily condoned.

The faculty response to the crisis at SFSC may be viewed in
this light. It is hard for a faculty member to see the educational system
which provides many benefits for him and for others in the society as
so repressive that counterviolence against it is legitimate. Instead one
is inclined to argue that the system should be maintained even if it is
occasionally put to discriminatory uses, for the cost of destroying the
system seems greater than the benefits to be gained by overthrowing
it. Those who do not personally experience the discrimination inherent
in the system can easily accept such an argument. In the past, when
liberals fought to extend the protection of civil rights, they fought
against discrimination they were experiencing—against the development of special rules to keep them from jobs and education. To the
degree that they have been successful in fighting this discrimination
they have gained "freedom from," and they now reap many of the
rewards society provides the successful.

What these liberals fail to recognize is that the application of
universal criteria is not enough to protect the civil rights of all citizens.
Those who through no fault of their own have been poorly educated
are now protesting against discrimination for which the traditional
guarantees of constitutional civil rights are of little help. Universal
standards applied for entrance to colleges or occupations inherently
discriminate against them; they are fighting for "freedom to." Not

    [4] L. Mayhew and A. Reiss, Jr., "The Social Organization of Legal Con-
tracts," *American Sociological Review*, 1969, *34*(3), 309–318.

having experienced this kind of discrimination themselves, many traditional liberals see the current violence as threatening the stability of a system they find adequate if not perfect. Consequently they believe such violence to be illegitimate. Thus we should not be surprised when we find many liberals joining the conservatives to protect the status quo rather than joining the battle to extend the rewards of society to those who are still disadvantaged.

CHAPTER 13

Aristocratic Workers

Sherri Cavan

ƒ♦

A style of life may be viewed as
a pattern of activity that characterizes the everyday social action of
some group. The everyday life of any given individual may be a collage
of varying components of different life styles. The longshoreman-
scholar is one example; the Supreme Court justice–mountain climber
is another. Although individuals may choose to meld different styles of
life for their own purposes, groups of individuals are described in
terms of those aspects of life style they share. In this sense, quite independent of their age, sex, income, political affiliation, or ethnic
background, what defines academicians as a collectivity, or social
group, is the style of life they share.

Styles of life—or any routine patterns of conduct—are made
possible when persons are located within institutional settings.[1] In

[1] E. Goffman, *Behavior in Public Places* (London: Collier-McMillan,
1964).

170

this sense institutional settings should not be narrowly interpreted to mean formal bureaucratic settings. Restaurants, barber shops, and grocery stores are institutional settings, for everyone who enters has generally similar expectations about what can be accomplished there. Everyone understands what behavior is and is not considered appropriate in that context. The institutionalized settings associated with particular status groups customarily provide the social stages, props, and backgrounds as well as the supporting cast of actors required to live out some particular style. For academicians, the settings are the institutions of higher learning—the college and university. Academicians are a status group to the degree that they share a common fate within those institutions and a common dependence on them for legitimate support of a common style of life.

The cap and gown of the academicians symbolize their generally privileged status in the social order—a status which has much in common with aristocratic status. Academicians ordinarily assume that such a style of life is proper and fitting for them. What the academician demands from the institutions of higher learning is essentially that they support him in the life style he wants to enjoy. Such demands are reflected in descriptions of academic positions found in employment ads in professional journals: "Salary range $10,000–$16,000 for nine months; . . . stimulating social, cultural, and economic change area. . . . Chance to develop new program. . . . Associate or full professor; undergraduate teaching; may lead to chairmanship of six-man department in near future. . . . Salary $9,000–$12,000 plus 20 per cent of noncontributory . . . retirement and fringe benefits—department growing and will shortly be giving the master's degree. . . . Flexibility according to specialization . . . high salaries, nine hour teaching load, removal expenses, and other fringe benefits." And here, from the applicants, are some of the characteristics desired of academic positions: "Desire associate or senior position in an urban area. . . . Prefer New England or West Coast. . . . Prefer Northeast. . . . Teaching-research university level. . . . Prefer location with opportunity to complete course work for Ph.D. nearby. . . . Will locate in warm climate."

Thus for academicians, salary and work load are but two considerations. As exemplified in ordinary professional gossip, other relevant considerations include the general standing of the institution; the social and intellectual climate in the surrounding area; and, often, whether student assistants are available for the academician's retinue. Furthermore, although academicians may be strongly committed to the goal of higher learning, such commitment does not necessarily extend to the specific institution of higher education where they are employed. Just like participants in other privileged occupations—sports, music, and art—academicians may be enticed from one institution of higher education to another by what the institution offers them for aggrandizing their particular style of life, including the nature of the position; the kinds of special privileges; the demands on time, action, person; and the opportunity to pursue individual interests.

Within the institutions of higher learning in America, the position the academician holds is officially a titled station, as is noted in rosters, bulletins, institutional announcements, and on the doors of faculty offices.[2] Thus, where honorifics are customarily employed, they are ordinarily used not only by the students in addressing the faculty[3] but also by the administrative personnel and their staff. Furthermore, academicians expect their position to be tenured, and the basis, legitimacy, likelihood, and outcome of tenure decisions are matters of serious consideration. The administration and its staff come and go for various reasons; the students come and go for obvious reasons. But once an academician has finally secured his niche in a particular institution, he expects to be free to abdicate it if he wishes to, while being ensured from deposition if he does not.

The privileges of both title and tenure reflect a general prestige which is supported by the opinions of the community. For American respondents, the college professor (as academicians are customarily known) ranks seventh out of ninety occupational categories.[4] In this social hierarchy, professors rank not only above the student in academic matters but also above the administrators in general prestige. Thus an academician can reasonably expect to be acknowledged as an authority in his dealings with students and as an object of respect in his dealings with administrators.

    [2] Cf. E. Post, *Etiquette: The Blue Book of Social Usage* (New York: Funk and Wagnalls, 1960), p. 28.
    [3] See, for example, T. Sebeok on naming and graduate students in *Style in Language* (Cambridge, Mass.: MIT Press, 1960).
    [4] National Opinion Research Center, "Jobs and Occupations: A Popular Evaluation," *Opinion News*, 1967, *9*, 3–13.

In addition to the general social honor accorded them, academicians often have special privileges within their institutions. For example, in most colleges and universities, facilities for eating and for personal hygiene are especially designated for faculty. Similarly, facilities which are generally for all members of the institution, such as the library and the book store, often employ special rules for the academician; for example, he is permitted to check out books for indefinite periods or to purchase his books at discount prices. Thus within institutions of higher learning, academicians can expect their position to be distinctive, if not decisive. For many and perhaps most academicians, their place of work is only partially defined by the administrative assignments of classrooms and offices. They expect to be free to take classes on field trips away from the institution, to meet in homes rather than classrooms, and to do as much of their academic work at home as they desire.

Academicians characteristically also expect other special privileges, so that what others in the institutions of higher learning are bound by in general the academician expects to be exempt from specifically. The relationship of the academician to the clock and the calendar of the institution provides one example. Although the academician's work may have a daily pattern to it, that pattern is at most only tangentially imposed on him by the organizational demands of the institution. The nine-unit teaching load essentially means that the academician's commitment to be present and accounted for in the institution is limited to nine hours a week, and even these hours can be canceled at will. A professor can also expect that variable amounts of time are to be spent with students and other faculty members. But he expects the scheduling of these other times to be either at his discretion or negotiable. Thus his office hours, when he is individually available to students, are typically set at his convenience. Departmental faculty meetings are usually arranged at the mutual convenience of the members of the department. Even the times of intracollegiate meetings can be negotiated, as when outside lectures and meetings conflict with local matters. Thus, at most, the institution of higher learning and the academician are only loosely joined by the clock and calendar. And from the perspective of the academician, such temporal arrangements are subject to his approval. This temporal flexibility in conjunction with physical seclusion from the institution exempts the academician from any sensible accounting of his activities to the institution. Like an aristocrat, he expects to be the final authority on whether he is living up to the responsibilities of his position.

The general autonomy which the academician has in deciding where and when he works is also found in the specific manner in which he chooses to work. Academicians are often exempt from the personal evaluations which ordinarily are made in large scale organizations. A male professor who has neglected to shave for three days is not assumed to warrant the social censure which an administrator or staff person may receive. Similarly, sartorial slovenliness, impracticality, aloofness, flamboyance, or pride can all be occasionally indulged because of the common understanding that academicians are occasionally eccentric, although essentially mild.

Academicians are also allowed to choose between two orientations toward their work. They may see themselves as scholars who are oriented toward their discipline or as scholars who are oriented toward their disciples. In the contemporary groves of academe, both Socrates and Einstein are legitimate role models; and hence each academician is free to choose his ultimate goals and interests. Once such a personal choice is made, the academician expects the freedom to act upon that decision. Departments and schools, as bodies of academicians, may have a reputation built upon one orientation or the other. But characteristically, each academician expects his colleagues to respect his right to choose between research and writing or teaching and advising.

In addition to these special privileges, academicians, as a status group, expect that the structural arrangements of the institutions that employ them will make their academic style of life possible. And, under ordinary circumstances, the bureaucratic arrangements do routinely meet this expectation. Insofar as the aristocratic style of life of the academician is, in the last analysis, much more a symbolic elaboration of the position than a matter concerning the practical bureaucratic tasks of the institutions, there is no discrepancy or conflict. In routine times, the academician never has to question whether he is officially, within the institution, any less powerful than he appears to be. However, Max Weber has made an explicit conceptual distinction between status groups and class groups.[5] In a status group members share a

[5] M. Weber, *From Max Weber*, H. Gerth and C. W. Mills (Eds.) (New York: Oxford University Press, 1958), p. 180.

common style of life. This style of life makes certain courses of action proper and fitting for group members and thus gives members some measure of worth, both individually and collectively. In contrast, a class is a group in that its members share a common fate. For Weber, as for Marx, the significant determinant of the fate people share is their opportunity in the economic marketplace.[6] This opportunity is determined by the particular relationship they have to the means of production. Thus a social class may be viewed as a particular structural arrangement between individuals and the resources, tools, and conditions of their work.

In contemporary American higher education these resources, tools, and conditions are found in the bureaucratic structures of institutions of higher learning and the physical plants in which those bureaucracies are housed. As distinct from higher learning, higher education is a bureaucratic enterprise specified in terms of institutional policy. In a well-run college or university—as in any well-run factory —the students (the raw materials) enter at one point in the system (such as the admissions office) and leave at another point in the system (such as the registrar's office). Between these two points, the faculty is expected to engage in a specifiable set of procedures which, in the bureaucratic records, attest to the fact that students are being educated. Thus, as members of a social class, academicians are salaried employees in the institutions of higher learning. And a salaried employee is, in the Marxian sense, a worker insofar as his control over his work is always superseded by the control which his employer has over him. To administrators the prestige of their scholars is not an important practical consideration. They make academicians "instructional staff," thereby bureaucratically transforming the academicians' privileged position. The work of this staff is to provide documentation of the job done by the institution. For administrative purposes, evidence that education is taking place is found not in the opinions of teachers and students but in the bureaucratic files where grades are recorded.

Thus regardless of the academician's choice of orientation toward his work, his freedom to define his job is limited by the institutional policies that define the essential tasks of the instructional staff.

[6] *Ibid.* See also K. Marx and F. Engels, *The German Ideology* (New York: International, 1947), pp. 7–8.

Matters such as how long it takes to give a particular course; how much credit (if any) those taking the course are granted; the appropriate times for evaluating student progress and performance; the number of students to be enrolled; and the legitimacy or illegitimacy of a student's dropping the course without penalty are all ultimately matters of institutional policy. They are at the same time matters which are directly relevant to the work of the academician.

However, as long as traditional patterns continue, the academicians need not ask themselves what the nature of their situation is. The routine organization of the institutions makes such questions superfluous. As long as the organization remains familiar, there is a good enough fit between the academic's expected style of life and the bureaucratic demands on his work so that he can reasonably believe that patterns are, in fact, as they ought to be. Only when events no longer occur within a familiar context may the discrepancy between academic prestige and bureaucratic control become manifest. And then questions about the academician's situation may well have to be raised. The crises at San Francisco State provide one example of this process.

The confrontation between the students of SFSC and the administration of the college related directly to the loci of power and control in the institution. In the process, a number of nontraditional events took place which made the dilemma of the academician explicit. Like their peers in other institutions of higher learning, the SFSC faculty had a particular conception of what an academician is and how he can expect to be treated. These general expectations provided a background against which the college faculty constantly evaluated their experiences.[7] Prior to the confrontation, matters such as whether their teaching loads were fair, their office spaces adequate, the perquisites of their position equitable were topics of frequent—albeit mainly informal—discussion. But insofar as their status was ordinarily paid due honor within the institution, the question of their power with respect to policy decisions was rarely raised.

Yet, this group was in no way immune from the campus turmoil. The student rebellion took place amid the buildings and grounds where the faculty worked and drew personnel from the same persons

[7] Cf. J. Roth, *Timetables* (Indianapolis: Bobbs-Merrill, 1963). Roth describes a parallel situation where patients in a TB hospital evaluated their progress against general expectations for patients in their stage of recovery.

necessary for the academicians' work. The rebellion thus affected daily work by making it physically, socially, and, for some, psychologically difficult to teach. So, regardless of his particular ideological positions, each member of the SFSC faculty had a practical interest in the confrontation.

Initially the faculty responded as a body of academicians in the usual sense of the term. In full faculty meetings they often deliberated about the nature, effects, and possible solutions to the student strike. When the disturbances on campus increased, the faculty voted to suspend its ordinary rules and to meet in continuous session. Even so, the extraordinary character of the situation was in large measure normalized by the academic character of the deliberations. After passing the ritual resolutions of censure (which few academicians would see as inappropriate to their social position)', they found it hard to agree on what to do next. And so, they continued to issue edicts, resolutions, and directives to the Academic Senate, the campus administration, the chancellor, and the trustees on the assumption that the prestige of their position carred institutional power. And to maintain their social honor while their voices were raised in dissent, such statements were couched in socially proper terms. In the course of one faculty meeting, a point of extended discussion involved whether a resolution of censure addressed to the chancellor and trustees should be worded "respectfully request" or simply "request." Such language stands in direct contrast to the terms employed by workers—"demand." During the full faculty meetings, about five or ten motions were passed, but few were implemented; and another fifty to seventy were submitted to a committee for preparation of an agenda. The meeting in which action on these latter motions might have occurred was canceled after the change in administration; and no further meetings of the faculty as a body were permitted until weeks after the turmoil subsided.

In the course of their academically proper activity, many faculty members realized that their effective power was nil. In no case were any of their motions acted upon by the administration; and, in most cases, the administration never even acknowledged receipt of the proposals. Thus small cliques of concerned faculty members began to form informal committees. These committees not only demanded action on the part of the administration but also considered threatening action—to withhold their services from the institution until a settlement was reached.

Such threats tacitly acknowledge that those issuing them do not expect that their claims can be satisfactorily met in an ordinary way by the institution.[8] Those who make threats also imply that they do not have available to them the institutional power to make and enforce decisions of policy.[9] Thus, for the college professor to threaten reprisals against the system of which he is a part is, for him, openly to acknowledge the discrepancy between his status and his power. For the faculty as a body, the general problem was to define themselves collectively either as persons of professional status or as employees with grievances.[10] Within this context, the specific question which each academician at SFSC had to answer was whether such extrainstitutional action as threatening to strike was proper and fitting for his social position. Reasonable arguments for both positions were available. And they were debated at length in formal, semiformal, and informal faculty gatherings. On the one hand, there was the understanding of how responsible professionals are ordinarily expected to act. On the other hand, there was the growing realization that the proper action attempted so far had been ineffectual.

During its meetings the faculty decided that the most pressing concern of the college was the student strike and, hence, that conflict should receive first priority from all responsible professionals. The faculty as a whole passed a motion on November 15 to begin deliberation with the administration, the chancellor, and the trustees, and to remain in continuous faculty meeting—thus suspending classroom instruction—until a satisfactory outcome had been agreed upon by the parties involved. The seeming advantage of such a motion was that it permitted the faculty to exercise power within the institution while in no way compromising their professional status. They were not striking against the institution; they were acting within a structure where faculty meetings are traditionally accorded priority over any scheduled

[8] Cf. G. Simmel, *The Sociology of Georg Simmel*, K. Wolff (Ed.) (New York: Free Press, 1950).

[9] T. Schelling, *The Strategy of Conflict* (Cambridge, Mass.: Harvard University Press, 1960).

[10] E. Goffman, *Presentation of Self in Everyday Life* (Garden City, N.Y.: Doubleday, 1959).

instruction. Thus the faculty could sustain a definition of its members as responsible professionals addressing campus problems.

The response of the administration to this action was effectually to redefine responsible professional on the SFSC campus. The newly appointed president suspended the faculty-endorsed convocation, adjourned the faculty meeting which had been in continuous session since November 12, and commanded faculty members to "meet their classes during the hours scheduled, in the scheduled places, except as approved by the president or his designee." As a responsible professional then, a professor at SFSC is one who remains in his designated classroom post, come what may.

Thus, the faculty members were divested of any institutionalized means to act in an organized manner as responsible professionals with an urgent interest in the campus dispute. This situation highlighted the problematic nature of the academician's position; irrespective of the privilege and honor associated with his status, the administration which employed him determined and delimited his power. As a responsible professional, he had no voice whatsoever in the decisions on policy and practice which affected the campus as a whole. To have an audible voice in those matters, he was required to consider himself as an employee with grievances. Within this definition of his position, extrainstitutional means for action could be legitimately established. Unless he assumed this definition, however, his views were, at most, an academic matter.

The basic dilemma the college professor encounters in the bureaucratic structure of most institutions of higher education is this incongruity between living his life as an academician and earning his living as an academician. However, since a style of life is much more visible on a day-to-day basis than is the control one has over one's work, the existence of the former may be frequently taken to imply the existence of the latter. Unless the question is raised explicitly, the college professor may well assume that as an academician he has not only a privileged but also a consequential position.

This notion that the college professor's importance is evidenced through his social status and class can be sustained as long as the academician does not question the bureaucratic definition of his job; and ordinarily he does not. His transition from student to professor is usually direct, and hence his long and constant familiarity with the typical bureaucratic arrangements of educational institutions vest the conditions of his work with the authority of tradition. In the depository of social knowledge of the American academician, classes are either fifty or seventy-five minutes long; the academic year always begins in September and ends in June; grades are assigned and submitted to the registrar by a particular date; and some specifiable number of class meetings must take place for credit to be given. Under ordinary circumstances, no one else questions the loci of power and control in the institution either. Hence the possibility that the college professor is as powerless as any other salaried employee is characteristically obscured.

Only after policy questions have been raised does the college professor discover how feeble is his power in the institution. Regardless of the privilege and honor associated with his academic position, the practical control of institutions of higher education is traditionally vested in the administrators and their superiors. The recommendations of the faculty, as a privileged status group, may be taken under consideration when policy decisions are made, but they are in no way binding on their institutionally more powerful superiors.

The paradoxical features of the academic position in contemporary American institutions of higher learning do not present merely another instance of role conflict, similar to that of the public school principal[11] or the foreman in industry.[12] Representatives of relevant interest groups are not making conflicting demands on the time, energy, or resources of the college professor. Rather, the college professor must reconsider the definition of his social identity. His problem is similar to that of youth facing adolescent identity crises. But this time the individual must decide not who he is socially but where he is socially: whether he occupies a privileged position or whether he is a part of the working class. This choice affects the future of academic participation in decision-making and policy formation for higher education. If the academic chooses to maintain his aristocratic image at any cost, he inevitably remains a mere functionary. If he acknowledges his position as worker, he accepts the fact that he has no special honorific status, but he wins the opportunity to creatively influence the definition of the job he is expected to perform.

[11] N. Gross, W. Mason, and A. McEachern, *Explorations in Role Analysis* (New York: Wiley, 1958).
[12] See, for example, D. Wray, "Marginal Men of Industry: The Foreman," *American Journal of Sociology*, 1949, 54, 298-301.

PART **IV**

⟨❈⟩⟨❈⟩⟨❈⟩⟨❈⟩⟨❈⟩⟨❈⟩⟨❈⟩⟨❈⟩⟨❈⟩⟨❈⟩⟨❈⟩⟨❈⟩

The professors at San Francisco State are again teaching and doing research. The students are attending classes. But the campus is certainly not back to normal; old assumptions and patterns of association are not easily reconstituted after a campuswide revolt. Disagreements surfaced which are hard to ignore now that they have been made public. In addition, some unhappy consequences of the disruption are constant reminders of how much was lost because of the struggle. Innovative programs have evaporated, student activities have regressed in the direction of former Joe College days by order of administrative spokesmen, many faculty who participated in the strike have been refused reappointment and tenure. Generally speaking, the centralized powers of the state college system have reaffirmed their control and exacted vengeance upon

182

AFTERMATH

critics with the determination of a political machine. In consequence, unresolved problems and old discontents are still seething and threaten to erupt again at any time.

Nonetheless many still consider themselves fortunate to have participated in the strike. They believe that they are working for improvement rather than providing an obstacle to the evolution of higher education. This view is sustained by a focus upon long-range changes rather than immediate successes (or failures) on the campus. It is also sustained by consideration of immediate, positive changes for the participants. Many who were accustomed to sedentary, cautious, and reflective lives were glad to discover that they could act when the need and the opportunity arose. Engaging in positive action brings considerable satisfaction to those who find their consciences burdened by the inequities of the modern world. If they cannot fight against injustices everywhere, they can at least do so in that area where they have both expertise and opportunity.

183

The opportunity for decisive action was, of course, not limited to those who joined the union. Equally decisive were the swift repressive actions of college authorities. President S. I. Hayakawa won great favor with the central administration and great acclaim from the public by his instant forays against critics. Perhaps the most striking and tangible consequence of the campus revolt has been Hayakawa's sudden rise to fame and notoriety, as described in the first chapter of this section. His activities on the campus and his other public appearances now receive wide attention in the news media. Perhaps he fits the mood of the time better than most college presidents do. When people are seeking clear, hardheaded answers to knotty problems, Hayakawa is the kind of leader who can satisfy them. He agrees with the public that the hard line is the solution to the problem of student-faculty revolt. And he does not hesitate to use the force of the city and state to support him when his own constituents rebel against an administration imposed by questionable procedure.

The new fame of Hayakawa was probably the single most widely known and publicized consequence of the strike and its aftermath. But the faculty are most keenly aware of some more general and less publicized consequences. The extent and the nature of polarization in their own ranks were their legacy from the conflict. Once life was disrupted, it was hard to reassert the old assumption that security and serenity are found on a college campus. Old colleagues are now potential enemies; promotion and tenure hearings are the source of more tensions and suspicions than these highly charged affairs normally emit. Everyone is ready for battle; everyone makes inferences from the most casual comments. Rumors are widespread about the atrocities committed by the other side—gossip concerns departments where members attack their political minority or where professors penalize students for espousing an opposing political stand. Long after the event, campus decisions are still affected by how a department split or united during the strike. The cautionary tales culled from the memoranda of a discreetly anonymous department reflect the mood that was pervasive at the end of the strike and which still exists.

The first preliminary analysis of research on the strike previews a more extensive effort in preparation by Naboisek and his students. The findings from their survey of campus attitudes and opinions are presented here to provide some evidence for just how much polari-

zation occurred during that strike. Much of the silent majority on the campus became more extreme than they were before. A particularly interesting finding is the extent to which isolation of the administration from the views of both faculty and students increased as a consequence of the crisis. Both the faculty and the students became more radical by participating in the events at State, while the administration became somewhat more conservative. These findings do not seem encouraging for future negotiation or compromise between conflicting interests on the campus.

Unfortunately the consequences of this strike also spread far from campus. Trials of students who were arrested on campus for participating in an illegal rally during the strike continued throughout the following year. Ofsevit reports his observations of those trials. He argues that inequities in legal procedures created bitterness and cynicism about justice in both participants and observers. And he argues that perception of these inequities can only increase the pessimistic convictions of those already suspicious about the viability of the political system in America.

In summary, what were the consequences of the strike? Agreements were eventually signed; does that mean the strikers were successful? In "Assessments" McDermid suggests that the agreements (see Appendix) were meaningless; they were merely formal ways to save face and end the strike. (Her analysis of the strike issues and the terms of settlement are presented in Chapter Nineteen.) The administration and faculty have still not resolved the issues which precipitated the crisis. Some specific problems may have been faced; but the crucial questions of legitimate authority in campus affairs are far from settled. Instead of encouraging faculty and student participation in decisions, the administration has tended to restrict both faculty and student activities. Dissent is not encouraged; it is defined as disruptive and deserving retribution. To criticize the president's refusal to abide by established and previously agreed-upon procedures is considered divisive. Many of the new procedures which suggest an atmosphere of repression rather than free and open inquiry are discussed in this chapter. In spite of this atmosphere, the author reaffirms the necessity to speak out in conscience against injustices. In this view she is supported by other contributors. The struggle to free the educational institution from the stranglehold of outmoded approaches will certainly continue.

CHAPTER 14

Making of the
President, 1969

Arlene Kaplan Daniels

꠸꠸꠸꠸꠸꠸꠸꠸꠸꠸꠸꠸꠸꠸꠸꠸꠸꠸꠸꠸꠸꠸꠸

This chapter discusses the attention paid to Acting President S. I. Hayakawa by the public media during the crisis at San Francisco State College.[1] The media coverage of his actions in the winter of 1968–1969 brought him national fame as a major educational figure. During this period, Hayakawa engaged in a number of highly unorthodox activities for a college president: he

---

[1] The data for this chapter were collected by students as part of their research for term papers. I wish to thank all of them for their esprit and perseverance. Particular thanks are due to Frank and Sherrilene Di Puma for their careful collection of material on Hayakawa. Kristin Johnson remained after the finish of the semester to complete all aspects of the content analysis. Without her assistance this paper would not have been completed.

leaped on to a sound truck and ripped out its wiring; he engaged in televised temper tantrums when questioned about his decisions; he participated in a number of "screaming matches" with his opponents; and he visibly lost self-control in a variety of public situations. He also made such widely quoted statements as: "I am sorry I have not been able to keep in better touch with you, but there really hasn't been time. Some days it was all I could do to find time to go to the bathroom" (in a letter distributed to the entire faculty at SFSC, February 10, 1969). " 'One of the things that gives me the greatest satisfaction,' he confessed, 'is that when the strikers go home and turn on their TV sets they find me, and if they switch the channels they still find me. It must drive them crazy, and this thought gives me a great deal of pleasure' " (*San Francisco Chronicle,* March 6, 1969).

The theoretical framework for the discussion here of the public response to such an unorthodox figure as college president is provided by Orrin Klapp's analysis of symbolic leaders.[2] In his view, these leaders emerge as the public responds to dramatic or otherwise important personages. These figures become symbolic in the sense that evaluations of their behavior provide indicators or barometers of public opinion. Once a public figure has elicited a strong response, the underlying values of those who have responded are revealed by their support or criticism of various aspects of his behavior. A dramatic figure may at one time be admired and respected for strength and ruthlessness, for example, while in another era or another society, these same characteristics may make a figure hated, ridiculed, or feared. This spontaneous emergence of symbolic leaders out of dramatic figures who catch the eye or the attention of the public (and become particularly idolized, vilified, or otherwise typed) is one of the clearest available processes through which to study widely held values in a society.

If we use Klapp's theoretical framework for the analysis of highly controversial symbolic leaders, we have an analytic tool for a study of response to social change. Competing interests strive to present their views; and they stress their interpretations of how strategic or dramatic events should be understood or evaluated by the public. In addition, special interest media or editorial sections of the general media directly champion their sides of an event. Each side appeals to

[2] O. Klapp, *Symbolic Leaders: Public Dramas and Public Men* (Chicago: Aldine, 1964).

the as yet unknown sympathies of the public and examines events to justify quite opposite courses of action. In this process, to some extent, the mass media are themselves influenced. They may reflect as well as formulate public opinion. Therefore, we may turn to the media for the ultimate evaluation of symbolic leaders and the criteria on which these evaluations rest.

Although some leadership positions have specific symbolic meaning invested in them, most, particularly those within complex bureaucracies, do not. In America today, the faceless bureaucrat— whatever his acknowledged competence—is not likely to become a dramatic figure. Current events are changing these traditional expectations, however. The public eye turns, first cursorily and then with greater interest, as disruptions and arguments in these sectors of modern life require public pronouncements and then highly publicized decisions from the organizational spokesmen.

These officials may become dramatic figures and receive evaluations as heroes, villains, or fools irrespective of their interest in becoming symbolic leaders. According to Klapp, this process occurs because public crises or interests—such as those currently generated in educational and other public agencies—can create pressures upon those seen as protagonists to do something. If their activity is judged successful, they may become heroes; if unsuccessful but pardonable, they may become tragic heroes; if ridiculous, they may become clowns. In the crisis at SFSC, for example, public values are indicated by the emergence in the press of President Robert Smith (Hayakawa's predecessor) as a weak, indecisive, wishy-washy figure. By other standards, certainly for many faculty observers, he was a tragic figure. The failure of his attempt to create an atmosphere of discussion at SFSC can thus be seen as ineffectual or fumbling from the start—governing officials found Smith weak and indecisive in his management of events prior to the crisis at State and stated publicly that they knew how to solve the problem (by firing Murray) even if he did not (*San Francisco Chronicle,* November 16, 1968). Or Smith's failure can be seen as a brave and honorable attempt to resist political pressures and to solve problems through discussion and maintenance of due process—as described by the former president of Sarah Lawrence College, Harold Taylor (the television program *Newsroom,* April 17, 1969).

Several issues precipitated the crisis which led to the emergence of Hayakawa as a symbolic leader. SFSC, like many other colleges in this country, had been emitting ominous volcanic rumbles for a number of years prior to the eruption. Continued difficulties in the funding of various programs, accusations of discrimination against minorities, administrative difficulties caused by an allegedly unwieldy and inefficient bureaucracy are examples of the problems. Generally, the consequences of all the preexisting difficulties at this particular educational institution combined to make the position of president untenable. The rapid and highly publicized turnover of incumbents in that position had created great local public interest, even if the finer points of the administrative and political difficulties leading to the turnover were not always clear. At the same time, public interest focused upon the problem of student unrest. Although the causes of unrest are debatable and the issues around which the dissidents rallied were sometimes obscure, the "facts" of the case were generally summarized in the news media. The consequences of disruption that could be seen and measured in terms of presidential resignations and firings or in acts of violence against persons or property were the key events in the drama portrayed through the newspapers. Thus, in the public view, the events precipitating the crisis at SFSC were administrative difficulties and student violence. Within this context, or definition of the problem, Hayakawa emerged as an important figure in the student and faculty strike against the college.

As often happens a hitherto unknown person became a symbolic leader by accident. Prior to the crisis, Hayakawa was a part-time, tenured professor in the department of English. His name was familar to both the general and the academic public as a popular semanticist. In the year before the campus strike, he had been active in attempting to promote an organized, conservative faculty group (the Renaissance). A basic tenet of this group was the legitimacy of current academic standards and academic disciplines. Those who do not meet the requirements—whether or not through their own fault—must remedy deficiencies before entering. Once they have entered, violators of the rules must be firmly treated. This has come to be known as the hard-line approach to campus disorder. But Hayakawa was not particularly esteemed for his academic contributions by many of his colleagues; by some, he was regarded as a popularizer of semantics rather than as an

independent or creative scholar.[3] Nor did he show evidence of administrative talent. He had never held an administrative position at the
college and was little known in local administrative circles. After
Hayakawa's sudden and unexpected appointment to fill the vacancy
caused by the Smith resignation, all groups in the amazed academic
community and the interested general public watched for further
developments.

Hayakawa's public images began to emerge from the very
moment of his appointment because he had news appeal arising from
the public focus on SFSC. His appointment was presented in the press
as a reasonable solution to an aggravating problem. Hayakawa offered
something to everyone. His strong line should appease the conservatives; and his description of himself as a liberal Democrat should
mollify the liberals. His academic qualifications, if considered marginal
by some of his colleagues, did look good to the public—his basic text
on semantics had been a favorite for years and had once been a best
seller. His Japanese ethnicity might appease the dissidents in the academic community who were accusing the administration and the trustees of racism. Finally, he was colorful and gave promise of offering
good copy because of both his outgoing nature and his apparent love
of publicity.

However, the Academic Senate raised some difficulties; various
members protested publicly that the sudden unilateral appointment by
the trustees was in violation of all precedents and agreements between
faculty and trustees about the share each would have in presidential
selection. It was also in specific violation of the agreement of the Faculty Selection Committee for President that one of its members—and
Hayakawa was one—accept the position of president. However, these
discussions were not at the forefront of the problem as it began to be
formulated in the public view. The legitimacy of procedures was not
as significant a concern as was the necessity to bring order to the
campus. The crisis was defined in public discussion as one requiring a
firm hand. The villains or the troublemakers were the student dissidents and their supporters. The script seemed to call for a strong hero
to deal with these bad guys. Once the trustees appointed Hayakawa to
this role, the media began to focus upon him intensively to watch the

[3] E. Shorris, "Hayakawa in Thought and Action," *Ramparts*, 1969, 8
(5), 38–43.

drama unfold between hard-line administrators and dissident students. Hayakawa's statements, actions, press conferences were all news.

In the first days after his appointment and before he took office, the news media gave much attention to his plans to reopen the campus after it had been closed in the course of rising student strike violence accompanying the collapse of a campus convocation and the resignation of Smith. Hayakawa planned to reopen the campus with music piped through the speaker systems, banks of flowers, and free distribution of blue arm bands to his supporters. It was said that through these means he hoped to quiet the violence shown in the early stages of the student strike. He also hoped to attract the "uncommitted majority" to help preserve peace on campus. In his view, this group was by far the largest segment of the student population. They would rise to his support and demonstrate the futility of further dissident action by the radical minority. During this early period (November 27 to December 2, 1968) Hayakawa was frequently photographed wearing flower leis, and his wide acquaintanceship in the world of jazz was mentioned to stress the areas in which he and youth—especially minority youth—might share common interests. His friendship with Mahalia Jackson, a noted Negro gospel singer, was also mentioned; and the possibility that she might join him on campus on the reopening day was raised. Descriptions of Hayakawa's colorful or sporty dress and his plaid Tam O'Shanter received broad coverage. Thus it could be argued that the news presented him as an amusing and interesting figure; one who perhaps might be considered a little odd for a college president but who had definite possibilities. At the very least he could provide the color Smith had not shown. And in addition the press stories suggested that Hayakawa showed promise for dealing firmly with dissident minorities and for coming to grips with the problems raised by student demands.

Beginning with the announcement of Hayakawa's appointment and continuing through his first months of office, the local and national press paid considerable attention to him. Aside from the many news stories in which he figured, the local morning paper coverage reflected the attention the entire community gave this acting college president. In the period studied (November 16, 1968 to March 17, 1969) the *San Francisco Chronicle* was filled with references to Hayakawa: eighteen letters to the editor, twenty-seven mentions by a famous local columnist, and fifteen other mentions, including lengthy articles in various magazine sections, women's pages, and editorial sections. Hayakawa was becoming a celebrity in his home town.

The descriptions and evaluations of Hayakawa appearing in the news stories in the *San Francisco Chronicle* indicate how the public viewed him: Two distinct and opposing images emerge. The positive evaluation stressed Hayakawa's academic credentials ("distinguished semantics professor turned president," "world-renowned semanticist") and mentioned the support for his appointment from the trustees and the governor of the state. (Ronald Reagan is reported as saying "we have found the right man.") It was suggested that this support gave him a greater chance to succeed at the job than previous presidents had.

Hayakawa's admirable or likable personal characteristics were displayed in the sound truck incident. They were described as audacity, courage, foolhardiness. It was a "bravura performance." He was "jaunty", he "plunged, wrestling" into the sound truck group. His gestures included a "crisp nod." He "leaped nimbly, despite a 5 foot 6 inch, 153 lb. frame, began enthusiastically throwing elbows." He showed "gusto"; he "popped into" the scene before police and protestors could stop him. He was "peppery" and "feisty." Finally, the positive evaluation of his policy and tactics stressed that he was "determined, firm"—"the man to take charge on the battlefield." He was taking the hard line and that was what was needed. He had a "firm grasp," a "keen perception"; he acted "bravely"; he was a "determined leader."

The positive picture of Hayakawa (a total of forty-six remarks) mentioned his academic credentials (eight times) and discussed the favorable regard he was receiving from state and national political leaders (seven times). He was described as calm, hard working, careful, articulate, optimistic (five times), and he was praised for his courageous stand, determination, hard line, vigor, firmness, and ability to put others in their place (eighteen times). His personality was described as jaunty, peppery, spunky, and sporty (eight times).

However, the press provided a parallel negative evaluation. Hayakawa's academic qualifications were questionable background for his new job as he was "by no means an experienced administrator or handler of people." His support from the trustees and the governor indicated only that he was a "puppet," "tool," "errand boy," or "pawn." In addition, his detractors deduced from the support offered him by the conservatives in the state that he was a "quisling," a "fascist," a "tool of the far right," a "big brother," a symbol of "white racism represented by a yellow skin."

His personal characterictics were also seen negatively. He acted "wrongfully," "willfully, and maliciously" when he "forceably defaced" the sound truck in the view of those who eventually sued him for these actions. He was described as "gleeful" after Bloody Tuesday, when many were injured on campus—in a news story bearing the caption "A Madman at the Helm." He was a "fussy little rationalist" who "had alienated many with his cool aloof manner and mocking wit." He was "incapable of understanding." His "brief shoving match" and the whole sound truck incident were "not a propitious start." Finally, his actions suggested that he was totally unsuited for the job. He had engaged in "unprofessional conduct." His "repressive action" had caused a "reign of terror." He was "administering the college terribly"; "a ten year old could do as well."

In sum, then, the negative picture of Hayakawa (a total of forty-seven remarks) impugned his motivation (thirteen times) and his ability and suitability for the job (twenty-three times). In addition he was mocked and ridiculed for his undignified and hysterical behavior (trembling with rage, screaming, walking out abruptly, showing vanity in reading his fan mail) eleven times. He was a maniac, fathead, and despot.

A simple tally of statements from news stories does not indicate a partiality to either evaluation of Hayakawa. Only when one considers where the evaluations came from—to what source they were attributed—does some idea of the trend of public opinion emerge. In order to show this trend, favorable and unfavorable assessments of Hayakawa were taken from news stories and all other features in the *San Francisco Chronicle* and the *San Francisco Examiner* (the only daily newspapers in the city) for the previously selected time period. Sources were classified into five types: respected community leaders (such as elected officials); identifiable special interest community groups and their spokesmen (such as the Young Republicans, Commonwealth Club, reporters); editorial writers and columnists; the general public (including otherwise unidentifiable sources); and special interest groups clearly identifiable as anti-Hayakawa (such as faculty, students, blacks, and other Third World leaders)'. Most (83 per cent) of the unfavorable remarks come from persons or groups easily identifiable as anti-Hayakawa. And these groups are also those which the public already tended to view with suspicion and alarm—students, militant leaders, and faculty. Virtually all the laudatory evaluations of Hayakawa (91 per cent) are identifiable as coming from respected or established officials, community leaders, and members of neutral or unidentified groups. Such sources may be considered opinion leaders and also representative of public opinion.

Reference Sources	Remarks about Hayakawa		
	Favorable	Unfavorable	Total
Respected community leaders	46 (27.0)	5 (2.3)	51
Special interest groups	29 (17.0)	12 (5.6)	41
Editorials and editorializing	50 (29.4)	12 (5.6)	62
General public	34 (20.0)	15 (7.0)	49
Anti-Hayakawa special interest groups	11 (6.5)	169 (79.3)	180
	170 (99.9)	213 (99.8)	383

The categories of assessment were simplified into positive and negative evaluations of the following: (1) Hayakawa as a hard-line president. Statements showing confidence in him were: "we have found our man," "has my support," "courageous stand," "take-charge man," and descriptions of standing ovations and cheers. Statements showing doubts were "destroyed my faith," "call for removal," "reliance on police power," "taken a repressive stance," and reports of boos and organized resistance. (2) Descriptions of Hayakawa's academic credentials and character. Descriptions showing Hayakawa in a favorable light included such adjectives as "prominent" and "spunky" and such statements as "lives by definitions of words and must act according to dictates of logic and reason." Unfavorable descriptions included words like "puppet," "madman," and statements like "words take on quality of incantations of a witch doctor who operates in the unreality of his own wishful thinking." The unfavorable remarks tend to focus upon Hayakawa's personal characteristics (62 per cent of the 213 total unfavorable remarks)', while the favorable remarks emphasize confidence in Hayakawa's ability to succeed in quashing the trouble at State through the hard-line policy (59 per cent of the 170 favorable remarks)'. Perhaps the explanation of these differences is that proponents of Hayakawa ignored his lack of previous qualifications and focused on the necessity and possibility of his achieving immediate results. But opponents of Hayakawa focused critically on his general background and character, throwing cold water on the notion that he had the temperament, training, or ability to achieve any long-term benefits for the college.

In the first months of office, Hayakawa reaffirmed and strengthened the images that both sides held of him in a variety of public statements and actions. The informal and sometimes incongruous nature of these statements made it difficult for even his most enthusiastic supporters to see him as a serious or dignified college president. But the demand by the public for a strong, hard-line president who would get quick results was very keen. Perhaps as a response to that demand, an image of Hayakawa began to form: he might not be dignified but he might still be construed as admirable and perhaps likable. He was plucky. You had to hand it to him. He was getting the job done. In this vein, Hayakawa received support from Republican and other conservative leadership in the state. (Hayakawa was commended by Mayor Sam Yorty in Los Angeles, by State Superintendent of Public Education Max Rafferty, and by the San Francisco Medical Society, December 13, 1968, *San Francisco Chronicle*. Hayakawa and Reagan had "an agreeable talk," reported on January 13, 1969, *San Francisco Chronicle*.) The growing numbers of incidents and skirmishes which became a part of keeping the campus open despite the student strikers all encouraged the view that Hayakawa was doing the correct thing: teaching those young rebels and hippies that there are limits. After all, his idiosyncrasies were less important in the long run than his attitude toward student dissent. (A Gallup poll reported in January showed Hayakawa to be the most admired man in education.)' And the public developed a similar position to that of the conservative leadership in the state in typing Hayakawa as a hero.

Despite defections and rebellion from faculty and students, Hayakawa rose to national fame as a successful, hard-line president.

Conservative groups at other schools facing similar rebellions were reported to wear Tam O'Shanters and blue arm bands and to take Hayakawa's name as symbols of their espousal of his position. (The conservatives at the University of Wisconsin were known as Hayakawans for a time; graffiti on the walls at Stanford University during difficulties there criticized the weakness of President Kenneth Pitzer and called for Hayakawa to subdue the radicals on that campus.) Hayakawa was later suggested as a political nominee for a variety of public offices; he dined with the President of the United States; he gave congressional committees his views on the causes of campus violence; and he generally hobnobbed with the mighty. Hayakawa jokes were abroad in the land ("the trouble with your wife is that you can't pull the wires out of her and turn her off"); graffiti reading "Hayakawa is an Uncle Tam" were reported; his home on the slopes of Mt. Tamalpais was renamed Mt. Tam O'Shanter; a bumper strip read "Hayakawa is an Uncle-San"; and the national newscasters reported his actions and the activities of SFSC almost nightly during crises throughout the strike. On one of these national news programs, Hayakawa received a generally favorable assessment for ending the strike without succumbing to the various demands made upon him by the radicals. His public image remained relatively unaffected by the invidious facets of his public presentation and by possible negative assessments which might be made on these bases.

The process of Hayakawa's selection as a symbol emphasizes, as Klapp suggests, that social typing is a cooperative process; people in the audience return cues to give a dramatic figure a view of how his image is developing. Of course, selective attention to those cues constrains an individual's appreciation of the responses he receives. In the case of Hayakawa, for example, he did not seek appreciation in the academic community but rather found acceptance and encouragement from the general public and those conservative business and political circles which support the hard line against educational rebellion. In becoming a national figure, then, Hayakawa was increasingly forced into the paradoxical position of being the antiintellectuals' intellectual, for he represented the apogee of the academic world to many who seem to threaten academic standards and values by their determination to suppress dissent and emphasize order. But, as he himself pointed out, it was the people who supported him and who approved his actions. And his stacks of fan mail apparently provided adequate evidence. Aside from the question of how much this image was technically engineered by public relations men (see Chapter Seven), public support was offered to a figure behaving quite differently—and with quite different values—from the usual college president. In this case, one might say that when the crisis at State produced a president like Hayakawa, the public was given the opportunity to show that peace, order, and respect for authority are their primary values in the choice of an educational hero. At the same time, this choice shows the public assessment that quick and decisive action, even at the cost of some repression, is more important than traditional academic values and the procedures traditionally used to protect them.

The effect of public assessment (Hayakawa became permanent president despite little support from his own campus) also suggests certain political lessons. At the end of the general crisis at State, the college and its constituents were in disarray. Everyone had experienced profound and demoralizing shocks from the police occupation, the mass arrests, and what seemed to be political firings. The experimental, student-initiated programs were virtually destroyed. The ethnic studies program was foundering before it began, and the rate of faculty resignations was rising. Only Hayakawa had prospered. His personal fame (or notoriety) as a celebrity in education seemed assured. There is no better way to state this consequence than to use Hayakawa's own words, as quoted in an interview with an investigator from the National Commission on the Causes and Prevention of Violence.

When, on December 2, I sort of blew my top and climbed that sound truck and pulled out those wires, it just happened that all the media were there. And after that dramatic incident, right to this day, television people and radio people and newspaper people are after me constantly because that incident made me a symbolic figure. And so, like any other symbolic figure, you're good copy, you're always news just because you're there. It wasn't anything planned. That was the luckiest thing that ever happened to me— that sound truck incident. It just suddenly, you know, just placed power in my hands that I don't know how I could have got it if I had wanted it.[4]

[4] W. H. Orrick, Jr., *Shut It Down! A College in Crisis*, a Report to the National Commission on the Causes and Prevention of Violence, June 1969, p. 59.

CHAPTER 15

Cautionary Tales for Exemplary Professors

A Department Chairman, A Hiring Committee

T̲he following documents are exerpted from memoranda distributed to members of a department at San Francisco State College. One is the chairman's memo to the department written a month after the end of the strike. The other is a statement made by the Hiring Committee a few months later. They are presented here to suggest the many discontents which disrupt a department in times of challenge and crisis.

The management of departmental affairs is difficult enough in ordinary times. There are always differences among colleagues over such matters as the best hiring, promotion, and tenure policies, or the

198

most appropriate education to offer students. And questions always arise about equity in the distribution of those limited rewards and perquisites available. But men of goodwill generally try to compromise on these matters, or else they overlook what they cannot change by democratic procedures. Unfortunately, disruptions like those at State have a tendency to reopen old controversies and to bring them out for discussion once more. But this time, the discussion is carried on in an atmosphere of repression and suspicion, with the ominous possibility that new opportunities have arisen to settle old scores. And so peaceful resolution of intradepartmental differences is seriously hindered by the fear of reprisals from opponents.

The sources of these threats range from opponents in the department through power enclaves at all levels of administration. For example, outvoted members in the department may have powerful allies in the division, college, or statewide administration; political views that are in the minority at the departmental level may hold sway at any of the other levels. In the emotional atmosphere of the crisis, members may decide to use their political alliances to affect departmental decisions. Thus the assumption that primary loyalties belong to one's departmental colleagues is now questioned, as are other patterns of behavior which may previously have been given little thought. This mistrust contributes to the inability of departments to achieve peaceful and permanent resolutions of differences. The political divisions thus contribute to a sense of insecurity over what plots one's colleagues may be brewing, and ultimately to the destruction of both formal and informal mechanisms for decision-making at the departmental level. Perhaps the most unfortunate consequence of polarization is that once it occurs, the distrust—and the futility of trying to reach those with opposing views—creates hopelessness and stalemate among colleagues who need to heal old wounds in order to work together.

Concerned professors may profit from our cautionary tales. They suggest that once the crisis erupts, the damage to prior understandings becomes virtually irreparable. Thus active participation may be required from all faculty members to resolve the general educational problems we face today before they reach crisis proportions in any particular institution. This endeavor is required as much in enlightened self-interest as in idealistic concern for the future of higher education.

Memo from a Chairman to His Departmental Colleagues

Last week was perhaps the most distressing week I've spent as department chairman. It illustrated all of the problems that face the department and showed me just what we are up against. I have talked to many of you in the last few days and heard from others indirectly. Let me take this opportunity to tell you what I see as our problems and suggest some things that we might do to begin to get out of this hole.

Despair, fear, hatred, resignation are harsh words, but they do not exaggerate the feelings that are conveyed to me as I talk with you. Fear and distrust are probably the most important factors leading us to the spot we are in today. These personal states of mind go hand in hand with what we might call the politicalization of the members of the department. Increasingly, we have placed each other in differing camps. There are the radicals and conservatives, and although these labels do not always fit, they are the ones that are being used. Those of us who thought of ourselves as liberals or moderates are constantly being pushed into either of these two categories. Because we have come to look at the world of our department as a political world containing only two categories, we have come to see all actions, both individual and collective, in this light. One group sees the other as attempting a departmental takeover as a launching platform for the overthrow of the Establishment and the destruction of higher education as we now know it. From the other perspective, the conservatives are reactionaries, opposed to all change, totally interested in maintaining the status quo, and protecting their position in the system at any cost.

Now, in reality we don't all fall in one of these two extremes. But we would be foolish to think that these fears and distrusts are not real and do not have real consequences for the future of the department. I have heard it said that the radicals are organized: they have control of the chairman and the Hiring Committee and have the support of the radical students in the college in order to enforce their demands. If this were true and if all these radicals aim to overthrow the establishment, those who have a stake in the status quo have reason to fear.

I have heard it said that the conservatives have control of the powerful Tenure and Promotion Committee, they have the support of the administration and will see to it that radicals are punished and that no real changes will occur. If one were really concerned about liberal changes and saw the conservative element of the department as I have portrayed it, there is reason for resignation and despair.

You may have noticed that I haven't said anything about the strike or about the AFT up to this point. I have not done so because I feel that the real issues that divide us (and they are *real* issues) go far beyond the strike. If there is one word that would convey my perception of the issue, it is *change*. How much? How soon? And in what direction? It is not that one group is against change and the other for it. It is more that we have come to perceive the world in far different ways and, as a consequence, have come out with differing orientations. What has happened this year is that the crisis that befell our college has caused us to stand up for our commitments. No longer can we drift along and hope that the academic enterprise will prosper. Those who feel committed to the established methods of education are threatened by those who are demanding immediate change; and those who have committed themselves to change are frustrated by those who insist on doing things as we always have. These are not just childish arguments, and because they affect our whole life organization, it is not surprising that feelings run deep and that bitterness and distrust are common. It is also not surprising that many are seeking other posts.

My guess is that some of you will remain unmoved by my plea. But others will see at least some of the same reality that I see, and so it is worthwhile trying to reach you. However, while I am convinced that many of us do perceive each other as polarized in opposition, I am equally convinced that our commitments are not that much at variance. The distrust is real and must be faced. Yet the ideological differences may not be as great as we think; if so, this can be our salvation.

There is no simple way out; and I have but one suggestion. I suggest that we launch a major review of our department and try to use our situation to make this a better place for all of us. Two factors suggest that this is a good time for reform of this sort. First, departures have created several openings for next year. Since we are no longer committed to existing personnel, we can be flexible and move into new areas that may better suit our current needs. The second factor is the growing size of the department. Now that we have almost twenty members, we must reorganize our administrative structure. Why can't we use this next year to move in a positive direction again? I realize that this will require compromise for most of you. For those who fear change, this will take faith. For those who would like radical reform, this will take restraint. For all, it will take trust in our colleagues— trust that the betterment of the department can be placed above ideological commitment or personal interest.

Statement of the Hiring Committee

1. Whether people have conspired or not is beside the point—there is a consistent pattern of bloc voting in this department going back to the hiring decisions a year ago, including the Tenure Committee voting of spring and fall and including the tenure decisions of the fall and the hiring votes of last Friday.

2. What we are about to say is not to be construed as implying a view that there is a little John Birch Society and a little Communist Party in the department with us good guys in the middle—it is an effort to say that we are in a bind and to suggest how we get out of it.

3. Probably the bloc voting reflects three things:
   a. For many reasons, the strike fostered personal antipathies which some individuals are still indicating symbolically through their votes on departmental candidates.
   b. These personal antipathies (and various other circumstances) have meant that individuals in both blocs are less often physically present in the department.
   c. The above creates the further effect of fewer departmental discussions of the type which leads to compromise. This effect was particularly evident in the voting on the tenure decisions in the fall. It was clear at that time that at least three totally different views existed before the voting; but we could not civilly nor intelligently discuss these views in order to arrive at a decision from the perspective: "what is good for the department as a whole."

4. Both blocs have been intentionally or unintentionally willing to use the middle group as patsies while they fight for their version of the department—versions they know to be impossible because of the polarization. The Hiring Committee says today that it will no longer be the patsy for this kind of no-win strategy. We have seen hundreds

of hours of work shot down for two consecutive years in order that the two groups—not doing the work—could preserve their views without compromise.

5. We offer you then the following three alternatives:

   a. We change the hiring procedure and get the rest of you to do the work that the Hiring Committee has been doing until now. Any four individuals will have the power to hire a candidate if they can convince the Hiring Committee to vote for him (or her). The Hiring Committee will accept two nominations from any four-man coalition. Each coalition should have its slate of candidates ready no later than two weeks from now. At that time we will agree to cast our votes with no more than one candidate from each coalition. If we get no more than one slate of candidates we will work out whatever compromises are necessary with that coalition to arrive at a total of two mutually acceptable persons to whom we may make offers. We believe this procedure to be the only fair and possible procedure given the present split in the department. It allows *us* to stop serving as straight men for the pie-in-the-face routine and shifts the responsibility for doing the dirty work in other directions. It guarantees an equal voice in the departmental hiring to any four-man (or woman) coalitions that can be assembled.

   b. These two groups of you who have been doing the bloc voting for the past year can get together with the other group and elect your own slate with a total of eight votes. We on the Hiring Committee would like nothing better than to see this happen because it would mean that for practical purposes, like running the department, the split would be over.

   c. The third alternative is to present no slates of candidates and to continue without any permanent appointments. In this case the Hiring Committee will continue as it did last year and this summer to make temporary appointments to meet our teaching needs.

CHAPTER 16

Changing Attitudes

Herbert Naboisek
George Crouch, Elizabeth Hollifield, Nancy Legenza,
Michael Cole, Anastasios Anastasiou,
Dianne Moore, Kitty Rinehart

In addition to joining the picket lines, members of the AFT used their professional expertise in a variety of other ways during the struggle at State. They engaged in community relations projects, wrote articles, made public speeches, and gave lectures at schools, colleges, and universities. My response, with the cooperation of my students, was to begin systematic research on the effects of the strike. Other chapters (Chapter Twelve, for example) describe the polarization on campus and the arguments of those who supported or opposed the strike. We wanted to collect responses from students, faculty, and administration about such matters as their views on the issues raised in the strike, how the strike had influenced their feelings, and whether an increased solidarity or increased division on the campus could be detected. Our overall purpose in conducting this study was to examine the state of campus opinion and campus morale. To this end, we wanted to discover by survey what issues divided the campus and how sharply and whether evidence would support or refute the general evaluations of what had occurred. The sample we used to supply this evidence included 194 students, 67 faculty, and 33 administrators.

To gauge the commitment to those issues at the heart of the strike on the part of these relevant campus constituencies, we developed a set of sixty-five items based on a list first suggested by M. E. Troyer of Syracuse University.[1] The items included college policy on disciplining students, control of the budget within academic departments, policy regarding adding and dropping courses, control of the operation of the Student Union, use of academic buildings, intercollegiate and intramural athletics, standards and quotas for special admissions, use of recreational fields and other areas, prices to be charged in book store and cafeteria, and college wide educational policies. We added to this list the substance of the demands from the Black Student Union and the Third World Liberation Front (hereafter summarized as the TWLF demands). (See the Appendix.) Scores for attitudes held before the strike (as remembered by respondents) and present attitudes (subsequent to the strike) were obtained using a five point scale. Respondents were asked What should the role of students, faculty, and/or administration be in making policies and regulations concerning [these issues]? They were then given five alternatives: student autonomy; faculty and students sharing power; administration, faculty, and students sharing power; faculty and administration sharing power; and administrative autonomy. The faculty were placed in an intermediate position on the scale for two reasons. First, the strike was initiated by students; the real protagonists were students and administration. And in day-to-day campus activities, the faculty has a foot in both camps and in many ways is split in its identifications. The students often consider faculty to be henchmen of the administration, and

[1] M. E. Troyer and Y. Owada, *Roles and Values of Students, Faculty-Administration in University Policy and Decision Making* (Mitaka, Japan: International Christian University, 1964).

the administration often sees faculty as accomplices of the students. For these reasons, the faculty is here considered in the context of the struggle and not independently. Second, decision-making power in the state college system flows in one direction—downward. This system was created by the legislature, which delegates some powers to the trustees, reserving other powers for itself. The trustees in turn delegate some of their powers to the chancellor and to local college presidents. On the local level, the college president has authority over two less powerful constituencies—faculty and students. The faculty have some power over students; and the students rest at the bottom of the hierarchy. Therefore in investigating attitudes about increasing or decreasing autonomy for various constituencies in the state college system, one must take account of this present distribution of power.

To test the validity of this scale we correlated the scores for a sample of students with their scores on a conformity scale and the F-scale (used in studies of the authoritarian personality).[2] Our hypothesis was that our scale did tap dimensions of radicalism and conservatism if those who were nonconformist and nonauthoritarian on already validated scales appeared radical on ours. This hypothesis was supported when the relationship proved significant at the 0.01 level.

In operational terms, we wished to discover how respondents were divided in their opinions or attitudes by examining their scores on the selected items. In future reports we will examine specific aspects of the differences that we found. However, in this first report we wish to show only what kinds of differences existed on the campus over issues and among interested groups of students, faculty, and administration. Our purpose, then, was to examine scores of all respondents in the three groups and to compare responses on remembered attitudes prior to the strike with those held at the time the survey was conducted (June to July 1969). We hoped to see whether we could explain any differences in perspectives through individual variables such as age, sex, and career line. In addition we addressed three main questions to the data: Was there a significant movement of students, faculty, or administration to radicalism or conservatism after the strike? Were there more or fewer differences in viewpoint among the groups follow-

[2] T. F. Pettigrew, "Personality and Sociocultural Factors in Intergroup Attitudes: A Cross-National Comparison," *Journal of Conflict Resolution*, 1958, 2, 29–42.

ing the strike? Were there different patterns of responses within the range of the sixty-five items?

We began by considering the composition of each group—students, faculty, and administration—in terms of which demographic features were associated with the tendency toward radicalism or conservatism on the after scores. We made analyses of such features as age, sex, ethnicity, political party, military status, marital status, school or major subject, and other categories especially relevant to status as student, faculty member, or member of the administrative staff. The special descriptive categories for faculty were AFT membership, experience in college administration, tenure, rank, full- or part-time status, highest degree attained, and years of service at the college. For administration, especially important categories were teaching experience, AFT membership, full- or part-time status, number and type of academic degrees, and number of years in position. For students, status categories of special importance were employment, receiving financial aid, and grade level.

Only two characteristics bear on differences within the faculty: AFT membership and school of the college. Not surprisingly AFT members were more liberal in attitude than were nonmembers at the 0.01 level of significance. The remaining important differences are that the schools of business and of health, physical education, and recreation were more conservative and the School of Behavioral and Social Sciences more radical than the others (at the 0.05 level of significance). These differences may be two manifestations of the same thing, of course, for the "conservative" schools were reported to possess only one AFT member each, while the "radical" school contained more AFT members than did other schools. However, commitment to a professional field precedes union membership; and so the former must be taken as important in understanding political tendencies on a campus.

Compared with the other two groups, the administration presents a remarkable homogeneity in both attitude and social characteristics. Respondents are almost uniformly male, married, over thirty, Caucasian, suburbanite, veterans, and members of either major political party (they are Democrats two to one). It may be argued that members of this group fit much of the stereotype of the WASP. All administration respondents are over thirty-one and most are over forty; yet the majority (twenty-two out of thirty-three) have held their administrative positions fewer than five years. This finding suggests that appointees may enter administration after an academic career of some duration. Perhaps they are culled from the rest of the faculty by a combination of their own interests in advancement or administrative work and the interest of the administration in persons possessing particular attitudinal characteristics. In this way, the process of self-selection and recruitment policy may produce the homogeneous product we have found. Administrators do divide slightly on one characteristic: number of years in position; persons in administrative posts for fewer than five years are more conservative than those in positions for more than nine years.

The students are the most heterogeneous of the three groups in social characteristics, so that conservative and liberal tendencies arise from many different sources. Statistically reliable differences are associated with age (older students tend toward conservatism), political party (both Democrats and Republicans are conservative), subject major, and grade level. There is a sharp change once a student passes his junior year from liberalism to conservatism. Perhaps students become conservative for one of the same reasons their elders do—to protect their investments in the status quo. In this case they may want to protect their opportunity to finish school and acquire their B.A. degrees. These findings run counter to studies of conservatism and radicalism at such places as Bennington, where students became more radical as they progressed through college.[3] Perhaps the crucial difference is the type of student body. Most students at Bennington had high socioeconomic backgrounds. For them, college was considered a time of free inquiry with a moratorium on real life struggles; and priorities in the educational system were not given to preparation for social mobility. Worry over future jobs is not such a keen problem for the seniors in such elite colleges as it is for their counterparts in commuter colleges like SFSC, which cater to students with low socioeconomic backgrounds. For them, the seriousness of the financial investment may create caution and conservatism through fear of risking that investment. The most significant polarizations in the students occur around school major.

[3] T. M. Newcomb, "Attitude Development as a Function of Reference Groups: The Bennington Study." In E. E. Maccoby et al. (Eds.), Readings in Social Psychology (3rd ed.) (New York: Holt, Rinehart, and Winston, 1958), pp. 265–276.

Students in social and behavioral sciences, humanities, and creative arts line up against those in business, education, and health-physical education. In these cases all but the education students follow the tendencies apparent in their professors.

A comparison across these three groups indicates very different profiles. The administrators show the most and the students the least homogeneity in social characteristics and political viewpoint. As often occurs, the faculty are in between. One interesting sidelight is that all the administrators live in surrounding suburban areas, the faculty are both city and suburban dwellers, and most of the students live in the city. A high percentage of all three groups are members of the two major political parties. But the students also belong to New Left groups, while the faculty belong to the AFT. Members of the administration have no political ties corresponding to these. The influence of time in position is curious: among students higher grade level is associated with conservatism; among faculty, time at the college has no effect; while time in position among administrative personnel tends to be somewhat related to liberalism.

Since we saw these definite tendencies for disagreement within segments of the campus population, we wanted to know how attitudes were affected by the strike. Was disagreement more or less extensive after the strike? We began by considering the before and after effect of the strike. On mean scores for all sixty-five items, the three groups were strikingly alike in their slight tendency toward conservatism prior to the strike. (Scores below 3 indicate a tendency toward radicalism; scores above 3 indicate a tendency toward conservatism.) Students (with a mean score of 3.32) remember themselves as being even more conservative than do faculty (3.17) and administration (3.23); and the faculty of SFSC (famous for its radical professors) initially tended toward more conservative views than one might have expected.

However, the after scores show considerable changes in the groups. Faculty and students (both with mean scores of 2.98) see themselves as becoming radicalized; they now approve of a greater sharing in decision-making by the students than they had before. (The changes in attitude by students and faculty are significant at the 0.01 level.) The administration, far from changing with the others, moves somewhat in the opposite direction (with a mean score of 3.26).

The potential antagonisms implicit in these changes of attitudes suggest an important finding—the growing disagreement among members of the campus community. A difference of 0.26 points or more in mean scores among the three groups was arbitrarily chosen as the operational sign of disagreement for comparison of the before and after scores. Before the strike, thirty issues met this criterion for disagreement, but afterward forty-eight did. In other words, before the strike the campus community was in tolerable agreement about 57 per cent of the issues, but afterward agreement dropped to 26 per cent.

Preliminary examination of the items on which there was agreement or disagreement among groups indicated no identifiable interest clearly unifying the students, faculty, and administration. But the trend toward radicalism of students and faculty is confirmed by the significant differences on the after scores. When the H-test was used to distinguish among students, faculty, and administration on their after scores for all sixty-five items, twenty-three issues showed significant differences. On all but one of these issues the students or faculty or both were more radical than was the administration. (The faculty aligned with the administration on the issue of salaries of the student officers; the students never aligned with the administration.) In general we could discover no pattern to distinguish those items which revealed significant differences. Our question of why change occurred as it did was not yet answered.

In order to discover patterns of responses we made a factor analysis from the scores of all sixty-five questions for each respondent. Our factor analysis revealed eight independent clusters of these sixty-five items. We have titled these factors to suggest the perceptions that respondents have of the underlying problems of the college. These eight factors are listed with the three items having the highest loadings in each cluster and the amounts of the loadings.

Factor I.   Who should determine current policy for higher education?

    0.69   Determination of faculty salaries

    0.60   Policy concerning official recognition of campus organizations

    0.64   Preparation and control of college budget and fiscal policy

Factor II. Who should control student government and activities?
    0.74 Salaries of student officers
    0.72 Dispensing student fees to various organizations and activities
    0.69 Control of student funds

Factor III. Who decides what is called education?
    0.71 Specific course requirements and units of credits for the major
    0.67 Development of new programs or majors within a department
    0.60 Determination of qualification for admission to graduate school

Factor IV. Who speaks for the campus?
    0.65 Publication of campus affairs to the community
    0.54 Staffing and control of campus publication
    0.54 Power and function of the Academic Senate

Factor V. Can the college be an independent social institution?
    0.56 Acceptance or rejection of money coming into the financial aid office from various organizations
    0.51 Allowing on-campus groups or individuals to do research connected with defense contracts
    0.51 Definition of academic freedom for the college

Factor VI. Who controls the financial resources available to students?
    0.57 Library fines
    0.57 Allocation of funds for research to both faculty and students
    0.54 Determination of qualifications for recipients of financial aid

Factor VII. Who should define the future character of the college?
    0.57 Tuition
    0.63 If and when to have a quarter system
    0.47 Collegewide educational policies

Factor VIII.   What is the appropriate public image for the college?

   0.59   Discipline within the college for students' off-
campus civil offenses

   0.54   Establishment of coeducational residence halls

   0.50   Use of liquor and drugs in residence halls

All but one of these factors are represented in the twenty-three
items that showed significant differences on the H-test. Since the factors
by definition are independent, this interrelationship proves that the
H-test differences, particularly those between students and administration, pervade and underlie the entire gamut of campus problems.

What issues do these factors tap? Since the same issues vex social
critics who review the conflicts within higher education today, both
observers and participants seem to have developed a similar focus on
where the problems lie. Factor I (Who should determine current
policy for higher education?) and Factor VI (Who controls the financial resources available to students?) suggest what the debate over the
allocation of powers and the distribution of resources may be. For example, criticism of governing boards or of the lack of Educational
Opportunity Program or scholarship funds for minorities are issues
which involve these factors.

The specific ends for which power should be used in the university suggest the general focus for three factors. Factor III (Who
decides what is called education?) considers the formulation of appropriate standards for student recruitment, student performance, and
curriculum development. (These issues were raised by the TWLF in
the student strike and are considered at length in Chapter Five.)
Factor V (Can the college be an independent social institution?) concerns the relations between the organization of the campus and the
specific interests in the broader society. (See Chapter Six.) Factor VII
(Who should define the future character of the college?) raises questions particularly crucial in California about the future structure of
higher education. The current California system designated by the
Master Plan is considered unsatisfactory by many. (See Chapter
Four.)

The remaining three factors (II, IV, VIII) revolve around the
issue of autonomy. In Factor II (Who should control student government and activities?) issues arise which have long been part of political

debates over emendation of Title V in the California education code. The legislature and trustees plan a revision to give college presidents control over the use of student body funds. Formerly the student body officers had this power, but as student activities entered political and off-campus areas (such as tutoring ghetto children and community mobilization in ghettos), college authorities defined these activities as misuse of funds. Factor IV (Who speaks for the campus?) is an issue on campuses throughout the country. For example, the power (or powerlessness) of the Academic Senate tends to create conflicts between faculty and administration. (See Chapter Ten.) And the information from the campus made available to the larger community is a concern of everyone on campus. The administration may wish to have dissidents portrayed as thugs; the dissidents may be angered if they think acts of police brutality have not been publicized. (See Chapter Seven.) This issue is related to that of Factor VIII (What is the appropriate public image for the college?). Clearly students and administration have widely varying views on this matter. The students want the rioting and demonstrations on campus reported because they see these activities as consequences of repression. The administration regards publication of these activities as endangering public relations and alumni support for higher education.

The existence of eight factors shows that the campus was not as polarized as many participants believed. Individuals varied their answers in response to the specific items rather than taking one overriding political position. Despite wide disagreements on the campus, areas of overlapping allegiances can still be found. Further examination of these factors suggests that the basic issues of the debate on this campus are similar to those on other campuses. Perhaps an understanding of them can lead to a greater understanding of the problems of the American campus today.

CHAPTER 17

Politics of Justice

Stanley Ofsevit

ͷͷͷͷͷͷͷͷͷͷͷͷͷͷͷͷͷ

The constitutional guarantee of equal protection under the law has long been considered an essential element of our society. A bipartisan thirteen-member National Commission on the Causes and Prevention of Violence, headed by Milton Eisenhower, issued the following statement: "Order is indispensable to society, law is indispensable to order, enforcement is indispensable to law. The justice and decency of the law and its enforcement are not simply desirable embellishments, but rather the indispensable condition of respect for law and civil peace in a free society."[1] Yet this constitutional guarantee is the one most often violated in the American social system. Although it is not at all clear how much violation of the hallowed principle of impartiality American people will tolerate, one thing

[1] *San Francisco Chronicle,* November 9, 1969.

is certain: it is becoming increasingly difficult for the citizenry to disregard these violations.

Today some of the most debatable legal procedures—which give rise to serious questions about the efficacy of constitutional guarantees—are related to the management of youthful protest. And one of the most serious efforts to punish or restrict this protest occurred in the struggle for what the participants saw as equality in education. The occasion was the mass arrest in San Francisco of approximately 450 strikers from State at the Free Speech Platform on campus on January 23, 1969. This event occurred during the faculty-student strike. The alleged offenses were failure to disperse when ordered to do so by the police, illegal assemblage, and disturbing the peace.

The Free Speech Platform had been the scene of many student gatherings prior to the strike without complaints to the police. Yet on this occasion, when the noise level was not particularly different from what it had been at past events, the police claimed a serious disturbance of the peace. The difference on this occasion was the violation of the president's ban on rallies. The police gave an order to disperse and then surrounded the crowd. Witnesses testified to the amazing speed of the police action. Two or three minutes after the order to disperse, the entire group was encircled by the San Francisco police tactical unit (Tac Squad). Thus, to many observers the action appeared designed more to seize and detain the assemblage than to urge them to cease and desist.

However, except for participation in the rally activity itself, the students demonstrated their willingness to be law abiding. Despite the sudden nature of the arrest, no resistance was offered. Those arrested waited quietly through the afternoon to be placed in police vans and taken to the Hall of Justice. One faculty member caught in the encirclement until well past the lunch hour stood serenely eating a sandwich—as evidenced by news photos. Many others called to friends outside the circle, giving instructions about whom to notify or how to move cars from limited parking zones. But not all were so serene. One student who was arrested told me how happy she had been to see me standing outside the circle, for I was a friendly face and she was quite scared. Others who were frightened were comforted, often by strangers. And those injured during the encirclement were given special attention by their fellows. A physician who asked to be allowed to attend to an injured student was told to "go right on in," and then he too would be placed under arrest. The policeman in question later testified that he told this to the doctor to test his veracity. Despite the difficulties and discomforts, the feeling of camaraderie among those encircled was very evident to those of us on the perimeter. At about five o'clock, four and a half hours after the encirclement, the last police vans were leaving. But one could still hear chants and singing as the persons were taken away.

For many of these people the first experience with American jurisprudence occurred when the courts refused them the opportunity of being released on their own recognizance (O.R.). O.R. is utilized in San Francisco and other localities to minimize expense and time-consuming responsibility for the court before defendants are brought to trial. O.R. also has benefits for the defendant, for it enables a low-risk defendant without funds to be freed until the time of his trial. But, at a meeting of all judges of the municipal court held soon after the first arrests at San Francisco State College in November 1968, it was allegedly agreed (and subsequent events seem to bear out) that O.R. would not be granted to anyone arrested at San Francisco State College, whatever the recommendation of the O.R. project. The judge in the cases of January 23 made no decisions regarding the possibility of suspending bail; he only honored the prior agreement.

Thus, the decision to deny O.R. to the defendants was an agreement based largely on political considerations. Certainly many of those who were arrested would otherwise have been considered low-risk defendants by the established criteria. They had strong ties in the community via family, school, jobs, and friends. Some persons believe that denial of O.R. was intended to divert the activists from strike activity into fund-raising efforts in the interest of their friends on trial. If this was the intent, it was partially successful; the strike was divested of considerable devotion and energy, while the leadership organized collections to pay bail bonds.

The news media publicized the arrests widely for several days. Charges and countercharges about guilt and innocence and proper and improper definition of civil liberties were discussed at great length on campus and in the larger community. But the full import of the event could be known only when the cases came to court. Officials tried to persuade those arrested to plead guilty on lesser charges in order to escape with probation or other minor punishment. The purpose was to save time and money in the court and public embarrassment for the arrested. However, at that time, the students believed that a fair trial would affirm their innocence and publicly vindicate them. They were soon disabused of such idealistic notions by the events which followed.

Six months later, during the summer interim, I took the opportunity to learn more about the outcome of these incidents than I could learn from the newspaper reports. I observed in depth four trials conducted simultaneously in the San Francisco municipal courts. During this time I was given ample opportunity to discuss the issues and proceedings with lawyers, defendants, police, reporters, witnesses, parents, and professional colleagues. I witnessed most of the court proceedings in each of the four cases, for the styles of the judges, prosecutors, and defending attorneys varied, and this variation resulted in different scheduling of court proceedings. For example, recesses were taken at different times in different courts. Prosecutors and defense attorneys often had to appear in other courts, and judges also had other responsibilities which caused delays in trials. Furthermore, much of the prosecution's testimony and many of the exhibits were identical from case to case. Therefore, it was possible to miss part of a trial and to have it repeated at another trial across the hall. The presentation of evidence was so repetitious that judges and lawyers who were trying more than one case said that it often seemed like seeing a movie for a second time.

These observations created frightening impressions and gave me, no less than the defendants, grave doubts that having one's day in court during this period of history results in justice. Doubts are particularly grave that defendants who have been associated with currently unpopular movements and activities receive an impartial hearing. Adding substance to the suspicion of political tampering in these cases was a disclosure by the *San Francisco Chronicle*. In a leading editorial (February 6, 1969)˙ the paper condemned the act of a California assemblyman (Don Mulford of Oakland)˙.

He has not only called for draconian punishment of the student demonstrators but has now overstepped the bounds by threatening judges who decline to hustle them into jail for six months or such other terms as the law allows. At his behest, judges from all sections of the state were recently summoned to Sacramento for a meeting with him and Assemblyman Frank Murphy, chairman of the criminal procedures committee. They were informed by Mulford himself that those who are guilty of leniency in such cases will find themselves up against heavily financed opposition when they next file for reelection.

Such disclosures are not likely to be forgotten by the defendants; and their desire for drastic social and political change in America will not be vitiated by the memory.

In addition to the political atmosphere of the trials, lack of resources was a problem for many of the defendants. The American system of jurisprudence guarantees the defendant the right of adequate counsel and one of his own choosing. It also guarantees him an individual trial so that the merits of his particular case can be judged independently of any categories or groups to which he belongs. In order for the city to minimize the expenses of such an unprecedentedly large number of trials, the students were brought to court in groups of ten. Such economizing did nothing to minimize expenses for defendants. Jury trials in these cases often involve several weeks of litigation. Few lawyers can afford to take time from busy practices to provide low-cost defense. And few defendants could afford the high cost of legal defense this situation would otherwise entail. Unlike students at many private schools, most students at San Francisco State College come from very poor, working-class or lower-middle-class families. As many as 75 per cent of the students at the college work full- or part-time. Most of the arrested students then were forced to seek counsel from the office of the public defender.

The public defender's office is understaffed and possesses inadequate resources under ordinary circumstances; and it was given no additional investigatory help for the added burden of these trials. Normally, the San Francisco office has only three full-time investigators. Contrast this staffing to that of the district attorney's office, which was given three additional investigators to work exclusively on the San Francisco State College trials. One of the unfortunate results of this inequity was that some defendants met their attorneys the day trials began; others raised funds to secure attorneys of their choice only after their trials began. It seems clear that without funds, a defendant is in essence deprived of the right to adequate counsel. Perry Mason's assistance from his investigator is possible in fiction, but in reality the defense does not have the same supportive resources possessed by the prosecutor, who has virtually unlimited investigatory assistance. Only the very rich can provide their defending attorneys with adequate money to assure a proper defense.

To remedy this situation, the delegates to the California Bar Association in its 1969 meeting issued a resolution supporting the demand that poor defendants be provided with the same services available to the prosperous. Criminologists have for decades cited this lack as a basic inequity in our judicial system. A proper defense is always costly. Lawyers often have to purchase photos of documents and events; they must hire investigators to find witnesses. In the SFSC trials sometimes these costs were personally met by lawyers with indigent clients. Only such valiant efforts prevented more defendants than were from being found guilty on all counts. Some of the efforts by lawyers included long discussions with students and others concerning the strike and its background. Several attorneys spent time on the campus to familiarize themselves with the area as well as to get the feel of the campus. During the recesses or on days when their own trials were adjourned, lawyers sat in on other cases being heard. Defense attorneys from different trials held countless conferences to get new ideas and insights. Most of these efforts were made on the lawyers' own time, for the system does not provide adequate compensation for the requisite effort to build a case. However, such efforts would not be considered beyond the call of duty by a lawyer who knows he will be compensated for his time.

Although the defendants were shocked to have been denied O.R. and to realize they had insufficient resources to secure a proper counsel, few had anticipated severe inequity in jury selection. Again, they were soon disillusioned. Jury panels are selected from voter registration lists, and the names of the poor, young, and black do not appear with the same frequency as do the names of older, white, middle-class people. Thus, juries, including those at the SFSC trials, are usually composed of unemployed older women without children, government employees, retired employees, and employees of large concerns. And this is the same cross-section of the population that contains the greatest number of those aligned against student unrest and activism.

While the voter registration lists by their nature eliminated many prospective jurors who might have been considered peers of the defendants, peremptory challenges by lawyers further reduced the possibility that a jury of peers would be selected. Judges discounted charges of racial bias in the use of peremptory challenges made by the district attorney's office. Yet those few blacks who did appear in jury selection panels were usually removed by the prosecutor. In one trial concerning a prominent newspaper man and physician in the black community, the defense protested the fact that the prosecuting attorney dismissed all ten of the black members of the jury panel under peremptory challenges. The judge declared a mistrial when the district attorney did not respond to a summons to appear to face the charges of racial bias in jury selection.

Although few blacks or young people could pass the tests for jury selection, the defense still sought those who might give their clients a fair hearing. They desired jurors who strongly supported the First Amendment and the principle of free speech it is supposed to guarantee. The defense lawyers challenged on the basis of clear-cut bias. For example, they excluded prospective jurors who had doubts about the efficacy of the First Amendment or thought that students and teachers did not have the right to strike or thought that long hair and "strange" dress were signs of poor character.

The prosecution used their peremptory challenges against blacks, young people, and anyone who appeared sympathetic with the new youth culture. The prosecution also had secured a list of all those organizations that had ostensibly supported the strike. Some of the organizations listed did, in fact, support it, but others did not. Some churches were listed because they permitted the strikers to hold meetings on their premises. Included in the list were political, civic, labor, legal defense, and church groups, among them the American Friends Service Committee, Sacred Heart Church (Roman Catholic), Painters Union Local 6, and the NAACP. To be excluded on this basis one need not have actually belonged to an organization; merely to have supported it in any manner or to have known a member was sufficient reason for challenge by the prosecution. Prosecutors, when challenged on the rationale for linking these organizations and a clear bias favoring the strike claimed to be determining only potential bias on the part of prospective jurors.

One consequence of prosecution tactics was the development

of concern about the propriety of the proceedings among defense lawyers. Several of these attorneys initially admitted little sympathy for their clients. Yet as the jury selection proceeded, many of them came to the conclusion that the trial was no mere criminal case but a political one. One of the defense attorneys has described some of the political characteristics.[2] For instance, he points out that in such trials public opinion and public attitudes on the social questions involved inevitably had an effect on the final decisions. Of course, the prosecution may argue that political issues are not relevant, for it is in their interest to avoid a political definition of the crime which may mitigate or explain the circumstances and make the act something other than a simple criminal one. But political issues must be faced directly for jurors to see how their personal opinions might affect their verdict. And the defense lawyers have to realize that to ignore these issues prejudices their cases.

The questioning of prospective jurors disclosed the major strategies of both the prosecution and the defense. The prosecution sought to establish the simple fact that a law had been broken and a crime committed. The jury had to determine only whether the prosecution has established that fact. Naturally, the prosecution sought to eliminate any prospective juror who might have concluded that a student rally was an exercise of constitutional rights, and the defense sought to eliminate any who could not see the connection between a student rally and those constitutional rights. In addition, the defense attempted to introduce as evidence such factors as the oppressive atmosphere on the campus and the problem of police brutality. The well-managed picket line formed by the students and the peaceful rallies were identified as exercises of democratic and civic responsibility. They made no attempt to deny that the students had been attending a rally on January 23.

Furthermore, the defense tried to establish that the defendants did not disturb the peace, that is, that the activities cited as peace-disturbing were normal for the campus and did not, therefore, involve an illegal assembly. In addition, the defense maintained that the order to disperse was improperly made. First, it could not be distinctly heard; and even if it had been distinct, insufficient time was allowed

[2] M. Burnstein, "Trying a Political Case," *The National Lawyers Guild Practitioner*, 1969, *28*(2), 33–40.

for those assembled to disperse. Second, the defense contended that the California Penal Code Section 726 clearly indicated that the order was improperly made. The order was given over an amplification system with loudspeakers about five hundred feet from the rally. Section 726 states:

> Where any number of persons, whether armed or not, unlawfully or riotously assembled, the sheriff of the county, and his deputies, the official governing the town or city, or the judges of the justice court and the constables thereof, or any of them, must go among the persons assembled or as near to them as possible and command them, in the name of the people of the state, immediately to disperse.

The prosecution argued that the law was old and should not apply in this case in light of modern electronic advances which make large public address systems possible. This argument strongly contradicts their oft-stated position—in opposition to defense arguments—that prosecutors do not judge laws and codes but only enforce them. The prosecution was in the strange position of asking the judges and juries to disregard the clear statement of the penal code. The judges, without exception, acceded to this request, and in their instructions permitted the juries to decide this matter at their own discretion as a decision of fact rather than law.

This example is just one of many involving biases of the judges. In order to secure justice for all, the American system of jurisprudence is supposed to provide an impartial judge skilled in judicial procedures. He is expected to restrict his comments to ruling on points of law. Many observers, witnesses, defendants, defense lawyers, and reporters were shocked by the extent to which judges verbalized value judgments concerning student and faculty strike activities. Thus, one judge remarked when giving instructions to the jury, "Ladies and gentlemen, the real issue is whether the colleges are to be run by the administration or a mob." Another, on several occasions, mentioned "typewriters being thrown out of windows," apparently referring to an incident when one typewriter had been tossed from a window; this action occurred months before the mass arrest occasioning the trials. When the juries were out of the courtroom, the judges were even freer in defining strikers, both teachers and students, as rabble-rousers who were "discourteous," "vicious," "cruel," and "immoral." It seemed

that the judges were adamant in their intention to punish the defendants for their general "sins" by convicting them for the specific alleged
sin for which they were being tried. Apparently, they were little concerned that public protest would be aroused by such judgments.
Clearly, such an assessment proved correct. No inquiry into these
judicial practices followed; and three of these judges were promoted to
the superior court.

   This pattern is a far cry from the standard that students of
civics expect to find. Ideally, our legal system provides that anyone
charged with a misdemeanor or felony is innocent until proven guilty.
In order to determine the truth, two adversaries, both lawyers, the
prosecutor and the defense attorney, are pitted against each other with
a neutral lawyer, a judge, present to assure that the rules of evidence
are obeyed and that due process of law is strictly observed. Where,
then, was the neutral lawyer in many of these cases?

   By November 1, 1969, 195 defendants had been tried under
these conditions. Of this number, eighty-two were convicted of all three
charges, thirty-six were convicted of one or two charges, forty-two were
acquitted on all charges, and thirty-five had hung juries. Thus, almost
all possible combinations of verdicts were rendered, although the evidence throughout the trials was essentially identical. Briefly, the important variables appeared to be the activities of the judge, the abilities
of the prosecuting and defense attorneys, the jurors, and the presentation of those defendants who testified on their own behalf. Jurors
seemed to listen intently to this testimony, not so much to consider the
statements in determining guilt or innocence but rather to find out
what kinds of people the defendants were. One could see jurors wince
at radical or irreverent statements.

   In interviews following the trials, jurors indicated they had
been deeply influenced by the length of a defendant's hair or the style
of his attire. Above all, they were influenced by the use of profanity
heard on a tape recording of the rally played during the trial by the
prosecution. One juror, in a trial where all defendants were found
guilty, commented that the jury was impressed when they heard someone shout "fuck California" on a tape recording. Other jurors indicated that they felt failure to convict might lead to more campus disturbances and that it was up to them to prevent such events. Others
felt that when defendants smiled during their trial, this was an indica-

tion of their taking the trial "too lightly," which should not go unpunished. Such comments clearly showed that jurors were convicting defendants at least in part on behavior exhibited during the trial and not on alleged behavior on January 23, 1969.

It appears, then, that many jurors who favored conviction were not as concerned with assessing what occurred during the mass arrest on January 23 as they were in expressing their distaste for the values expressed by the youth involved. Some of the observers (professors, lawyers) were stunned by the irrationality of these decisions; they, no less than the students, left the courtrooms convinced that only a massive overhaul of the means of administering justice in our courts can forestall violent confrontation. Indeed, many feel that time has already run out.

Only the sentences imposed by the judges were more inconsistent than the verdicts. Sentences ranged from thirty days suspended sentence to one year in jail for those with identical convictions. Generally, but not always, convictions for first time misdemeanors involve a maximun of thirty days in jail; again, usually, this is transmuted to a suspended sentence and perhaps one-year probation. Yet some of those given suspended sentences were placed on probation for as long as three years. It could be argued that those who insisted on due process were punished for the trouble to which they put the court.[3] The approximately 255 defendants who pleaded *nolo contendere* (waiving the right of trial) were generally put on probation for one year; however, even ten from this group received jail sentences. Generally a plea of *nolo contendere* is encouraged on the grounds that both defendant and court system will profit from a swift conclusion to the case. The assumption, in omitting adversary proceedings and jury trials, is that defendants who are guilty will see the reasonableness of a procedure which is likely to offer them the lesser penalty. An attempt is made to weight the system against abuses by those who are guilty but request a jury trial in hopes of obtaining a verdict of innocence. The courts are likely to impose stiffer sentences on those ultimately found guilty than on those who plead *nolo contendere* in the first place. In this view any "irresponsible" use of the courts will be limited, for only those who

[3] M. Mahoney, "Some Lessons from S. F. State Trials," *San Francisco Chronicle*, January 5, 1970, p. 8.

genuinely feel that their innocence would be upheld in a trial will brave these potentially serious consequences.

The sacrifices to secure one's day in court are considerable. The students were required to give up wages from summer jobs, family vacation trips, or attendance at summer school. No provision in our judicial system allows compensation to persons for such sacrifices even when they are found innocent. Although people are presumed innocent until proven guilty, they are in fact punished while the state attempts to establish their guilt.

Two additional areas in which politics affected the trials can be found in examining the system of parole and appeals which applies to students. In the United States, it has been customary in most juris-dictions to place first offenders on probation, especially if they are charged with a misdemeanor. Prior to a decision on probation, trained probation officers do a social case study of the defendant and present their report and recommendation to the judge, who ordinarily follows the recommendation. Given this procedure, one would expect many recommendations for probation in this case since most of those on trial had no criminal backgrounds. It was astonishing, therefore, to hear probation officers testify that they had been instructed by their super-visors to recommend jail for all defendants. And so the extent of the misuse of the system of justice became clear. In the courtroom, where the focus is upon standards of evidence in order to minimize irrelevant idiosyncratic criteria, the verdicts and sentences were highly variable and apparently influenced by such criteria. Yet, in the probation pro-cedure, established to consider individual differences, the defendants were treated as a political category rather than as individual cases.

In the spring of 1970, between 130 and 140 people from twenty-one group trials were appealing their cases. In order for a lawyer to be effective in his appeal to a higher court, he must have a trial transcript, the cost of which is usually borne by the defendant. If the defendant is indigent, then the city, in order to assure equality for rich and poor alike, pays the costs. However, the trial judge decides whether a convicted person is indigent, on the basis of the person's income and financial responsibilities. As noted, most of those convicted in this case were working students with incomes sufficient for only basic subsistence. Almost all the convicted defendants had filed indi-gency reports. In addition a judge usually automatically grants indigency to those originally eligible for counsel from the public defender's office. But only one free transcript was granted. And seven months after this award was made, the defendant had yet to receive it. The city refused to pay for it; and the judge had not ordered the city to do so.

One reason for refusing to give defendants free transcripts was that judges knew that if they granted a transcript to one defendant in a group, all in the group would have access to it. Judges stated that those who could pay for the transcript (as determined by the judge) should pay their shares before the city paid the shares of those the judge determined to be indigent. But the judges overlooked the original responsibility of the court in creating the situation whereby one transcript could be useful for a whole group. In all these cases, although each person was independently tried, they were placed in groups of ten as a convenience to the court. It does seem that judges used the denial of a free transcript as a punitive measure. Students were told by the court to sell their cars, borrow money, use their $100 bank account, or to figure it out themselves. But if they did so, they would relinquish their claims to indigency status and their rights to the services of the public defender.[4]

What insights can be gained from this analysis? Part of the American creed is that the innocent will be protected. A necessary corollary is that all will receive this protection whether or not they are attractive and meritorious citizens in other respects. Such protection generally involves guarantees of due process irrespective of politics, and for this reason the courts are established and maintained as a structure independent of the political system.

Many frustrated or disappointed by injustices perpetrated within the political system may yet retain their belief in the ultimate justice of the democratic system. Their confidence in the court system permits this faith to remain unshaken. But, as the Eisenhower and Kerner commissions have reported, recent experiences with the judicial process may be seriously undermining that faith today. The analysis of the San Francisco State College trials presented in this paper should lead any citizen to understand why dissident youth have little faith in the American tradition and why so much criticism of current practices within that tradition is expressed by men of good faith.

[4] *Ibid.*

CHAPTER 18

Strike Settlement

Nancy McDermid

ʃ❋ʃ❋ʃ❋ʃ❋ʃ❋ʃ❋ʃ❋ʃ❋ʃ❋ʃ❋ʃ❋ʃ❋ʃ❋ʃ❋ʃ❋ʃ❋ʃ❋ʃ

To settle the strike, student members of the Black Students Union (BSU) and the Third World Liberation Front (TWLF) entered into negotiations with the college Select Committee. Faculty members of the AFT, Local 1352, entered into negotiations with representatives of the Board of Trustees and of the college administration. On the basis of signed agreements, the teachers ended their strike on March 2, 1969, and the students ended their strike on March 21, 1969.

An analysis of the somewhat equivocal terms of these two agreements and a study of the lack of meaningful, good-faith implementation of the often obfuscated promises may explain one cause of the strike. Even when students and faculty attempt to use processes appropriate to democratic organization such as negotiation, com-

227

promise, and agreements, they soon realize that institutional change is achieved by these processes only at the whim of those in authority.

Because of such a whim, S. I. Hayakawa did not even sign the agreement negotiated by his Select Committee with the BSU and TWLF. Nor did the Board of Trustees sign the agreement which their representative, Louis Heilbron, made with Local 1352 on February 16, 1969. Some members of the AFT argued that such signing was unnecessary, that the trustees had only to ratify Item 3 of the agreement, which provided for a chancellor's Review Committee for grievance and disciplinary appeals. However, the trustees blatantly disavowed any settlement at all. On January 6, 1970, Mansel Keene, assistant chancellor, wrote to the executive officer of the San Francisco Labor Council, tersely stating: "No strike settlement was ever entered into by the Board of Trustees. . . . (It)' was never adopted by the Board of Trustees nor signed by it or on its behalf." Thus, neither settlement has been treated as an agreement by the nonstriking nonsignatories. Therefore, the holding of the California Court of Appeals that a strike settlement is binding upon a public agency (*East Bay Municipal Employees, Local 390 AFL-CIO* vs. *County of Alameda*)' is probably not a decisive precedent for the students and teachers at San Francisco State. If there is no settlement, there is nothing to which the public agency can be bound.

Signed or unsigned—illusory or binding—have the promises made in the two agreements been implemented? This question can perhaps be answered by evaluating the action (or inaction) taken on each item. (See the Appendix for a full statement of student and faculty demands and settlements.)'

The BSU Demand 1 for a Black Studies Department had already been met—on paper—before the strike settlement. The response of the Select Committee to BSU Demand 2 for the hiring of Nathan Hare as chairman of the Black Studies Department was to agree that "the department chairman shall be selected by the usual departmental process and Dr. Hare shall be eligible for selection." By this process, Hare was chosen as chairman of the department and recommended for early tenure and promotion. Hayakawa refused to accept this recommendation and succinctly explained his veto during one of his after-dinner speeches: "Dr. Hare's contract expired in June."

BSU Demand 3 asked for "sole power of the chairman, faculty, and staff to hire faculty and control and determine the destiny of the Black Studies Department." The Select Committee promised that the Black Studies Department would have "full faculty power commensurate with that accorded all other departments of the college." However, all six of the full-time faculty members in the department were summarily denied reappointment by the administration, even though four of them were recommended for reappointment by the hiring, retention, and tenure (HRT) committee of the department. A letter dated March 10, 1970, to Hayakawa from the council of the School of Third World Studies describes bitterly the emptiness of the BSU-TWLF agreement: "The refusal of the administration to recognize the legitimacy of the black studies HRT committee and its recommendations for rehiring is a direct attempt to impose irregular and unprecedented supervision over the School of Third World studies through having non-Third World school staff involved in processes and decisions which are normally reserved to a school." (If one studies the status quo on campus, he might argue cynically that the agreement relating to BSU Demand 3 was implemented. Faculty power in the Black Studies Department may be commensurate with that accorded other departments, for at least sixteen teachers in other departments were similarly fired by the administration in negation of departmental decisions. Perhaps, commensurately speaking, all departments are equally impotent.)

The clear intent of the fifteen demands was that students have some part in making decisions within the Black Studies Department and the School of Third World Studies. Less clear was any such intent in the strike settlement, although the agreement did speak of "cooperation of ethnic minority students," a "belief that self-government in student affairs is desirable," and a Planning Group and Advisory Committee with BSU and TWLF students as members. However, the administration attacked student power and publicly cited it as causing a "reign of terror" within the Black Studies Department. In some instances, the administration refused to meet with groups unless students were excluded; in other situations, the administration declared decisions made by committees with students as members invalid. Fear and distrust of students will probably lead to the enactment of oppressive laws in California. Senator Alfred Song has introduced legislation which would add to the education code a section prohibiting delegation of authority for appointing, dismissing, or suspending of faculty to any student, group of students, or organization which contains student voting members.

The intent of BSU Demand 3 and TWLF Demand 1 was to develop close ties with the community and to formalize such ties with the creation of community boards. The Select Committee paid lip service to this intent and recommended, approved, and urged the formation of a plethora of groups which were to function as think tanks, negotiators, roving ombudsmen, junior civil rights commissions, and crisis decision makers. Community groups are working with students and faculty in some of the ethnic areas. Occasionally, Hayakawa brings persons from the community to his office or appears at news conferences with some of his Negro minister friends. However, Hayakawa and the School of Third World Studies faculty and students could not agree on appointments to the community board. One year after the settlement, there was no ombudsman, no racism study committee, and no machinery for peaceful resolution of disputes, even though all of these were promised by the terms of the agreement.

BSU Demand 4 and TWLF Demand 3 that "the unused slots under the special admissions program be filled" were implemented by the admission of 128 students under the Educational Opportunities Program (EOP) in the spring semester, 1969. However, the rhetoric of the Select Committee in response to BSU Demand 5 and TWLF Demand 4 that "all applications from nonwhite students be accepted in the fall semester, 1969" remained devoid of meaning. About four hundred students were admitted under the EOP program in 1968–1969; the program was drastically curtailed by the legislature in enrollment and in financial support for 1969–1970. The college administration was accused of aggravating these problems of EOP by gratuitously adding its own restrictions. Local policy mandated discontinuing spring admissions and firing many of the student assistants who were involved in the strike. The legislature requires all EOP candidates to be approved by their high school or by one of sixteen Sacramento-based state agencies. This requirement was harshly interpreted by local authority to mean that the EOP on campus could have no role in recruiting. "The Tribulations of the EOP" were accurately described in the February 20, 1970, issue of the *Daily Gater:* "The high school authorities are, in short, the very people who made the EOP necessary in the first place, through their hostility or indifference to student needs; the only students whose applications they can be expected to approve are those with high grades and no money who would be better off applying for a state scholarship." Thus, the selection procedure closes the door to college admission before there is even a chance to knock.

BSU Demand 7 asked that a black person be placed in charge of the Financial Aid Office. This part of the agreement was implemented; a black man was placed in a decision-making position on financial aid packages developed for black students. That black man, Ron Boyd, resigned in May 1970 because of a "repressive and racist" climate at the college and because of an "adminstration interested in pleasing only the chancellor and the governor." Barriers almost as insurmountable as this alleged racism are created by the paucity of funds (the legislature is considering a 1.6-million-dollar slash in the EOP budget), the imposition of tuition, and the get-tough regulations which eliminate as recipients of the grants and loans any student who ever has been or is now a campus disrupter. Each student applying for financial aid must certify that he has not been convicted of any crime "which involved the use of, or assistance to others in the use of, force; disruption; or the seizure of property under control of any institution of higher education to prevent officials or students in such institution from engaging in their duties or pursuing their studies."

These repressive guidelines for all financial aid are just a part of the spectrum of punishments for those who were involved in the strike. The faculty and the student settlements contained some assurances against the imposition of punitive measures for strike-related activities. BSU Demand 8 asked for amnesty—"no disciplinary action for participation in the strike." The Select Committee merely recommended to the president certain prescribed penalties for various categories of acts—violent, nonviolent, and disrupting. Arrangements were made that allowed many students to plead *nolo contendere,* waive any hearing, and receive a written reprimand in their files for strike-related activities. However, this deal was not accepted by some of the students who believed that they were innocent and who had perhaps read *Black's Law Dictionary* definition of the plea of *nolo contendere* as "having the same legal effect as a plea of guilty." Other students were advised by their attorneys not to participate in any campus hearing while their cases were pending in the criminal courts. Some students could not complete the spring semester because their trials for misdemeanors lasted as long as seven weeks. One year later, the student disciplinary procedures were still being reviewed and amended as recommended by the Select Committee. However, the amendments allowed no student participation on the panels and made no provisions for delaying the hearing until criminal court action had been resolved.

In response to BSU Demand 6, the Select Committee promised 11.3 faculty positions to the Black Studies Department and, "if the need is demonstrated, the allocation could well exceed twenty." Enrollment in the fall 1969 demonstrated such a need, but no additional positions were allocated. The enrollment dropped in the spring semester, 1970. The causes for this decrease in student enrollment are not known, but members of the various ethnic studies areas suggested explanations. In October 1969 the college officials charged "a reign of terror" in the Black Studies Department. Constant threats by Hayakawa and his faithful deans indicated an almost irresistible urge to dissolve the department and to scatter courses to other departments. Such threats understandably had a chilling effect on many students concerned about completing their majors and getting their degrees. They may have wondered, as they registered for the spring semester, whether the administrative violence inflicted upon the School of Third World Studies might be merely the prelude to complete destruction of the program. The faculty and students in other area studies also were involved in numerous hassles with the administration for approval of new courses, allocation of additional faculty positions (TWLF Demand 2), and provision of space and staff for program planning. The council of the School of Third World Studies wrote to Hayakawa on March 10, 1970: "These firings (of the entire full-time faculty of the Black Studies Department) coupled with the continuing administrative harassment of the other Third World instructional units—Asian studies, La Raza studies, and native American studies—demonstrate clearly the intent of the San Francisco State administration to first cripple and then to eliminate the School of Third World Studies."

BSU Demand 9 asked that the trustees "not be allowed to dissolve any black programs on or off campus." This demand referred not specifically to the Black Studies Department but to the many experimental community-based, tutorial, work-study, and student-run programs supported primarily by student body funds. The agreement promised that the college "will resist any revisions to the California Administrative Code, Title V, which intend to abridge the decision-making role of students in student affairs. . . . New regulations should be provided, if necessary, to clarify areas of financial responsibility." However, the Associated Students funds are still partially controlled by the office of the attorney-general and by a court appointed trustee. The Select Committee recommended that the college intervene legally in the dispute over Associated Students funds. This intervention was the interference by the administration in the Associated Students election in spring 1969, when several strike leaders were elected to office. The second and administration-sponsored student body election was denounced by the Academic Senate, which called for a third election in fall 1969. There was no third election because the court upheld the administration-run election, relying on the indisputable reality that the president had power over everything. The student body fees were reduced to one dollar per student per semester causing virtual bankruptcy of the student body government. This decision by the college administration made the issue of how the funds should be allocated and whether programs would be dissolved by the trustees entirely academic.

The final Demand 10 of the BSU and Demand 5 of the TWLF was that George Murray be rehired. The agreement simply said, "Personnel matters of the Black Studies Department are a concern of the community board." No community board is recognized by the administration. Even the hiring, retention, and tenure committee of the Black Studies Department would have had problems rehiring Murray since he spent almost six months in jail awaiting trial and then was given probation on the condition that he not return to the San Francisco State College campus.

This analysis of the status of the student-administration joint agreement should explain why the students are examining that agreement and wondering whether those ten typed pages are anything more than scraps of paper.

The faculty agreement did not even pretend to address itself to the original strike demands of Local 1352. The February 16, 1969, agreement, cosigned by representatives of the trustees and the college administration, was accepted by a very narrow majority of the AFT members. An examination of the document explains the reluctance of many to consider it a strike settlement. Several sections of the agreement merely repeat already existing policies and procedures. For example, in Item 1, the trustees promised to meet with representatives of employee organizations, including AFT—this promise was merely a restatement of policy. In Item 2, faculty grievants were told that they had access to local campus grievance machinery—such permission to use existing campus procedures was not necessary. Item 4 referred to funding for faculty positions which had been completed at least two months before this document was even written. Other provisions in the AFT agreement, such as Item 6, relating to the nine-hour teaching load, and Item 7, providing for open personnel files, are similarly meaningless. These promises simply reiterate that "prevailing college procedures," "regular staffing formula," and "Academic Senate recommendations" will continue to be followed.

The only two controversial terms of the agreement are those which clearly have not been implemented in any way. The trustees are still trying to select the members of the chancellor's Review Committee, which was promised in Item 3 of the agreement. The Review Committee may never meet to make a decision because the chancellor has already proposed revisions that would return final authority to the chancellor. Item 9 of the AFT agreement was much more explicit than the Select Committee–BSU-TWLF agreement in its no-reprisal assurances: "There will be no reprisal against a returning teacher simply because he participated in the strike." This promise has been contemptuously violated and absolutely disregarded. For example, Morgan Pinney was not reinstated by the School of Business after the strike, even though members of a faculty hearing committee unanimously recommended "that Morgan Pinney be considered as being equal with all other returning faculty strikers and be treated as having been employed during the spring 1969 semester and be awarded back pay." Hayakawa vetoed this finding and added, "I personally have grave reservations about the propriety of the grievance panel considering the case of a nonemployee." With this illogic, no fired teacher could ever use the grievance procedures because he would be a nonemployee. Almost thirty other faculty members have been denied tenure or reappointment by the administration; many of these teachers plan to pursue their grievances through campus channels, the State Personnel Board, the Labor Council, and the courts, charging that their firings were political reprisals for their strike activities. The no-reprisal promise has not been implemented.

Like the students, the teachers are looking at their scrap of paper called an agreement and are charging violation of that agreement and a vendetta by the college administration. The AFT attorney has labeled the reprisals against certain members and officers of the union "an outrage that is not to be countenanced—an agreement is an agreement." An agreement *is* an agreement. Vagueness and even equivocation may at times lend flexibility and breathing space to such agreements. Negotiated settlement of disputes is usually a desirable process for resolving differences so that antagonists can begin to work together at the end of the conflict. However, the value of such agreements, negotiations, and conflict resolutions depends on acceptance by both sides of the binding nature of the settlement and willingness to implement the promises in good faith.

Little evidence exists of acceptance of these agreements or of good-faith implementation by the San Francisco State administration. One year after the strike, the council of the School of Third World Studies indicted the college administration for its "irrational, racist attacks" and its "irresponsible and violent attempts to impose plantation paternalism and regimentation upon the School of Third World Studies." The AFT has charged that there is a campaign of political repression to crush the union and to get rid of "innovative, active, and outspoken teachers." The strike was not settled.

CHAPTER **19**

Assessments

Nancy McDermid

¡ﬂ¡✽¡ﬂ¡✽¡ﬂ¡✽¡ﬂ¡✽¡ﬂ¡✽¡ﬂ¡✽¡ﬂ¡✽¡ﬂ¡✽¡ﬂ¡✽¡ﬂ¡

After his one-night confinement in the county jail in Concord for his refusal to pay state taxes, Thoreau sought to explain his act of civil disobedience:

> If the injustice is of such a nature that it requires you to be the agent of injustice to another, then, I say, break the law. Let your life be a counterfriction to stop the machine. What I have to do is to see, at any rate, that I do not lend myself to the wrong which I condemn.

Over one hundred years later, Martin Luther King, Jr., who had studied Thoreau's essay, wrote from the Birmingham city jail his own message on civil disobedience:

> History is the long and tragic story of the fact that privileged

236

groups seldom give up their privileges voluntarily. . . . We know through painful experience that freedom is never voluntarily given by the oppressor; it must be demanded by the oppressed. Frankly, I have never yet engaged in a direct action movement that was "well timed," according to the timetable of those who have not suffered unduly from the disease of segregation. For years now I have heard the word *wait*. This *wait* has always meant *never*.

As I walked on the union picket line at San Francisco State College—engaged in my own act of civil disobedience by ignoring a court injunction and defying the rules and regulations of my employers—I considered and reconsidered these two manifestos. Now, in attempting to assess the state of the campus, I continue to find the real meaning of those days and decisions from November 6, 1968, to March 3, 1969, in the words written by these two men.

Perhaps the influence of such men and their ideas made my reasons for going out on strike seem different from the prevailing rhetoric on the line and somewhat unrelated to the official statements of the union. I never considered the strike an optimal tactic or strategy. I did not go out on strike because I thought it would be the first line of a massive resistance to the insensitive interference of the trustees in our local campus affairs. I did not lose my salary for those months because I thought that my witness would miraculously change the priorities of the system and bring to pass a black studies program, a school of ethnic studies, and increased admission of Third World students. I knew without a Gallup or a Roper poll that my sign reading "Local 1352 on Strike" would not educate the public, the labor movement, or the legislature. I have never argued that this was the best time or even a good time to strike. One can never exhaust all the remedies—referring to committees, appealing to higher courts, remanding to lower courts, amending the amendments, questioning the quorum, waiting for the right time. I did not walk the line to expiate my guilt, to find inner peace, to put my body where my rhetoric had been. Therefore, I cannot assess the strike as a strategy, an expedient tactic, an educational process, or an exculpatory ritual. My reasons for striking were less practical, logical, and convincing than these: I felt I could no longer stay inside without lending my voice to the monologue and becoming a part of the institutional racism and repression which I condemned. I simply could find no place inside that I could be.

When we became especially despondent and discouraged on the picket line, we used to say half jokingly, "Let's declare a victory and go home." Yet even when the union voted on March 2, 1969, to accept the agreement and return to the classrooms, I could not pretend that the scrap of paper signed by one trustee and by an assistant to Hayakawa was a victory or even an agreement. (See Appendix.) The settlement letter is so cautiously and ambiguously worded that it means whatever any one of us—or any one of them—says it means: "It has been and is the long-time policy of the college administration. . . ." "The college has stated that it will recommend reinstatement on a nondiscriminatory basis for persons who have been absent simply due to the strike in proceedings brought before the Personnel Board." "There will be no reprisal against a returning teacher simply because he participated in the strike. . . . The college so advises." Such illusory terms as *long-time policy* and *will recommend* are so abstract that each party to the settlement may choose his own interpretation—lesson one in semantics. So I went home—back inside—not because of victory but because of defeat. I am back, working with students, teaching, serving on committees, yet finding it imperative to speak out, to describe the state of the campus, to assess the aftermath.

As I look about now, I see oppression, repression, defeat on all sides. Following the strike, the California legislature drafted over one hundred bills in its determination to suppress and punish dissent. These proposals express the hard-line view; they deal with crimes, controls, and penalties, not with causes, inequities, and injustice. Four of these campus unrest bills which were passed authorize the college president to declare a state of emergency on campus as he sees fit; to cut off financial aid to students who are convicted of causing campus disturbances; and to prohibit those ordered off campus by school officials from returning without permission—with a penalty of fines up to $500 and six months in jail. Other proposals would abolish academic tenure; severely restrict the amount and distribution of funds in the Educational Opportunities Program; provide for dismissal of teachers who strike; require a campus safety commission authorized to discharge any administrative officer who fails to act effectively to curb campus violence; and barricade the campus, with identification cards needed for entry and exit. Such harsh legislation may temporarily preserve peace, but only in the governor's sense of "keeping the campus open at the point of a bayonet."

Governor Ronald Reagan has been even more blatant than these measures suggest in some of his variations on this repressive theme. He saw the four bills passed by the legislature as "giving the college administrators more muscle to deal with hard-core campus troublemakers." During the strike, Reagan proclaimed, "Campus disorder has to stop, and it has to stop the day before yesterday. And it is going to be stopped with whatever it takes." Whatever it takes was the subject of another Reagan tirade when he said that statewide student unrest amounted to "guerrilla warfare" and that the solution in guerrilla warfare is "to eliminate and kill your enemy." The "enemy" seems to include those "heretics" who dare to criticize a governor, a college president, or a trustee. It also includes those "anarchists" who peacefully march on a picket line and those "traitors" who advocate a reshuffling of institutional priorities or who demand academic freedom.

The trustees of the California State colleges have left little breathing space for academic freedom. They are now attempting to delegate to themselves power to appoint and promote all tenured faculty members, to regulate student government, and to set decency standards for campus newspapers. Such patent interference with campus autonomy will virtually destroy the faculty tenure system and the right of students to initiate and allocate their own funds to community action and experimental programs. Such disruptive meddling by the trustees raises specters of censorship of the press, political tests for teachers, and the death of academic freedom. Paul Dale Bush, president of the Association of California State College Professors, accurately assessed the political realities for the trustees: "The tragic fact is that the Board of Trustees has not only failed to protect the California State colleges from attacks on academic freedom and due process, it has initiated many such attacks of its own. Furthermore, it gives such wide publicity to its own forays that it has contributed directly to the public's belief that such ideological interference with higher education is not only desirable but quite necessary." If the trustees are the guardians of the colleges, who is the enemy?

The legislature, the governor, and the trustees have found the judiciary, on and off campus, to be an ally in campus repression. On campus, the faculty grievance and disciplinary procedures have been violated by S. I. Hayakawa in his new robes of chief judge. The chairman of the faculty disciplinary panel accused Hayakawa of "overruling, by administrative fiat, the action taken by the faculty when it established the Grievance and Disciplinary Action Panel. . . . Your action not only short circuits the process with respect to this case but reserves for your sole discretion the decision as to which requests for disciplinary action will be allowed to proceed." Hayakawa's Louis XIV-ish cry, "I am the institution. I have all authority—incipient, intermediary, and final," should not have been so shocking to the panel chairman, who must have remembered that Hayakawa had already denied the legitimacy of the panel. On May 27, 1969, the panel had severely reprimanded Hayakawa and had recommended that he be removed from office. He had been charged with unprofessional conduct for destroying private property and physically assaulting individuals when he ripped out the wires on a sound truck operated by student dissidents and for accepting the position of acting president in violation of the normal and agreed-upon procedures for such appointment. The ouster vote was laughed off by the accused and ignored by Chancellor Glenn Dumke, who contemptuously labeled it "inappropriate and legally improper." Urban Whitaker, panel chairman, was quoted as saying, "It seems to me the impact of Dumke's decision is that the president, the most important faculty member on the campus, is placed above the law which the faculty has developed to govern itself." On June 17, 1969, Whitaker submitted his resignation as chairman of the panel, admitting that one of his reasons was his inability "to retain the level of respect from the office of the president which is necessary to the successful faculty-administration cooperation which this process requires."

So, the faculty disciplinary procedures are a sham—operative on a case-by-case basis, depending on the whim of the administration and the identity and loyalties of the accused. A union leader, William Stanton, was acquitted by the disciplinary action committee of charges based on strike-related activities; his tenure was recommended by the Tenure Committee of his department (economics) and by the school and college deans. Hayakawa reversed all these decisions; Stanton does not have tenure. Nathan Hare was cleared of all charges in two disciplinary proceedings; but he was fired by the president. On the other hand, the administration refused to allow charges of unprofessional conduct to be processed against certain professors who were participating in the kangaroo courts for student strikers. These charges were brought by some of Hayakawa's "enemies"—members of the AFT—and were filed against some of Hayakawa's "friends"—faculty members who served on the disciplinary courts in defiance of the recommendations of their own Academic Senate, the majority vote at a faculty meeting, and the written opinion of a federal judge. The chancellor has prepared drastic revisions which are to replace all procedures. Faculty participation in grievance and disciplinary proceedings is systematically removed by these revisions. Each college will have a hearing officer drawn by lot from a panel of retired Superior Court judges, and the college president will complete this usurpation of faculty rights with his power of veto in all cases. Thus, the accuser himself will sit in final judgment of the accused.

The student disciplinary procedures are even more offensive than are the faculty procedures to the values of fairness and freedom in the academic community. Hayakawa instituted his own student disciplinary procedures, which were in direct opposition to the procedures adopted by the Academic Senate and the general faculty. A suit filed under the Civil Rights Act (42 U.S.C. "Section" 1983) charged that the college "courts" combined some of the most objectionable features of the House Un-American Activities Committee, a military tribunal, and a juvenile hearing: The police report was used as evidence; there was no right to confront or cross-examine witnesses; the student's advisor was permitted to address the panel only "at the discretion of the panel"; and Hayakawa or his designee doubled as prosecutor and appellate judge. A select faculty committee on student disciplinary procedures reported that its was not able to reconcile the differences between the Academic Senate and the administration in three major areas: (1) Whether the president or the hearing panels should have final authority. The Academic Senate had insisted that the hearing panels should have final authority. Hayakawa refused even to discuss with the trustees the delegation of his authority in these proceedings, although many of the students were charged with violation of emergency rules instituted by Hayakawa. In some cases, he also signed the initiating complaint. (2) Whether the college should postpone hearings in cases where criminal charges are pending. The Academic Senate had urged that the college postpone disciplinary action against any student who faced criminal court proceedings for the same or related acts. If the college summoned him to appear at a hearing, he risked being whipsawed between the court and campus hearings; his attorney advised him to refuse to testify in the college hearing because of the risk of jeopardizing his criminal court case. To suspend this student would be in violation of at least the spirit of the constitutional privilege against self-incrimination. (3) The composition of the hearing panels. The Academic Senate had objected to panels of only faculty; the panels should include students, as the American Association of University Professors recommends in its guidelines on student rights.

In spite of these critical and unresolved differences, the report contains tribute from the select committee chairman to his committee members for their understanding, hard work, and spirit of compromise. The chairman concludes that all our problems may fade away if only the rest of us can attain the level of understanding and the spirit of compromise of this committee. Such a statement may seem reasonable to some, but it is meaningless to me. The committee accepted not compromise but defeat. The issue of final authority has been summarily settled by Hayakawa's benevolent statement that he will "normally" accept the recommendations of a panel. This is the preemptive promise of all men who wield final authority. Procedural and substantive due process must apply not only for those accused of panty raids or cheating but also for the controversial, foul-mouthed, loud-mouthed troublemaker.

Of course, I too applaud the select committee on student disciplinary procedures for their labors. I offer mixed praise to the committee for effecting a reduction in the number of hearings through substitution of the letter of reprimand given to certain students charged with minor offenses such as unlawful assembly, disorderly conduct, and failure to disperse. This generous option obscures the responsibility of the college for having originally set the stage for the mass arrests for minor offenses. Without the emergency regulations, there would have been no illegal assembly (see Appendix). The letter has helped this college community to forget that these reprimanded students are going through criminal trials for the same minor offenses. They are receiving fines, jail terms, and probation sentences because the administration swept away First Amendment rights by issuing emergency regulations and then invited the Tactical Squad to arrest students and faculty members who were at an assembly. In many cases, college authorities signed the warrants for the arrests. I am jubilant that those one or two hundred students will not be expelled or suspended for exercising their constitutional rights on their own campus; yet I am ashamed that they have been reprimanded for this activity.

The courts are coconspirators in this same masquerade of mercy by their urging students to cop a plea to help reduce court congestion. Woe unto those who demand juries and justice! During the strike, restraining orders and injunctions against picketing, striking, holding rallies, and passing out leaflets were freely granted to "the management" by the judiciary. The injunction is the weapon the courts often use to make a legal strike illegal. New judicial artillery was used during this strike. One judge ordered a freeze on the spending powers of the student government, which supported the strike. The court also upheld the second election for student body officers run by the administration after students who supported the strike won the first election. Thus, the court found still another pocket of ultimate authority presumed to be vested in the college president. Now, with the blessing of the court, the president may preempt the constitution, by-laws, and election procedures of the Associated Students.

What does the campus look like after the strike? Hayakawa now wields the final-authority bludgeon to harass and even purge those who defy him. Hare is gone. Although he was chosen by recognized procedures to be the chairman of the new Black Studies Department, he was fired by Hayakawa in violation of the strike settlement. Other black administrators are gone. Those who resigned in June 1969 said they were sick of being "niggers in residence," functioning in an atmosphere of racism, and reduced from being administrators to being powerless advisors kept around to help quell student unrest. Some of the good teachers are gone. Ruby Cohn, Jordan Churchill, James Schevill, and others resigned in the spring because of frustration, repressive policies, and a feeling that "there is nothing that we can do." Others are soon to leave: over twenty-one union professors have been refused tenure; and an unusually high proportion of this group have been terminated by the administration over the strong recommendations of their respective departments. The *Daily Gater* is still suspended as campus newspaper even though the suspension order by Hayakawa on March 1, 1969, was widely recognized as an act of censorship. (This act was labeled "the most blatant attack on the rudimentary expression of free speech yet seen at San Francisco State College" by the U.S. Student Press Association.)

I suppose that a brighter side of the campus should be described. Hayakawa continues to bask in his great public acclaim. He spoke at his own commemorative dinner and donated the "take" to "the programs cut by the legislature"—receiving for himself only his standing ovations and his media coverage. Black studies and Asian-American, La Raza, and native American courses are now listed in the catalogue. Of course, the student planning committees that provided the initiative and the creativity in these programs are being speedily phased out. The Third World professors remain without autonomy in hiring their own faculty. There are additions to the campus—a new dormitory completed and more buildings being built for more students. Changes can also be found in the key personnel of the college; white men have replaced black men as dean of activities, dean of undergraduate studies, and advisor on student discipline procedures. The Academic Senate has a new conservative majority who seem to listen carefully to the five representatives of the administration before lining up their vote. The Executive Committee of this senate sounds a cautious refrain of "compromise" and "let us not be divisive" when opinions differ from those of the administration. And there are flowers blooming on campus—daisies and petunias and marigolds planted where police made their arrests, where a medic knelt to wash away the mace, where striking students and faculty walked on their picket lines.

For the moment we have returned. We try to minimize the difficulties we face by working from inside. But many of us will go out on strike again if we find that inside we can only be a part of that which we condemn. We know we can go outside to act if we must. During the strike many of the faculty for the first time stood shoulder to shoulder with strangers from other departments and acted from deepest convictions. The feeling was good; it gave us enough strength to overcome the fear of personal and professional reprisals, of police harassment and arrest, of retreat or even defeat. Strangers are now friends, and they speak out in conscience more often. The good feeling and the solidarity engendered during those long days of the strike are today the bond which unites us as we fight within the institution for human rights and educational progress; and that same bond will mobilize us tomorrow if we find that we must again move outside the institution to the picket line.

Appendix

A. Declaration of Emergency by the President

In order to enable faculty and students at San Francisco State College to resume their classroom instructional program and other activities the following regulations are hereby declared to be in effect on this campus or at any college sponsored event:

1. Firearms, loaded or unloaded, or other deadly weapons may not be carried by any person other than an authorized peace officer.
2. The use of amplification equipment, except as authorized for normal classroom activities, is forbidden without the express permission of the president of the college or his designee.
3. The Speakers Platform shall be available to only those persons or groups who have scheduled the use of the facility with the dean of students office. The use of the facility will be at such times and under such conditions as shall be announced by that office.
4. There shall be no interference with scheduled classes or with any other educational or administrative processes of the college.

Those who are charged with a violation of these rules are subject to immediate temporary suspension. Due process will be furnished any student so suspended within seventy-two hours of such suspension by a hearing officer appointed by the president. Those found to have engaged in such disorderly behavior may be disciplined, suspended, or expelled.

Faculty members shall meet their classes during the hours scheduled in the scheduled places, except as approved by the president or his designee.

December 2, 1968

B. Ten Black Students Union Demands

1. That all black studies courses being taught through various other departments be immediately made part of the Black Studies Department and that all the instructors in this department receive full-time pay.

2. That Dr. Nathan Hare, chairman of the Black Studies Department, receive a full professorship and a comparable salary according to his qualifications.

3. That there be a department of black studies which will grant a bachelor's degree in black studies; that the Black Studies Department, the chairman, faculty, and staff have the sole power to hire faculty and control and determine the destiny of its department.

4. That all unused slots for black students from fall 1968 under the Special Admissions Program be filled in spring 1969.

5. That all black students wishing so be admitted in fall 1969.

6. That twenty full-time teaching positions be allocated to the department of black studies.

7. That Dr. Helen Bedesem be replaced from the position of financial aids officer and that a black person be hired to direct it; that Third World people have the power to determine how it will be administered.

8. That no disciplinary action will be administered in any way to any students, workers, teachers, or administrators during and after the strike as a consequence of their participation in the strike.

9. That the California State college trustees not be allowed to dissolve the black program on or off the San Francisco State College campus.

10. That George Murray maintain his teaching position on campus for the 1968–1969 academic year.

C. Five Third World Liberation Front Demands

1. That a school of ethnic studies for the ethnic groups involved in the Third World be set up with the students in each particular ethnic organization having the authority and control of the hiring and retention of any faculty member, director, and administrator, as well as the curriculum in a specific area study.

2. That fifty faculty positions be appropriated to the school of ethnic studies, twenty of which would be for the black studies program.

3. That in the spring semester, the college fulfill its commitment to the nonwhite students in admitting those that apply.

4. That, in the fall of 1969, all applications of nonwhite students be accepted.

5. That George Murray and any other faculty person chosen by nonwhite people as their teacher be retained in their position.

D. Strike Issues of AFT, Local 1352

I.   Strike issues directed to the president and administration at San Francisco State College:

   A. Negotiation of and adoption of comprehensive rules and regulations governing:

     1. Grievance procedures related to faculty affairs.

     2. Personnel decisions (hiring, firing, tenure, promotion, demotion, suspension, lay-off).

     3. Conditions under which pay can be reduced or docked.

     4. Sick leave and other fringe benefits.

     5. Unit and class load assignments for full- and part-time faculty.

     6. Stipulation of prerogatives and delineation of authority at various administrative levels.

     7. Guidelines and standards for professional perquisites (sabbaticals, travel, research leaves).

     8. Faculty involvement in decisions on academic matters (curriculum selection, assignment of faculty and staff, grading, graduation requirements, determination of calendar, admission requirements).

     9. Faculty involvement in decisions governing all local administrative matters (office space, parking).

      10. Recovery of faculty positions bootlegged for administrative purposes.

  B. Protection of constitutional rights.

      1. Amnesty for all faculty, students, and staff who have been suspended or have been subject to other disciplinary action and/or arrested, and withdrawal of outstanding warrants as a result of activity to end racism at San Francisco State College.

      2. No disciplinary action for exercising constitutionally protected rights.

  C. Black Students Union and Third World Liberation Front grievances must be resolved and implementation assured.

  D. All agreements on the above to be reduced to a written contract.

II. Strike issues directed to the trustees of the California State College:

  A. All agreements made with the local administratons under (1) above shall be binding upon and accepted by the trustees.

  B. Sufficient funds shall be provided from current reserve and emergency funds to:

      1. Maintain the present faculty positions (this will prevent the lay-off of 100 to 125 faculty in the spring semester, 1969).

      2. Gain new positions to replace those given by various departments and schools to staff a Black Studies Department and a school of ethnic studies.

      3. Protect the revised work loads presently scheduled in many departments for spring 1969 and assure the same for everyone who requests it.

  C. Rescission of the ten disciplinary rules passed by the trustees on November 26, 1968.

  D. Approval of the student union plan presented by the Associated Students at San Francisco State College.

  E. Cancellation of proposed changes in Title V that would take away student control of student body funds.

  F. Recognition of college constitution that emerges from the Constitutional Convention called by the Academic Senate at San Francisco State College.

III. Strike issues directed to the governor and the legislature:

    A. That a special joint committee of the California State Assembly and Senate be appointed to conduct negotiations with the state college Board of Trustees and the union to agree on systematic and continuing financing for the proposals under I and II above and to provide the necessary increases in salary required to maintain a qualified faculty at San Francisco State College.

    B. That when the special legislative committee, the Board of Trustees, and the union have reached agreement, the committee report to the next session of the legislature so that necessary monies may be provided to put the agreement into effect.

E. Joint Agreement Concluding Student Strike

We agree to the following responses to the fifteen demands.

Several of the responses are written to enable immediate action toward strike settlement, and they should be understood as taken without prejudice to future development along quite different lines. For example, one response is the establishment of a school of ethnic studies. This is an important first step to take, but other alternatives are not precluded for the future. Several of the unaccomplished implementations are due to the unwillingness of the college to proceed with planning without the active cooperation of ethnic minority students, faculty, and community representatives.

BSU Demand 1: 1. A memo to President Smith from Vice President Garrity, October 21, 1968, stated that existing black studies courses then in session were to be transferred to the Black Studies Department in spring or fall 1969. *Implementation by college:* All courses have been transferred with the exception of one in anthropology and one in drama. At this writing it is not known whether the plan is to maintain these courses in the departments or transfer them to black studies.

2. All instructors employed full-time will receive full-time pay. *Implementation by college:* Accomplished.

BSU Demand 2: The apparent failure to rehire Dr. Hare is irrelevant to the institution of the Black Studies Department. The de-

partment chairman shall be selected by the usual departmental process
and Dr. Hare shall be eligible for selection.

BSU Demand 3: 1. The department of black studies was
created by President Robert Smith on September 17, 1968. The
Bachelor of Arts Degree in Black Studies was approved by the trustees
on October 24, 1968. Through its actions of December 5 and December 17, 1968, the Council of Academic Deans provided the resources
needed to begin the black studies program in the spring semester of
1969. On December 5, 1968, the Council of Academic Deans recognized the Black Studies Department as having "full faculty power
commensurate with that accorded all other departments of the college." *Implementation by college and the trustees:* Accomplished.

2. The college approved a community board without specifying
what form it shall take. This board will recommend to the president;
that is, it will not *legally* have the sole power to hire faculty and control the department. One point, however, of having a community
board is to provide support from the community for the minority programs. *Implementation by the college:* Not yet accomplished. The college has so far been unwilling to institute the board without the active
cooperation of ethnic minority students, faculty, and community representatives. It is agreed that appointments to this board be agreeable to
the college, the Third World faculty, involved Third World students,
and Third World communities.

BSU Demand 4: This demand was met by the admission of
128 EOP students in the spring 1969 semester. *Implementation by
college:* Accomplished.

BSU Demand 5: 1. Admission and entrance requirements are
law, not subject to change by the college. The staff of the bipartisan
Legislative Joint Committee on Higher Education recently called the
state's Master Plan for higher education a failure and included among
its recommendations, the following: (a) Lower entrance requirements
for the university and state colleges until the percentage of minority
students enrolled throughout the system was the same as the percentage
of minority citizens of college age in the state as a whole. (b) Have the
state colleges accept the top 40 per cent instead of the top third of high
school graduates. (c) Raise the percentage of applicants for whom the
colleges may waive admission requirements from 4 per cent to 10 per
cent. Changes in the law take time to bring about, and we do not know

what changes will take place. The college has already committed itself (Position Paper on Issues, 2/26/69, VI, 3) to do its part in the study and revision of the Master Plan.

2. Parallel admission standards for Third World people, having the status of equivalents to regular admission requirements, are a basic necessity at San Francisco State College if the College is to fulfill its educational responsibilities as an institution of higher learning in an urban environment. The college shall develop parallel admission standards for Third World people and others and shall recommend them to the trustees for enactment in Title V. One responsibility of the Planning Committee for the school of ethnic studies shall be to develop, together with the dean of admissions, such parallel admission standards by October 1, 1969.

3. Under existing law, the college has initiated procedures for the active recruitment of nonwhite students, and we present the following information as evidence of good faith in this regard. For the fall 1969, (a) about the same number as for the fall of 1968 of *special* admittees (four hundred) is expected. The total college enrollment is expected to decrease by about five hundred, so that no increase in special admissions is possible without a change in the law; (b) five hundred *regular* admissions are being filled by qualified nonwhite students who are being actively sought and admitted when found; (c) it is estimated that about one hundred additional nonwhite students will enroll through *regular* admissions channels; (d) the expected total of new nonwhite student admissions for fall 1969 is therefore one thousand (out of a total of 4,670 new students expected to enroll). In fall 1968, the number of nonwhite students enrolled (including two hundred foreign students) was about 3,750 out of a total enrollment of 18,230, or about 20 per cent. For fall 1969, the estimate is an enrollment of 4,250 to 4,750 nonwhite students out of a total of 17,700 students, or from about 24 per cent to 27 per cent.

4. The college has committed itself additionally to seek the necessary finances and staff for the EOP (Position Paper on Issues, 2/26/69, IV, 2). The college also commits itself to seek funds, both within the state college system and outside of it, for students, counsellors, and tutors; and we recommend the drawing together in one office of the college all such activities devoted to acquiring the funds needed for the education of Third World and other students.

5. The college shall explore the feasibility of pooling at San Francisco State College the special admissions quotas not used by other state colleges.

BSU Demand 6: 1. 12.3 positions (11.3 unfilled) have already been allocated to the Black Studies Department. *Implementation by the college:* Accomplished.

2. Additional staff will be allocated in accordance with need and available resources; and it is expected that there will be additional staff allocated by fall 1969. In addition to faculty needed for course additions and increased enrollments, some staff time should be available for teaching and research assistants. If the need is demonstrated, the allocation to the department could well exceed twenty. *Implementation by the college and trustees:* In process.

BSU Demand 7: 1. The college has established a new position of associate director of financial aids, and a black administrator has been appointed to it. He is in charge of and responsible for the final decision-making in the College Work Study Program, and for the final decision-making on financial aid packages developed for all black students who wish their decisions made by a black administrator. The college already has in the Office of Financial Aids a Spanish-speaking administrator. He has the same final authority of decision for nonwhite students who wish their decisions made by a Spanish-speaking administrator. The respective administrators shall be directly involved in determining the final decisions on the obtaining of funds for financial aids. *Implementation by the college:* Accomplished.

2. The respective administrators shall be included among the appointments with which the community board is concerned.

3. The college needs additional staff and space support for the Financial Aids Office. Such support will be sought immediately from state sources. *Implementation by the college and trustees:* Not accomplished.

BSU Demand 8: The signatory parties are aware of the president's intention to continue scheduled disciplinary hearings but, in recognition of this agreement, to withhold his final decision on disciplinary penalties beyond probation until April 11, 1969. The members of the Select Committee and the representatives of the TWLF-BSU join in recommending to the president on all cases pending on March 17, 1969 that:

1. Students charged solely with acts of nonviolence shall receive a written reprimand. Students so charged may request a hearing after the receipt of the reprimand and in the event they are found guilty the penalty shall stand.

2. Students charged with "violent acts" shall, if found guilty by the hearing panel, receive a penalty of not more than suspension through the end of the fall semester of 1969–1970. ("Violent acts" are acts of physical aggression against persons or the use of or attempted use of explosives or incendiary materials.)

3. Students charged with "instructional disruption" shall, if found guilty by the hearing panel, receive a penalty of no more than suspension for the remainder of this academic year. ("Instructional disruption" is the disruption or the attempt to disrupt by force or violence or the threat of violence or force within the situs of the threatened act of any part of the instructional program of the college.)

4. All other acts are deemed to be nonviolent.

5. Probation shall be defined so as not to prevent full student activities or affect student financial eligibility or affect his hiring eligibility within the college.

6. No further charges will be brought for antecedent acts of instructional disruption or nonviolent conduct.

7. A review of current disciplinary procedures should commence immediately. This review should involve, among others, TWLF-BSU students, and should include consideration of (a) due process and (b) student judicial participation.

BSU Demand 9: 1. The college affirms its belief that self-government in student affairs is desirable and will resist any revisions to the California Administrative Code, Title V, which intend to abridge the decision-making role of students in student affairs. The college also believes that all persons involved in handling student funds should be held accountable in all fiscal matters. New regulations should be provided, if necessary, to clarify areas of financial responsibility. *Implementation by trustees:* Not accomplished.

2. It is urgently recommended by the Select Committee and the representatives of the TWLF-BSU that the college intervene legally in the current dispute of Associated Students funds. The college shall recommend to the trustees that they require the colleges to fulfill their obligations under existing Title V regulations rather than add new

regulations affecting the controls of student funds. The college shall
further recommend to the trustees that any action on changes in Title
V be postponed until a representative group of Third World students
from San Francisco State College has had an opportunity to present its
case to the trustees. It is expected that some programs now being
financed by Associated Students funds can be supplementarily financed
in the future through the school of ethnic studies without diminishing
its accredited program. *Implementation by college:* Not accomplished,
awaits planning completion.

BSU Demand 10: Personnel matters of the Black Studies Department are a concern of the community board. Refer to the response
to Demand 3.

TWLF Demand 1: 1. The College will endeavor to establish a
school of ethnic studies to begin operation in the fall semester, 1969.
The college recognizes that in order to mount a truly significant program to meet the needs and aspirations of the ethnic communities,
additional funding must be secured. The only alternative available to
the college is to recommend to the chancellor's office and the trustees
the building or purchase of appropriate facilities for the development
of a school of ethnic studies. *Implementation:* Will require approval by
the trustees and the Department of Finances. A very large planning
job faces the college, and the work must start immediately.

2. In status and structure the school will equal existing schools
of the college. *Implementation by the college:* Follows implementation
of 1 above.

3. Staffing will be provided from presently existing funds for
planning the school during the spring semester, 1969, and funds will be
sought for summer 1969. There shall be a Planning Group and a Plan-
ing-Advisory committee. The Planning Group shall be composed of:
(a) A full-time director appointed by the college with the advice and
consent of TWLF students. (b) Three associate directors, half-time,
nominated by the TWLF students with the advice and consent of the
college and appointed by the college. They should preferably be either
faculty members or graduate students. (c) At least one student from
each subdivision of the TWLF (including the BSU) appointed by the
TWLF. The students shall be paid. The functions of the Planning
Group are: (1) to do the actual planning for the school of ethnic
studies, in consultation with the Planning Committee; and (2) to pro-

pose plans for consideration of the Planning-Advisory Committee.

The Planning-Advisory Committee shall include the planning director as an ex-officio member and twelve members of the faculty or administration as follows: (a) four chosen by the Academic Senate, (b) four chosen by the president with the advice and consent of CAD, (c) four chosen by the BSU and TWLF students. The functions of the Planning-Advisory Committee shall be: (1) to work closely with the Planning Group in reviewing plans for the school of ethnic studies; (2) to inform the college community of the needs, difficulties, and problems encountered in planning stages; (3) to recommend to the appropriate college committees, the Academic Senate, CAD, and the president the final plan for the school of ethnic studies. The college will endeavor to obtain funds in order to enable planning to continue during the summer. *Implementation by college:* Not accomplished, but it can be immediately.

4. The college will take immediate steps to review its own academic Master Plan with the purpose of considering the following issues: (a) Raising the FTE ceiling for the college to accommodate the school of ethnic studies, if new facilities are built or purchased. (b) Reserving an FTE allotment for the growth and development of a school of ethnic studies. *Implementation by college:* Not accomplished.

5. A community board representing the several ethnic areas involved has been approved by the college to assist and supplement the administrative operation of the school of ethnic studies. This board will recommend to the president; that is, it will not *legally* have the sole power to hire faculty and control the department. *Implementation by the college:* Not yet accomplished. The college has so far been unwilling to institute the board without the active cooperation of ethnic minority students, faculty, and community representatives. It is agreed that appointments to this board be agreeable to the college, the Third World faculty, involved Third World students, and Third World communities.

TWLF Demand 2: The allocation of faculty positions to the school of ethnic studies will follow upon spring planning and resources acquired by the college. The number of such positions for the fall semester will be determined during the spring and will depend upon the nature of the programs developed, the FTE allocated to the school and the capacity of the facilities allocated. We commit the college now, in advance of planning, to ten positions for the fall semester 1969, without prejudice to the needs for additional positions. If need is demonstrated, the allocation to the school could well exceed thirty. *Implementation by college and trustees:* Not accomplished.

TWLF Demand 3: Same as response to BSU Demand 4.

TWLF Demand 4: Same as response to BSU Demand 5.

TWLF Demand 5: Same as response to BSU Demand 10.

We further agree to the following:

1. That a committee of students, faculty, and staff, ethnically mixed, be formed immediately to advise the college on how to deal with the charges of racism at the college. A first task for this committee will be to recommend procedures for dealing with claims of racism within the college.

2. That the procedure for appointing an ombudsman be started again and pressed to as rapid a conclusion as possible.

3. The college shall establish, through its Academic Senate and the Council of Academic Deans, a small committee to expedite decision-making and action concerning all aspects of this agreement. Its chairman shall have direct access to the CAD, the vice-presidents for academic and financial affairs, and the president. The committee will make monthly progress reports to the president, the Academic Senate, and the Council of Academic Deans and will recommend any steps necessary to facilitate the development of the program.

4. In recognition of the urgency of the present situation, we recommend that the chancellor and trustees expedite in every way possible the consideration of any requests for special resources presented by the college president which arise from the extraordinary needs of the college at this time.

5. In instances where differences of interpretation occur in the precise meaning of any part of this agreement, final and mutually binding decisions upon all parties shall be made by a three-man group composed of one person named by the president of San Francisco State College, one person named by the dean of the school of ethnic studies, and the chairman of the various ethnic studies departments, and a third person selected by these two. If no agreement can be reached as to this third person, the third person should be Bishop Mark Hurley.

6. Staffing and admission policies of the school of ethnic studies shall be nondiscriminatory.

7. Police should be withdrawn immediately upon the restoration of peace to the campus.

8. The state of emergency on campus should be rescinded immediately upon settlement of the strike, together with the emergency regulations restricting assemblies, rallies, etc.

9. The college shall resume planning for a Constitutional Convention and for a student conference on the governance of the urban campus.

10. The students and the administration together recognize the necessity of developing machinery for peaceful resolution of future disputes, arising from conditions or needs outside the terms of this agreement.

11. The student organizations signatory to this agreement and the college agree that they will utilize the full influence of their organizations to ensure an effective implementation of this agreement.

F. Letter Concluding Faculty Strike

February 16, 1969

Mr. George W. Johns
Secretary-Treasurer
San Francisco Labor Council
2940 Sixteenth Street
San Francisco, California 94103

Dear Mr. Johns:

In view of our several meetings, exchange of correspondence, and supplementary advice received from the chairman of the statewide Academic Senate regarding an appellate grievance procedure which the Executive Committee of that body is making to the entire Academic Senate, and on the assumption that such recommendation will be favorably acted upon by the senate, the majority of the trustees, individually, of the Regional Committee are prepared to make recommendations to the full Board of Trustees in accordance with the contents of this letter.

You will appreciate that any recommendations required to be made to the board will go through the usual board procedure of committee hearing and that other official bodies and other organizations may be heard thereon and that no group of trustees can assure the adoption of any particular recommendation or limit the sphere of action or contrary action by the board. To the extent that board action may be required on any of these matters (i.e., Item 3), we will urge adoption of our recommendations. If necessary, the recommending trustees will support the right of the college to make the decision on rehiring and reinstatement indicated in Item 8. It is our understanding that union and council action are not dependent on what the board may or may not do with the recommendations.

Nothing in these paragraphs affects such commitments as have been made by striking teachers and others to the college to return to work and meet assignments per independent correspondence held with the college.

1. The Board of Trustees itself or through a committee, officer, representative, or employee is authorized by law on proper request to meet with employee organization representatives. The AFT at San Francisco State College is such an employee organization within the law. Accordingly, insofar as the demands of this group relate to employment conditions and employer-employee relations, including but not limited to wages, hours, and other terms and conditions of employment, they are germane to such a meeting. Accordingly, a proper request by AFT, Local 1352, has been and will continue to be honored. Any future meetings with the union would have to be consistent with the obligations to meet and confer with other employee organizations. The relationship of Local 1352 and the trustees shall be governed by the above.

2. Any matters of amnesty, arrests, and warrants affecting members of the AFT, Local 1352, will be referred to meetings of representatives of San Francisco State College and such local. The right is reserved to any grievant or his representative to submit grievances covering retention, reappointments, reassignments, tenure, promotion, and discipline to the appropriate grievance or disciplinary procedure. It is understood that an administration member or other faculty member usually brings the charges in disciplinary cases, but for reference herein regarding appeals the party charged is regarded as the grievant and both the retention *et al.* and disciplinary procedures are called "grievance procedures."

3. In grievance procedures, as particularly referred to in the last two sentences above, an impartial panel for appeals would be selected on a statewide level. It would be provided that the chancellor augment the existing panel on grievances (and any disciplinary panel to be selected) with ten or more members as may be necessary, acceptable to the chairman of the Academic Senate, drawn from the state colleges and the University of California, with particular consideration to the principle that academic matters are involved.

For any particular appeal the chancellor may select from the panel a committee of three; or, if the grievant prefers, the committee may be selected by lot, or the chancellor or the president may select one, the grievant one, and these appointees select a third member, all members to be from the panel. In the event agreement cannot be reached, the third party shall be selected by lot.

4. Present faculty positions will be maintained and sufficient funding has already been provided to prevent the layoff of 100 to 125 faculty members in the spring semester of 1969. The provision of this funding to meet the budget deficit was set out in Vice-Chancellor Brakebill's administrative letter to President Hayakawa dated December 16, 1968.

5. It has been and is the long time policy of the college administration that the staffing and budgeting of the Black Studies Department and the school of ethnic studies shall be made by independent budget and the academic positions shall not be taken from presently assigned department positions or budgets.

The present situation of voluntary allocation from other departments will not extend beyond the spring semester.

6. No academic employee who has been assigned a reduced teaching load during 1969 and after would be docked or otherwise have his pay reduced as a result thereof so long as said assignment was made in accordance with college procedure and the staffing formula.

7. The personnel files in the college shall be open to inspection by the faculty members, upon consent of the college, as provided in Academic Senate resolution AS 176-68/FA. The college administration is prepared to follow the recommendations of the local senate in this matter.

8. The rehiring and reinstatement procedures of striking persons who have been absent will be as set forth by the college in a

memorandum transmitted to you by the college. The college has stated that it will recommend reinstatement on a nondiscriminatory basis for persons who have been absent simply due to the strike in proceedings brought before the Personnel Board.

9. There will be no reprisal against a returning teacher simply because he participated in the strike; there will be no reprisal against any member of any other labor organization who participated in or supported the strike. The college so advises.

The foregoing administrative statements of the College and recommendatory statements of the recommending trustees are on the basis that the return to work and meeting of class assignments according to the spring schedule and other professional obligations will take place, all in good faith, at once; also that strike sanction of the San Francisco Labor Council will be withdrawn at once.

In reviewing this communication you will note that it mostly deals with matters as determined by the college. However, to the extent that recommendations are to be made to the board, the majority of the trustees of the Regional Committee individually will make such recommendations under the conditions as set forth in this letter.

Very truly yours,
LOUIS H. HEILBRON, Trustee

S. I. HAYAKAWA, Acting President
By FRANK D. DOLLARD

With respect to striking faculty who have been notified of an absence without leave for five consecutive working days and of consequent automatic resignation pursuant to Education Code Section 24366, the college will review specific statements by these individuals claiming that they have not been so absent. Each person wishing to present such a statement must do so within the next three days. The statement must be signed by the person who claims that he was not so absent and should specify the basis for that claim including a full statement of any assigned duties performed and the times each such duty was performed. These statements will be immediately reviewed. Should it be entirely clear in any instance that such absence did not take place, the individual will be so informed. In all other cases the persons concerned will be given an opportunity within the next two weeks to discuss the matter with a college representative. In any case in which the college concludes that such absence did not take place, college records will be adjusted accordingly.

Any person who differs from a college determination regarding such absence on his part may request the state Personnel Board to reinstate him pursuant to Education Code Section 24311.

The foregoing does not constitute an undertaking by the College to "toll" or postpone the running of the time periods within which to make such request pursuant to Education Code 24311, and it is suggested that anyone who claims that he has not been absent without leave for five consecutive working days, who has been notified by the college that he has been so absent, and who wishes to be reinstated to his former position at the college should file a request with the state Personnel Board within the times specified in that section.

FRANK D. DOLLARD

Index

265